HEART and SOUL

The Character of Welsh Rugby

To Graham
Best wishes

To Graham
Best wishes

To Graham,
Best Wish,

HEART and SOUL

the character of Welsh rugby

Edited by

Huw Richards

Peter Stead

and

Gareth Williams

University of Wales Press

Cardiff

1998

© The contributors, 1998.

First published 1998
Reprinted 1998

All rights reserved. No part of this book may be reproduced, stored in a retrieval system or transmitted, in any form or by any means, electronic, mechanical, photocopying, recording or otherwise, without clearance from the University of Wales Press, 6 Gwennyth Street, Cardiff, CF2 4YD.

British Library Cataloguing-in-Publication Data
A catalogue record for this book is available from the British Library.

ISBN 0-7083-1472-4

Typeset at University of Wales Press, Cardiff
Printed in England by Bookcraft, Midsomer Norton, Avon

CONTENTS

ACKNOWLEDGEMENTS vi
CONTRIBUTORS vii

INTRODUCTION Peter Stead 1
WRITING THE CHARACTER
   OF WELSH RUGBY Gareth Williams 7

CLIFF MORGAN Peter Stead 15
CARWYN JAMES Gareth Williams 29
BILLY BOSTON Phil Melling 45
DAVID WATKINS Chris Williams 59
GARETH EDWARDS David Parry-Jones 75
BARRY JOHN Hywel Teifi Edwards 93
JOHN TAYLOR Peter Stead 107
PROSSER'S PONTYPOOL Edward Butler 121
IEUAN EVANS Gerald Davies 135
ROBERT JONES Huw Richards 147
JONATHAN DAVIES Siân Nicholas 161
NIGEL WALKER Rhodri Morgan 179
SCOTT GIBBS Huw Richards 189
NEIL JENKINS Tim Williams 203

AFTERWORD Huw Richards & Peter Stead 217
SELECT BIBLIOGRAPHY 225
INDEX 229

ACKNOWLEDGEMENTS

All photographs by courtesy of the Western Mail and Echo Ltd, except for John Taylor and the Pontypool front row (both by courtesy of Colorsport) and Ieuan Evans (by courtesy of John Harris). The editors wish to acknowledge the support of the University of Wales Press and, in particular, the help of Susan Jenkins.

CONTRIBUTORS

EDWARD BUTLER Journalist and broadcaster. Rugby correspondent of *The Observer*. Sixteen caps for Wales, captaining the side in 1983–4, and a British Lions replacement in 1983.

GERALD DAVIES Chairman of HTV and rugby correspondent of *The Times*. Won forty-six caps for Wales, scoring twenty tries. A British Lion in 1968 and 1971.

HYWEL TEIFI EDWARDS Research professor, department of Welsh, University of Wales Swansea. Broadcaster, literary critic and cultural historian.

DAVID PARRY-JONES Television and radio commentator and journalist. Author of many volumes on rugby history including (with Mervyn Davies) *Number 8*.

PHIL MELLING Novelist, playwright and senior lecturer in American studies, University of Wales Swansea. A native of Wigan, former manager of British and Welsh student rugby league teams and author of *Man of Amman: The Life of Dai Davies*.

RHODRI MORGAN MP for Cardiff West since 1987. Former civil servant and head of the European Community's Office in Wales. Author of *Cardiff: Half and Half a Capital*.

SIÂN NICHOLAS Lecturer in history, University of Wales Aberystwyth, and the author of *The Echo of War: Home Front, Propaganda and the Wartime BBC 1939–45*.

HUW RICHARDS Journalist and historian. Writes on sport for *The Financial Times*. Author of *The Bloody Circus: The Daily Herald and the Left* (1997).

PETER STEAD Writer and broadcaster. Formerly senior lecturer in history, University of Wales Swansea. Author of biographical studies of Richard Burton and Dennis Potter.

CHRIS WILLIAMS Lecturer in history, University of Wales Cardiff. Author of *Democratic Rhondda* and *Capitalism, Community and Conflict: the South Wales Coalfield 1898–1947*.

GARETH WILLIAMS Reader in history and Welsh history, University of Wales Aberystwyth. A leading historian of culture and sport, his books include *1905 and All That* and, with Dai Smith, *Fields of Praise*. His latest book is *Valleys of Song: Music and Society in Wales 1840–1914*.

TIM WILLIAMS Barrister, consultant, historian and journalist. A columnist for *The Scotsman* and the author of *The Patriot Game*.

INTRODUCTION

Peter Stead

Rugby, like all great sports, is much more than just a game. Out of the pattern of play emerge structures, seasons, loyalties and heroes. Individual players, officials and supporters combine to create a culture to which they then give themselves to a greater or lesser extent. Often deepest friendships are determined within the game, but only individuals will know the precise degree to which the culture of the game has helped define and shape their very sense of self. We each carry with us our own idea of the game: we choose those parts of it which correspond to what we think meaningful in our own lives.

That process can operate in different ways. The most socially potent of all sports cultures has been that generated by American baseball, and yet for millions of fans their strong emotional attachment to the game and their sense of its crucial role in defining their relationship both with their own family and with the United States as a society was dependent for decades on radio commentators and newspaper box-scores. Mickey Mantle was a god to countless millions who had never seen him play, and Yankee Stadium was the true melting-pot for generations of Americans who had never sat in its stands. Sport has worked like this in Britain too although the role of sports cultures within the national framework has always been more complex. Earlier in the century there were many street cricketers who pretended to be Hobbs, Hutton or Compton merely on the basis of hearsay, just as later enthusiasts could claim to be experts on the relative merits of fast bowlers just through listening to *Test Match Special*. Today, the phenomenon of parents in Llanelli, Plymouth or Norwich buying replica Manchester United shirts is identified rightly as evidence of a new age of commercial exploitation in which manufacturers, clubs and the media seek to control patterns of sporting loyalty, yet the need for individual fans to develop and express loyalties, even for teams unseen, is nothing new.

Welsh rugby culture has developed rather differently. Welsh parents are now as ready as most to buy those replica soccer shirts for their children, just as they are prepared to subscribe to satellite and cable television in order to watch the best of their own sport being played in England or the southern hemisphere. But, they do these things knowing that something has been lost. What has gone is the immediacy of a sporting culture where true excellence was associated not only with all the great international arenas but also with the field at the back of the house. Nothing has ever rung so true for Welsh readers as C. L. R. James's explanation of how he suddenly understood, not only the nature of cricketing excellence, but also the essential character of the British Empire by merely looking at the skills being deployed in the game that was going on outside the window of his Trinidad home. Certainly Welsh fans love to be at the big game: 'We were there!' they used to chant to each other and to anyone else in sight as they clambered out of buses and trains after victories in Edinburgh or Paris knowing full well the credentials that the journey had bestowed. Yet that big-match mentality, that predilection for the trip, was only a refinement of a confidence and expertise that came from the deeper knowledge that the most promising players in Wales were to be found just down the road.

Essentially, the culture of Welsh rugby was intimate. For most of the century that intimacy held the danger of parochialism at bay, for world standards were applied and only the truly great were admitted to the pantheon. Yet there was always more to Welsh rugby than mere agreement about quality and greatness, since the true character of the game was determined by nuances relating to personality and place. Children who now wear Manchester United or Liverpool shirts have fathers whose first loyalty has always been to Penclawdd, Seven Sisters or Garndiffaith RFC. Youngsters who stick up posters of Ryan Giggs have grandparents whose first rugby heroes played for Llanelli Grammar School, Tondu or Mountain Ash. Within such a culture the pleasures that come from a shared history and an often recited consensus are always surpassed by the enjoyment of a knowledge that is above all private and personal.

We come to love the superstars in part because they remind us of those first heroes we spotted making tackles or breaks on unenclosed fields or on those slightly more formal school pitches which would not have been unfamiliar to Tom Brown and his schoolmates. We took pleasure in the great national teams because we had first come to appreciate flair and victory at a more humble level. Those were thrilling days when the school beat a South African touring team or when once again in the mud there would be victory over Neath Grammar School, Brian Thomas and all. Was there ever a better team than, say the Gowerton Grammar side of the late 1950s? Were there ever faster more creative back-row forwards than those short, dark, intense heroes of ours who would exchange a word with us even though they were prefects? And as we graduated from school and village games to the terraces at St Helens and the Gnoll we always expected that same quality of play and also the same immediacy and familiarity. We always supported players and teams because they were good and because we knew them.

A first visit to the Arms Park often came about because a local hero had been chosen to play for a select schoolboy or youth team. Buying the programme in Quay Street we rejoiced to see his precise roots identified. Thereafter there was always the thrill of buying the big-match programme to confirm that the national team would be made up of players whose backgrounds we knew so well. We loved to read the pen portraits, to see the club affiliations listed: the majority of players as always came from Newport, Llanelli, Swansea and Cardiff, but we were all silently proud that there were representatives too from Maesteg, Abertillery and Newbridge. There was an additional pleasure in looking up the details of any Neath or Aberavon players selected for, incredible as it now seems, we would often have seen them earlier that morning travelling to the game on the same train as us.

Those international days at Cardiff were always, in essence, outings for one extended family. That ritual reading of the programme notes was an exercise in which the details absorbed amounted to a definition of the identity both of the Welsh and their opponents. That a Welsh prop could be described as 'a bulldozer driver' was a matter of great satisfaction as was the information that his opposite number in the Scottish team 'was frequently prevented from appearing for the South of Scotland because of his activities as a sheep farmer'. Both men incidentally were British Lions. We were not surprised that another member of that Scottish pack was both a native and resident of Buenos Aires. We always checked to ensure that amongst the inevitable sales reps and schoolteachers that there were at least some genuine workers in our team (that 1965 front row of two steelworkers and a fitter always represented an ideal) before going on to guess what percentage of the

French team would be bar and restaurant proprietors. We loved it that an English scrum-half was born in Jammalamadugu India and that his world-class centre was 'reading history at Trinity'. Most astonishing of all were the Irish, most of whom seemed to have the qualification to be university vice-chancellors and to have been recruited from all parts of the globe: the Irish team that came to Cardiff in 1991 had a back division of which three were born in England, one each had been in Kenya, Zimbabwe and Australia and one unbelievably was a native of Jerusalem. By this time fuller programme notes were revealing some elements of the exotic and the utterly nondescript in Welsh careers, but what we were looking for primarily was that Wales was still dependent on the favourite sons of Nantyffyllon, Hebron, Tiger Bay and Mamhilad. The more we knew the more proud we could be. For aficionados of the Welsh game that eventual discreet dropping from the pen portraits first of places of birth and then of occupations marked not only the end of an era but quite possibly the beginning of the end.

There are those of us who are of an age to treasure memories of victories at Twickenham and Paris and can even recall at least one New Zealand team that lost a game somewhere in Wales. In our hearts though we know that the beauty of the Welsh game was that it was a village game played by village boys and that in those villages, both urban and rural, talent was nurtured initially in school and youth sides. In the recent dark days of national failure and in an era when television attempts to seduce us away from our primary loyalties many Welsh supporters have found solace in going back to their roots. Games are lost at Cardiff and Wembley, and even attractive traditional fixtures at Stradey and Rodney Parade may be abysmally attended, but there is still pleasure to be gained from dropping in at games at Merthyr or Dunvant. There have been afternoons at Abertillery when the valleys have never looked so lovely, and during games at Bonymaen one has looked up at the familiar, ancient and snow-capped moors and realized yet again that it is from those hills that we will derive our strength.

Our authors too write from within their culture. They write not necessarily to confirm a pantheon – other writers may have chosen different players – but rather to explore the nature of a sport that has been shaped by a tremendously close and intense interaction between personalities and their supporters, between if you like, entertainers and their audience. They write to evoke men whose actual play has been memorable and whose careers both on and off the field have become part of our history. They write to celebrate individual players but also their own memories and their experience of a culture to which they are indebted.

From the outset all the contributors realized that they wanted to examine the role that rugby, and in particular their chosen subjects, had played in their own lives. Throughout the exercise subjectivity was encouraged. Whatever their backgrounds, whether it be in academia, journalism or politics, the contributors came together in debate just like any group of friends after a game. Everyone had favourites, subjects they 'just had to do', but in several cases choices rapidly changed as authors realized precisely what it was they wanted to say about the game and themselves. We were sorry to see some great favourites lose their place but soon realized that they would reappear as supporting players in several essays. Our chosen few are firmly discussed in context and the necessary comparisons are made.

We took pleasure in the patterns that emerged: the ways in which authors were fascinated by the village backgrounds of their subjects, their schooldays, their teachers and by their early fascination with the ball-skills picked up in games of soccer. But we welcomed too the different perspectives that the changing nature of the game in Wales would necessarily induce. As we reconstructed the history of Welsh rugby from Cliff Morgan, the first star of the television age, down to players like Scott Gibbs and Neil Jenkins who have to strive to retain their own dignity and well-being in the midst of commercial and administrative chaos, we realized that a number of approaches would be needed. In any discussion of this game there has to be room for dewy-eyed nostalgia. But hard-headed realism and anger are called for too. These qualities are all here. We wanted to recall golden moments and first pleasures, but we also wanted to make it clear that it is time for things to get better. Now more than ever Welsh rugby has to find and show its character.

WRITING
the CHARACTER of
WELSH RUGBY

Gareth Williams

Given the centrality of sport in the Welsh cultural landscape, it is surprising that we have so few Welsh sports biographies. It is no disrespect to John Harding, Andrew Hignell and Bob Lonkhurst, the authors of fine accounts of the careers of, respectively, Billy Meredith (1985), Wilfred Wooller (1995) and Tommy Farr (1997), to wish that we had more serious historical biographies to compare with William J. Baker's of Jesse Owens (*An American Life*, 1986) or Randy Roberts on Jack Johnson (1986) and Jack Dempsey (1987), life-stories that manage to combine penetrating social history with meticulously researched assessments of their subjects as sportsmen.

The particular achievement of those authors is that they explain their subjects in terms both of the social conditions that produced them and of the concepts of sporting excellence they represented. On a more modest scale, the contributors to this volume are also aware of the determining context of community, class and culture. Each has written an essay on a sporting legend. But legends have lives too, and if they have enjoyed extraordinary careers they are still ordinary people; while their sporting success intrigues, what they are like *off* the field as citizens, fathers, job-holders, even voters, can be as revealing as any appraisal of their performance *on* it. The reader ought not, however, fear that he, or she, is in for any fancy dancing. The writers who appear here are well aware that fancy sports writing is some of the worst writing of any kind; yet, at its best, writing about sport can carry symbolic overtones, address human relationships and engage with human frailties. And it will situate those relationships and those frailties in the essential and formative context of period, place and tradition which have not been the concerns of much past rugby writing; least of all of the two fundamental texts which legitimately command classic status and three-figure price tags in the sales-rooms.

Football – The Rugby Union Game (1892) edited by that intransigent defender of uncompromising amateurism and, in the late 1860s, vice-principal of Trinity College, Carmarthen, the Revd Frank Marshall, is like the present volume the work of many hands, including that of W. H. Gwynn, the Swansea and Wales half-back of the 1880s and secretary of the Welsh Rugby Union 1892–6, who contributed a chapter on 'The Four Threequarter System'. A decade and a half later appeared one of the most profound – though, on account of the slow acceptance of its lessons by the home countries, uninfluential – rugby books ever written, Gallaher and Stead's *The Complete Rugby Footballer* (1906). Dave Gallaher and W. J. (Billy) Stead were captain and vice-captain of the legendary 1905 All Blacks whose defeat at the Cardiff Arms Park, one of the defining moments in Welsh cultural history, alone came between them and invincibility. With overtones of Izaak Walton's *The Compleat Angler* in its title, Gallaher and Stead's penetrating discussion of the game – lines of running, angles of packing, miss-moves, compiling statistics on different phases of play – brought a startlingly new technical discussion to rugby literature, raising it to a level of sophistication previously unheard of and rarely exceeded since. Yet for all their modern thinking, Gallaher and Stead had little to say about individual players. The already obsolete 'Marshall' was readier, in appropriately antique language, to identify players' characteristics: if one was 'a capital drop and sure tackler', another was 'a player whose dropping skills and powers of shoving off were deficient'. When it came to individuals, it was to the heroes of that deathless December afternoon in 1905 that Gallaher and Stead looked for their examples, so that 'the best British swerver we saw was Morgan of Wales – a thoroughly clever man' (a reference guaranteed to secure Dr Teddy a fellowship at rugby's All Souls) – for 'either a man can dodge well or he cannot and never will and that is an end of it', pure *How Green was my Valley*.

When it came to piercing the defence, according to Gallaher and Stead, 'nobody we have seen on a football field is more of the past-master in the art of cutting than our redoubtable Welsh opponent Gwyn Nicholls'. Within a few years the 'redoubtable Welsh opponent' had written his own manual, *The Modern Rugby Game* (1908), which was soon translated into French. Gwyn Nicholls was the only one of the first Welsh Golden Era (1900–11) to write a book so it is all the more disappointing that he has so little to say about the great players around him at that time. Yet in publishing at all, and in his preference for discussing practicalities over personalities, he was a decade ahead of a field that was about to be over-run with coaching books.

9

There was a reason for this sudden sprouting. The refusal of the soccer authorities, unlike their counterparts in rugby union, to abandon playing on the outbreak of war (they carried on until 1915), branded the professional association game as unpatriotic, particularly in the eyes of the middle and upper classes. These now rallied to the defence of the perceived traditional values of amateurism, selflessness and loyalty which they believed were best upheld in the public schools and embodied in rugby football. As a result, and from motives that were more social than sporting, the post-war years saw a pronounced swing by scores of minor public schools (and the larger, socially ambitious grammar schools that copied them, like Cardiff High School) towards the adoption of rugby as their main winter game. This was reflected at the international level by the dominance of England who won four Grand Slams in the 1920s, their stranglehold on the championship broken only by Scotland whose own Grand Slam side of 1925 consisted entirely of public-school educated players. In these years a raft of former predominantly English international players, a hitherto reticent breed, were persuaded to launch into print with how-to-play rugby 'grammars'. This unprecedented flurry of instructional texts and practice manuals – by J. E. Raphael (1918), J. M. B. Scott (1922), D. R. Gent (1922), P. C. Trevor (1923), W. J. A. Davies (1923), C. J. B. Marriott (1924), L. R. Tosswill (1924), R. Cove-Smith (1925), I. M. B. Stuart (1926) and W. W. Wakefield (1927) – suggests that something like a concerted campaign was being mounted in the cause of what Hylton Cleaver called, in the title of his book of 1927, *Rugger: the Greatest Game.*

Welshmen, while they agreed that 'rugger' *was*, made no con-tribution to this ideologically driven feeding-frenzy. The very end of the decade, however, saw the appearance of one of the classics of Welsh sporting literature and of rugby writing generally. This was no dehydrated handbook but the highly readable *Rugby Reminiscences and Opinions* (1929) of the former Welsh international Rowe Harding (1901–91), as elegant as the author's play on the wing where he won seventeen caps, and as decisive as his judgments in the law courts later. His verdict on the WRU of his day, for example, would have a resonance fully seventy years on: 'There are one or two grave constitutional defects in the administrative body which controls Welsh Rugby . . . [where] a mild tyranny by second-class clubs exists.' Now, and for the first time, we are given lively vignettes, sharply but affectionately drawn, of players on the Welsh scene in the 1920s, lion-hearted forwards like Tom Parker (Swansea), Steve Morris (Cross Keys), Cardiff's Tom 'Codger' Johnson and the irrepressible Dai Hiddlestone of Hendy and the Gnoll. Here, drawn to the life, is the great Albert Jenkins, as much an idol to Rowe as he was to the Stradey faithful; and here too is the Swansea full-back Joe Rees, 'a thin, frail-looking man with curly hair and a curious habit of picking loose stones on the field and throwing them away. People who saw him shuddered when they saw a big fast wing tearing down upon him, but they shuddered for the big fast wing.'

In support of his Darwinian assertion that 'all first-class rugby players are, in a sense, freaks of nature because they have some peculiar qualities which fit them for the particular type of game they play', Rowe Harding brought a zoological eye to bear on an international gallery that resembles more a safari park than a hall of fame: Wavell Wakefield, for instance, had 'the strength of a buffalo', Scotland's Ian Smith had 'the speed and strength of leg of an ostrich', and George Stephenson of Ireland 'the swiftness and grace of a gazelle'. Harding recognized too, and earlier than most, the enormous potential of France, at that time the whipping-boy of the other countries, and he was forthright in his condemnation of the social exclusivity (which left the best players at home) and crass hooray-henryism of his fellow British Lions of 1924 who showed a blithe disregard for their hosts and their results alike.

It was twenty years before another rugby writer brought players to life with comparable verve. The *Rugby Recollections* (1948) of W. J. T. Collins (1868–1952), 'Dromio' of the *South Wales Argus*, extended over eight decades. To Townsend Collins, for whom Rodney Parade was (as it is to one of our contributors) the hub of his universe, no team would ever match the collective greatness of the invincible Newport side of the early 1890s. Read him on Arthur Boucher, read him on Tom Graham, read him especially on Arthur Gould. Even the cultivated aesthete Townsend Collins was totally unembarrassed by his admission that 'all of my life I have had a capacity of hero-worship', and sixty years after first seeing him play Gould was still 'to me the greatest Rugby footballer who ever played'.

To employ his own favourite formulation, 'one believes . . .' that the late J. B. G. Thomas (1917–97), whose interest in rugby began when as a small boy he was once lifted on to Albert Jenkins's meaty shoulders *at half-time* in a match at Pontypridd, ought to have made an exception in favour of including Gould among his *Great Rugger Players 1900–1954*. This was published in 1955 by Stanley Paul, whose list of sporting autobiographies in the 1950s reflected increased media attention, a new consumerism and a changing youth and popular culture; reverently shelved copies of Bleddyn Williams's *Rugger My Life* (1956) and Trevor Ford's *I Lead the Attack* (1957) bear well-thumbed testimony to a burgeoning interest in sports literature on the part of two of the present editors schooled in that decade. Before his later descent into repetition, cliché and self-parody, the indefatigable J.B.G. was able to draw on his deep love and already encyclopaedic knowledge of the game to write with vigour and enthusiasm about the exploits and occasionally the personalities of 'great rugger players' like Stoop and Corbett of England, Bannerman and Wilson Shaw of Scotland, Clinch and Crawford of Ireland, as well as, naturally, the Welshmen who make up a third of the book. This agreeably devotional 'lives of the saints' approach was soon taken up in the wider rugby world by A. C. Parker, *Giants of South African Rugby* (Cape Town, 1955) and many others down to Joseph Romanos' *Famous Full-backs* (Auckland, 1989) and *Famous Flankers* (Auckland, 1990) – only a New Zealander would dedicate entire works to those specific positions. The British prosopographical tradition of rugby writing, by contrast, is more inclined towards three-quarters and half-backs, like *The Great Number Tens* (1993) where Frank Keating, the nawab of nostalgia, shows the predatory instincts of an open-side flanker in capturing the fleeting essence of a pride of pivots from Percy Bush to Michael Lynagh. One of them, Cliff Morgan, anticipated this present volume (where a new attempt is made to define *his* teasing essence) by assembling a multi-authored collection called *Rugby: The Great Ones* (1970). There, the balance between backs and forwards is properly respected and the best portraits the unexpected, like Denis Lalanne's of Michael Crauste and Andrew Mulligan's of the Irish flanker Ronnie Kavanagh.

What makes for good *sports* writing, mostly, is good *writing*. That sport is a fundamental part of human aspiration, which only language can make intelligible, was intuitively grasped by that remarkable generation of American writers of the 1920s that included Ring Lardner, Grantland Rice, Damon Runyon and Paul Gallico. They wrote about boxing and baseball with, among other things – knowledge, humour, sympathy, wisdom – a style heavy in hyperbole. We are back to style. Lewis Gannett of the *New York Herald Tribune* once claimed that 'most sports writers suffer from a hyperthyroid congestion of adjectives and are dope fiends for forced similes and metaphors'. Several of the contributors to this volume are sports journalists (most of the others are an even more cynical bunch, academics). What they have in common is a care for language. One or two of them even manage to write shimmeringly about the game with something of the style and generosity of spirit with which they played it.

All the contributors have, too, a sense of sport as a mode of excellence and as social drama. They sense its meaning beyond the field of play. Sporting personalities and performances are 'texts' susceptible to varieties of readings, especially given rugby's status as a key component of Welsh popular culture in the twentieth century where it embodies some of the most meaningful constituents in the formation of our identity, personal and collective, social and national. Yet writing about sport is more than an exercise in meanings and identities. It is also about celebration, which is why so much of the most effective and evocative sports writing is often nostalgic and sometimes, as here, frankly autobiographical. That is the secret of Neville Cardus and Frank Keating, of Hugh McIlvanney and Geoffrey Moorhouse; it is what the best American writers have always grasped. Potently combined with a sympathetic but unsentimental 'then and now' approach favoured by the finest exemplars of collective sports biography, the results can be riveting. If Roger Kahn's weaving of the lives of fifteen Brooklyn Dodgers into a narrative that is as much about ourselves as about Jackie Robinson and company (*The Boys of Summer*, 1972), then David Halberstam's *Summer of '49* (1989) is next up, brilliantly capturing the same glorious era in American baseball when a war-wearied nation was transfixed by Joe DiMaggio and Yogi Berra's New York Yankees' World Series with Ted Williams's Boston Red Sox.

Each of these is a dazzling, bases-loaded homer and there is no exact rugby equivalent. In his recent *The Beautiful Team* (1998), Garry Jenkins, a Pembrokeshire writer, has tracked down the survivors of the fabulous 1970 Brazilian side that played football with such a dazzling blend of skill and spontaneity. Would not a similar retrospective portrait of the 'beautiful' Welsh rugby team of 1971 yield both a sobering human document and a contribution to the social history of Wales in the last quarter of the twentieth century? There *is*, in fact, a rugby prototype for this approach in Warwick Roger's *Old Heroes* (Auckland, 1991), in which the author, a New Zealander, explores what made the tour of his country by the 1956 Springboks so special. Though barely into his teens at the time, Roger's recollections and those of his contemporaries, older fans, sports commentators and the 'old heroes' themselves – players from both sides like Peter Jones, Tom van Vollenhoven, Don Clarke, Ron Jarden, Chris Koch and Basie Viviers – are interwoven into a compelling social profile of New Zealand at a cultural moment in its history. Warwick Roger was concerned to distil a spirit that brought his country's identity into focus. He recognized, like the writers of these essays, how heroes epitomize qualities their societies esteem; for in truth, in identifying with our sports heroes, we are really spectators of ourselves.

CLIFF MORGAN

Peter Stead

On weekdays consciousness now comes with the sudden awareness of the *Today* programme, but on Saturdays in early 1998, as for the previous eleven years, an awareness that things were special, that the day would be good, that the eagerly awaited weekend had arrived, was announced by Cliff Morgan as he introduced *Sport on 4*. His highly distinctive and utterly familiar voice was comforting, warm, intimate and above all enthusiastic. It was the weekend, a time to play or to attend sport, to listen to it or watch it, to think and argue about it and more than anything to celebrate it. Nothing in the twenty-five minutes that followed really surprised: Cliff's voice would almost break with emotion as we were asked to share the privilege of joining in reminiscence with superstars of the past such as Sir Tom Finney, Sir Bobby Charlton, Mary Peters or Rachel Heyhoe-Flint. We listened attentively and soberly as a disabled athlete explained how difficulties had been overcome and medals accrued, and almost certainly there would be an old friend, an old broadcasting 'pro' on hand who would be prompted by Cliff to evoke what was absolutely special about Aintree, Lords, Lansdowne Road, Newlands or the Melbourne Cricket Ground just a few hours before the action there was due to commence.

For some listeners and especially perhaps for some genuine sports fans this was all just a little over the top. Cynics had been known to enquire as to whether *Sport on 4* was produced by the BBC's religious programmes' unit, for the tone was that of a morning service; this was a time for testimony, for asserting the essential brotherhood and sisterhood of sport and for bearing witness to the character-building that underpins all the best athletic effort. This was no bland, easy introduction to the weekend, for with most editions one sensed that the mission was to raise a moral challenge, to make something give and even to induce a tear.

Regular listeners, however, were quite prepared to accept and even indulge in the programme's undoubted sentimentality and occasional mawkishness. Most true lovers of sport all too readily accept their membership of a national and even international family; nostalgia is their favourite mode and the identification and subsequent cherishing of heroes is a natural form of worship. We are what we are because we have learnt, more often than not initially from our parents and friends, that there are sporting saints, and at 9.05 a.m. every Saturday as we were reminded of Nat Lofthouse, Henry Cooper, Derek Randall, Viv Richards and Tessa Sanderson it was our membership of a communion rather than a community that was confirmed. The experience was authentic, and perhaps ultimately it was the obvious charm and sincerity of the moderator that made it so. In a world of sponsorship, sporting millionaires, opportunism and cynicism Cliff Morgan was there to remind us that the essence of sporting endeavour has not changed. The spirit and ethic that we learned from The Tough of the Track and Roy of the Rovers were still unblemished. And, furthermore, although there are many sports, many codes, that spirit and ethic was common to them all.

It was the popularity of *Sport on 4* that guaranteed the commercial success of Cliff's 1996 autobiography, written in association with Geoffrey Nicholson and very revealingly subtitled *Beyond the Fields of Play*. A well-established convention of the *genre* of sporting biography is an opening chapter which celebrates to the full the star's greatest moment of triumph, the career's defining moment, whether it be the Wembley hat-trick, the Melbourne double-century, the world-title fight or the Olympic gold. But Cliff's first chapter graphically recounts how 'at a stroke everything changed'. In 1972 he suffered a serious stroke which led to a lengthy period of convalescence and rehabilitation at hospitals in Germany and England. He concedes that his reputation and contacts brought distinct advantages in terms of the quality of treatment, but what one remembers from this chapter is the shocking extent of physical damage (he needed extensive therapy to ensure the recovery of physical co-ordination and speech) and the extent to which a prominent freelance broadcaster could be seriously embarrassed by such an interruption to his means of livelihood. Cliff was not insured and his wife had to borrow money from the family to fly to the hospital in Germany. A body and a career had to be rebuilt.

A note explains that the book's front-cover illustration of the author shows him at a rugby international, but the portrait is not of a player but rather of the later personality, the middle-aged man in tweed cap and riding mac, the man who recovered from a stroke and who, against all the odds and to the surprise of many, was able to pick up the pieces of his career as a television producer and go on to greater things. Before his stroke he had edited *Grandstand* and *Sportsview* for the BBC and the Rediffusion current affairs programme *This Week* for ITV; now he was to become BBC's Head of Outside Broadcasts, responsible not only for major sporting occasions such as the Olympics but also royal funerals and weddings. All great sporting heroes have to redefine themselves when their playing days are done but Cliff had to do it twice. It was this added dimension that made him into more than just a sporting celebrity like the many other athletes who had either joined him or followed him as a team member on *A Question of Sport*. Twice he had to justify himself as a professional television producer, and it was the tenacious way in which he did this that enabled him to establish a degree of authority as an exemplar of what organized sport means in our culture. Very appropriately, illustrations in his book show him displaying his prestigious decoration outside Buckingham Palace and on other occasions enjoying the company of Lord Tonypandy, Sir Anthony Hopkins and Sir Geraint Evans. The presenter of *Sport on 4* had undoubtedly become an institution.

All of this was made possible because Cliff Morgan was once a very good rugby player. There were some who thought that his rugby prowess was the sole cause of his rise in the world of broadcasting, and Cliff himself willingly concedes that there were jealous and disgruntled colleagues who had thought that there were others with better credentials. Certainly it was rugby that brought him to prominence, and it was rugby that also confirmed and developed many other qualities which he came to appreciate as essential to success in his new career. On the field of play itself he had always shown that urge and ambition to do just that little bit extra, not just to ensure victory but to give the spectators something special to treasure. And both before and after the game he would display a clear need to play a distinctive role in pleasing team-mates and confirming their essential *esprit de corps*. At the core of the performance there was this imperative to be a personality, a tenacious professional and yet an entertainer, a mood-setter, a facilitator, a catalyst. Perhaps his skill, energy and charm would have made him a star at any time and in any place, but in this case one is tempted to suggest that this phenomenon of the sporting hero with distinct and remarkable social and communication skills, not to say a national sense of purpose, came about because Cliff Morgan played the very singular and idiosyncratic game of rugby football in a particular place at a particular time.

In the British Isles of the early 1950s an age of austerity was gradually giving way to an era of consumerism and comparative affluence. The Tories were sanctioning enterprise and the accession of a new, young queen had prompted thoughts of a second Elizabethan age. In time, something called youth was to create its own culture, but for the moment full employment breathed life into the well-established pastimes of cinema-going and spectator sports. Suddenly, however, there was television, a new medium which significantly brought together economic and cultural enterprise and which in a dramatic way was prepared to highlight and celebrate cultural significance. In what was dubbed the 'Royal Year of 1953' we all knew about Hillary and Tensing on Everest, of Stanley Matthews winning what would always be *his* Cup Final and of how the last glamour boy of the pre-television age, Denis Compton, had survived long enough to win the Ashes at the Oval. In that same year Cliff Morgan was playing at outside-half for Wales and he, as much as Matthews and Compton, was a hero for his time. In a very perceptive and memorable passage the journalist John Billot talked of how 'the fifties brought Britain back to life' and of how in Wales Cliff Morgan, 'Mr Magic', was an essential part of that process. Courtesy of television and of the place that sport had been given within the culture, that magic was appreciated in Britain as a whole.

As a child I grew up in the 1940s in a home where the radio was a constant companion, an arbiter of family routine, and where soccer dominated the conversational agenda. In the early 1950s one became aware of other possibilities: I discovered television and rugby at the same time. A year or so before the Coronation it was reported that there were two or three people in our fairly large town with television sets capable of receiving pictures from somewhere called Sutton Coldfield. One Saturday I was taken to one of those homes to see my first television programme, a rugby international, Wales v. France. What I remember best were the excited crowd scenes at the end. Soon I was at grammar school and had to come to terms with rugby's prime place in the new scheme of things. Within the red brick wall that defined the school there was a huddle of old buildings and the rugby pitch, the two halves, really, of one world. 'Is that where the First XI play?' I stupidly and pushily asked the track-suited PE master. 'First XV, lad', he contemptuously replied. Soon the men (as I saw them) of that XV were my heroes, especially when they defeated a touring South African side. Soon too that PE master, who during games walked the touchline bellowing the advice 'Tackle low, school', was placed firmly in a context that invited us to broaden our horizons. He was Haydn Morris who played on the wing for Cardiff. We all took pride when it was announced that he would succeed the great Ken Jones in the Welsh team. On television we saw him score a winning try in Paris with a leap which, commented another teacher, Gwyn Thomas, 'almost brought him home to Barry'; and some of us were in the gym when he received the telegram informing him that he had been picked for the 1955 Lions tour. Once more his leap was impressive. As a recent convert to the game I had acquired my rugby supporter's credentials in double-quick time.

The school XV, Cardiff, Wales, the Lions: the hierarchy was clear, but in all truth it was Cardiff which initially seemed the most glamorous and vital link in the chain. On living-room floors we sat or lay reading programmes, sensing the historic significance of the blue-and-black colours, learning the teams and statistics off by heart and looking carefully at each face that stared out from team photos. We realized that we were living just seven miles from the home of the best club side in the world. This was confirmed when one father came home with the programme of a game in which he had already recorded that on that day Cardiff had beaten the All Blacks. After that we returned even more eagerly to our collection of programmes. One photo always stood out: in the souvenir programme of Cardiff's 75th Anniversary game against the recently returned 1950 British Lions side there was a photograph of Cardiff's own representatives on that Lions tour. For all the world Rex Willis, Jack Matthews, Bleddyn Williams, Billy Cleaver and Cliff Davies look like a complete team in themselves: they stand (all much the same size and height whatever their position) with the confidence of gentlemen, some with hands in pockets, Bleddyn holding the ball, not unlike a group of army officers who have just won a regimental tournament in Penang.

From the start the streets of Cardiff had impressed ('Just like London', my mother reported) and now we came to appreciate how those streets led to Cardiff Arms Park, not just a rugby ground but an imperial port of call, a key fortress in Britain's strategy of global control. The old North Stand was the dominant structure which announced that this was an important place, especially as glimpsed in profile from the Gwyn Nicholls gates at the bottom of Quay Street. Straight away we related that stand to the other buildings in Westgate and St Mary's Streets, to the hotels and clubs in particular, and we noted the way that men in overcoats and suits with college scarves and pipes passed readily from the stand into an exclusive civvy street. Cardiff Rugby Club was different from almost everything else in our south Wales lives; it had style, confidence and urbanity; it belonged to the world of affairs; there was something almost parliamentary and governmental about it. I doubt if at that time we would have used the word 'establishment', but we never doubted that this was the most important place in Wales, a defining institution. Yet for all its grandeur we could see that it was a club that drew its sustenance from the towns and villages of the hinterland. Cardiff even took two players from our town: our PE master played on the wing, and their hooker, Geoff Beckingham, we saw every day cycling to work in local parks and gardens. Now, as rugby programmes expanded and television coverage became fuller, we all became more interested in the personalities of the game and their backgrounds, more aware of how village boys were being offered the chance of stardom, first for Cardiff and then for Wales. Enter Cliff Morgan, who seemed to constitute, as Dai Smith and Gareth Williams have suggested 'an amalgam of the social and cultural forces that had shaped modern Wales, and of the currents that were defining Welshness anew in the second half of the twentieth century'. In short he was a working-class, grammar-school educated, Noncon-formist, music-loving, home-loving boy from the Rhondda who travelled by bus to Cardiff to play at outside-half for the most famous team in the world. It was a wonderful opportunity and Cliff had made the most of it.

He was not initially the star of the Cardiff team. As we have seen, it was a team bursting with talent, but one always ready to recognize a presiding genius. Scrum-half Haydn Tanner was the gaffer in the immediate post-war era and then that 'Prince of Centres' Bleddyn Williams became 'both the rugby brain and the crowd pleaser of Cardiff's greatest years'. In all his writings Cliff Morgan was to make clear that his whole career was made possible by the way in which he was brought on in a team that was shaped by Bleddyn's sense of what rugby was about. Tanner and, even more, Williams, the Denis Compton of Wales, were household names in rugby clubs but they were never really national personalities. Williams, having captained both Cardiff and Wales to victories over the All Blacks in 1953, played his last game for Wales in 1955 and somehow just missed the phenomenon whereby rugby internationals became more prominent in the nation's sporting calendar. The star-studded nature of the Cardiff team meant that the contribution of every player was greatly valued; the outside-half was there as the link between the pack and the scrum-half on the one hand and the brilliant three-quarters on the other. There was another tradition, however, and perhaps the time had come for it to be revived. The notion that Wales could produce outside-halves (or fly'a'ves in pub parlance) of genius who in the twinkling of an eye could win a game had been well established in the 1930s by the rivalry between Swansea's elusive Willie Davies and Cardiff's thoroughbred sidestepper, Cliff Jones. In the post-war world the search was on for a successor to that tradition. In his brilliant analysis of fly-half play Alun Richards has made clear his admiration of Pontypridd's Glyn Davies, a classic breaking matchwinner whose short international career suggested (both to Alun and Cliff Morgan) that he was the most naturally talented of all Welshmen in that position. Cardiff's Billy Cleaver, a safer but less spectacular tactician was now normally the man in the number- 6 shirt for Wales and this led to the general notion that Cardiff players were always highly favoured by the selectors and that at half-back it was always best to have a club pair. In that sense there was an inevitability about Cliff's initial selection for Wales. Rex Willis was a great, powerful scrum-half, successor to Tanner, and quite naturally he took his stand-off into the Welsh team with him. As Alun Richards has explained, the Welsh love to argue about fly-halves and every village and every individual fan will have a favourite son. Cliff was good, that was clear, but there were equally good players with other clubs: Carwyn James at Llanelli, Bryan Richards at Swansea and Roy Burnett at Newport. The point is that Cliff was playing in a context, but he sensed his chance and he had the determination and the personality to rise above it. He breathed new life into what then was the number-6 position, encouraging once again the thought that this was the quintessential Welsh position, and in the process he became, as the international programmes always pointed out, 'the greatest personality in British rugby today'. Consciously Cliff was wanting to emulate and surpass Ireland's Jackie Kyle, undoubtedly the star stand-off of his day. From the moment Cliff had claimed the succession everything seemed right in the world of Welsh rugby, for it can be argued that fans in the Principality only feel comfortable with themselves if they can boast of fielding the best outside-half in the world.

Cliff's remarkable presence on the field of play and his demonstration that the Welsh were entitled to expect that something extra from their outside-half has not surprisingly inspired some of the finest writing about rugby. Smith and Williams memorably captured him as the 5'-7" Celtic terrier 'with the ball held at arm's length in front of him, his tongue out almost as far, his bow legs pumping like pistons, eyes rolling, nostrils flaring and a range of facial expressions seldom seen north of Milan'. Writing more or less at the same time Alun Richards, too, referred to La Scala-like facial expressions and the impression Cliff gave of 'playing whole teams on his own'. For these authors, then, the Cardiff outside-half was a classic example of Gwyn Thomas's assertion that 'Welshmen are Italians in the rain' although, for me, Cliff's facial and body language owed more to the souk than the opera house and I am sure I have seen his twin selling camels in Tunisia. In one action portrait taken in South Africa such is his agonized grimace that it is surprising that the shot was not reproduced on Amnesty International posters. Alun Richards recalled his 'aggrieved stance' and 'accusing stare at a late tackler' and I can confirm this; on the occasion of his last international I stood just ten yards from him and his sharp, angry stare frightened me more than it did the retreating French forward. But the anger was all part of the show, of the restlessness, of what his great successor Barry John remembered as a repertoire of 'moving, twisting, turning, thinking with or without the ball'. There is a purely rugby explanation of his behaviour, for every cell in his body was partaking in the process of seeking an advantage, of twinkling to some effect, but equally Cliff was just being himself for off the field too he was rarely in repose.

He was a small man from a humble home in an undistinguished village above the Rhondda but Welsh homes, like Welsh chapels and Welsh schools have a way of encouraging, of prompting and of 'spoiling' any of its own whom they take to be special. In particular, they indulge those who have the capacity to entertain, those who have the gift of making any occasion, whether it be a concert, a religious service, a match or even a pub conversation, into something memorable. Live-wires displayed a constant stream of vocal, facial and emotional responses for the audience whether it be at home, in the chapel and the choir, at school and in the village that lived so much of its life on the street. All the while schoolteachers were paid to identify and channel various energies. Soccer was Cliff's first love but he qualified for the grammar school and in any case was probably too stocky to be as good a player as his father. Then it had to be scrum-half or outside-half; too small and probably too much the show-off for the former so the number-6 shirt it was. Meanwhile, of course, before and after games any team needs a joker, a catalyst, an entertainment manager just as much as any family or choir. The energies that had been given free rein in Trebanog were well suited for the rugby clubs in Cardiff and Ireland, for Wales and above all for the British Lions. Cliff was always the man for the sing-song, providing piano accompaniment and all the words, the man for the joke and the anecdote and, most indispensably in a group, the man who could spot immediately the mythic in any colleague: 'the marvellous Tony O'Reilly', 'the one and only Tom Reid', 'the unforgettable Stan Bowes'. And one thing about young men who are licensed to set themselves up as special entertainers is that there is little pressure on them to become cynical; boyish innocence, moral convictions, personal values and most of all enthusiasm and expectations of pleasure can be retained.

Cliff has been deservedly well-served by his chroniclers and also by his photographers. My all-time favourite rugby photograph, and arguably it is one of the best ever taken, is Pat Smith's shot, used as a cover illustration by Vivian Jenkins for his *Lions Rampant*, of the bald-headed Springbok flanker Basie Van Wyk resigning himself to the fact that Cliff is about to score a vital Test match try; in the background is the huge Ellis Park crowd. The photograph records one of the most celebrated and important tries in rugby history and in the process it captures all the tension, atmosphere and sheer sense of occasion of a major Test match (the 95,000 in Johannesburg's great stadium was a record) even as it classically defines the essential pleasure that a stand-off is there to provide. Ultimately what is best in rugby is the out-of-the-blue stand-off break that ends with a try. And that is what Cliff's career was all about. Again, Smith and Williams are felicitously cryptic for they recalled a Cliff who 'spent his whole rugby career working endlessly for an extra yard of space'. Someone who often tried to deny him that space was the Swansea flanker Clem Thomas who accompanied Cliff on that 1955 Lions tour and who was subsequently to remind readers that in those days before the rules were changed flankers 'had a licence to kill outside-halves' for 'it was legally possible to arrive at the outside-half before the ball by taking a flyer as the ball came out of the scrum'. For Clem it was Cliff's 'vitality and effrontery' which allowed him to flourish even in an age of flying flankers. Cliff must have been tackled in every match, but photographers preferred their man in space and that is why their collective work allows him to thrill us even now. In shot after shot we see him in the space that he has earned, his opponents well and truly 'frozen', as much by surprise as by the camera, whilst Cliff, gasping with anxiety, is still quite obviously on the move. My favourite example of the *genre* is the *Western Mail*'s photo of the Dublin game in 1952; Cliff looks not so much as if he is making a break but rather as if he has stolen the ball and is running home with it. Has the rugby ball ever been clutched so tightly? 'It's my ball, so there! You're not having it!'

Of course Welsh rugby fans are parochial; it is usually a matter of nostalgia and loyalty as well as a deep distrust of power structures. We all saw a better quality rugby at our old schools than has ever been served up since; our deepest loyalty is to our first village clubs; we all know of truly great players whom blind selectors ignored and there are teams either from across the border or from ten miles down the road that we want to see smashed whatever the circumstances. But we have standards too: we hate to see 'caps' given away and we have never doubted that selection for a victorious Lions Test side is the greatest honour the game can bestow. The 1955 Lions were my first Lions. I fully identified with them from the moment I shared in Haydn Morris's joy at his selection. For the first time too there were television newsreel pictures and we could all share the drama as an epic series was shared two tests each. The Lions won the First Test in Johannesburg 23–22, a game universally regarded as one of the finest ever, and the Third Test in Pretoria 9–6. These were both great team efforts but what we remembered was that at Ellis Park in front of a crowd of 95,000 Cliff had, in the words of Vivian Jenkins, 'three times bamboozled the home defence with lightning outside breaks', one of which led to that photogenic try, whilst at Loftus Versfeld, in what was largely a tactical low-key game, Cliff had been masterful and what is more he had captained the side. One South African cartoon had an old Boer arguing with a Lions fan and offering a deal: 'You give us Cliff Morgan and we'll give you back Simonstown'. For South Africans Cliff was 'the General'. This confirmation of our own Welsh stand-off's place at the very top, or indeed heart, of world rugby, did more than anything to make the game a truly national one in a new era when television and radio were combining with affluence to create a fuller, more inclusive, sense of Welsh identity. Rugby was no longer a sub-culture: speculation about selection, the weather and result was on everyone's lips. Expectations, not to be fulfilled immediately, were now enormous. When Cliff announced his retirement from international rugby in 1958 such was the debate that there should perhaps have been a referendum to choose his successor.

There is always a 'Cliff' story: 'he could stretch them', commented Danny Davies. When he went to South Africa, Cliff relates, he was on unpaid leave from his job but 'Mamie collected coins in a glass jar' and that helped to defray expenses. Cliff, even as the greatest personality in British rugby was always an amateur, and from the perspective of the 1990s it is almost shocking to read of the sacrifices that leading players had to make in those days and how perfunctorily they were treated by officials. But that was all part of the very appeal of the game in the 1940s and 1950s: rugby union football was an Imperial game played by gentlemen and even though its audience was growing appreciably and more and more men and women were becoming expert in the game, its ethos, its culture, really had all the intimacy and style of a club. As a working-class grammar school boy Cliff had set out on the ladder that would earn him full membership of that club. There was one slip up; he failed his exams at Cardiff's University College and there had to be a change of plan. A career had to be forged in industry. Undoubtedly, it was his year learning how to make and sell wire rope in Ireland that gave him the independence to succeed as an executive in any walk of life, whilst at the same time it was the informality and sheer human quality of Irish rugby that confirmed his passion for and his ability to express all that is socially best in rugby. He was ideally suited to represent the sheer wholesomeness, and indeed fun, of the one club that all international rugby really comprised. As a stand-off he stood between the big men and the fast men, and similarly as an articulate extrovert factory manager who could play the piano, carry a tune and pull a leg, he was ideally placed to bring together in laughter the school-teachers, farmers, salesmen, doctors, steelmakers and policemen with whom he had to share so much time. That social secretary's job he did for the 1955 Lions, and is precisely what he went on doing at 9.05 a.m. every Saturday morning for many years until Radio 4's misguided and unnecessary overhaul. What Cliff had uniquely offered was sporting fellowship.

Cliff was my first Welsh outside-half and everything about his being in post seemed right to me. 'Rhondda coal, Cardiff's gold', someone has said; this was the mainstream: Trebanog, Tonyrefail Grammar School, Westgate Street Cardiff, Ellis Park Johannesburg was Route 1 and Cliff had carried the ball two-handed all the way. Both the young Barry John and Phil Bennett had made a point of looking at him carefully when he visited Stradey Park: Barry noted that he was 'pure box-office', whilst for Benny he was 'the first twinkling super-star in my experience'. Clifford Isaac Morgan, more than anyone, had helped launch rugby into a new era of popularity, whilst unknown to him he was pointing some talented youngsters the way to what would be the most golden of all Welsh rugby eras. Forty years after his retirement he was still deservedly a public figure, still the best-known voice in rugby, and if the tone of that voice was just a little nostalgic then perhaps sport today is not quite as wholesome as it was in his day.

CARWYN JAMES

Gareth Williams

'A riddle wrapped in a mystery inside an enigma.' A lover of Chekhov and Gogol, one who had learned their language, Carwyn James was doubly qualified to appreciate Winston Churchill's verdict on the Soviet Union. For whatever insight he had gained into the Slav soul from his reading of the Russian classics, no one outside his immediate family can claim to have penetrated let alone understood the complexity of Welsh rugby's philosopher-king, 'a legend to all those who did not really know him', in the words of his friend and biographer Alun Richards, 'but at the same time a mystery to those who did'.

His entire upbringing and career are riven with unexpected ironies and colliding contradictions. The youngest of the four children of Annie and Michael James, he was born in November 1929 on the edge of the western coalfield of south Wales in the village of Cefneithin, and raised in a solid semi-detached stone house not in a terraced row of miners' cottages, although that was his father's occupation. The family roots, however, were in south Cardiganshire from where just prior to Carwyn's birth they had migrated, in the secluded hamlets of Beulah and Rhydlewis whose inhabitants had provided the much-vilified Caradoc Evans with the material for his lurid stories about the cunning, avaricious and lustful peasantry of Nonconformist rural Wales. Carwyn, by contrast, young and easy under the apple boughs on his summer holidays there, ran green and carefree through what were to him Elysian fields of unalloyed joy and spiritual refreshment. They were soccer fields too: the young Carwyn played for Rhydlewis in the Cardiganshire League and was offered a trial by Cardiff City, for rugby was the game of the proletariat of industrial south Wales, and hardly an identifying characteristic of the rural parish of Troed-yr-Aur. His later serious study of Welsh literature, notably of the poet Gwenallt who celebrated that proletariat before making the reverse move from the industrial Swansea Valley to pastoral Carmarthenshire, reinforced his deep affection for that older, more tranquil dispensation, peopled by a pious, literate Welsh-speaking *gwerin*, the bedrock of a well-ordered, civilized society that was at once democratic and firmly structured. The search for a similarly patterned perfection, as elusive in the playing of rugby football as it was unattainable in the living of life itself, informed Carwyn's thinking and whole outlook; his quest for a glimpse of it took him from the ferned hills of the Edenic Welsh countryside to the classic slopes of Stradey and on to the pitiless paddocks of Carisbrook, Dunedin, and Eden Park, Auckland.

If an essentially conservative world-view underlay Carwyn's pursuit of excellence, it was the democratic egalitarianism of his upbringing that impelled him in the late 1960s to fight the National Coal Board in the courts on behalf of silicosis sufferers like his father. Nothing gave him greater pride than to lead the Welsh Lions, most of them like himself products of the coalfield, on stage at the 1971 Porthcawl Miners' Eisteddfod to the acclaim of the large audience whom he then enthralled by reciting from memory a substantial section of Cynan's evocative description of a rugby international, 'Y Dyrfa' (The Crowd). It was, nevertheless, an untypical mining household which took the *Daily Express* and where the children called their parents by their Christian names.

The language of everyday life in and outside the home was naturally and unselfconsciously Welsh. It is a commonplace that the 'best' spoken Welsh – that is, the purest, most idiomatic form of the language, uncontaminated by English borrowings and insertions – is to be found on the borders of north Carmarthenshire and south Cardiganshire. It was certainly a belief to which the James household subscribed, and the children were encouraged to avoid the vulgar street patois of the Cefneithin natives in favour of the unpolluted vernacular the family had brought from Rhydlewis, and which could be revitalized by summertime return journeys.

At Gwendraeth Secondary (later Grammar) School between 1941 and 1948 Carwyn Rees James achieved precisely the kind of rounded excellence that such schools, at their best, were designed to identify and nurture. His was one of the last of those generations of Welsh secondary schoolboys who owed their confidence in public expression and their careers, like his own in education and later the media, to the competitive, performed culture in which they were reared in chapel and eisteddfod. Strongly attracted by the pulpit in his youth, a chapel secretary and deacon for much of his adult life, he might easily have been a candidate for the ministry; in an earlier age he would have been a boy preacher. But there were by now other avenues open to the recipients of the public acclaim that working-class communities proudly bestowed on their children who achieved academic distinction and sporting prowess.

At the Gwendraeth there was little he could not do, from verse recitation to writing well-crafted essays, in both languages. He was the product, too, of a society whose meritocratic cultural conventions embraced the sporting as enthusiastically as the scholastic. They were exclusive spheres to, perhaps, the sons of Nonconformist ministers, but if 'Rose Villa' was hardly a terraced house, it was not a manse either, so that by the age of eleven Carwyn was sufficiently expert at 'the table' to be invited, with parental approval, to play against a visiting world-class snooker celebrity who was giving exhibitions at the Cross Hands Welfare Hall. Carwyn's parallel scholastic progress gave the lie to the old cliché, that a crafty cue was evidence of a misspent youth. If he was bookish he was no swot, and despite, or to compensate, for his slender frame he possessed considerable athletic technique. Suddenly asked to throw the cricket ball at the school sports, he threw it nearly ninety yards.

He was a stylish cricketer, a sport for which west Walians have generally more enthusiasm than those reared in the narrower valleys to the east. He later taught cricket at Llandovery College, its spotless whites on carefully manicured grounds, like the sedate Anglicanism of the secluded environment, complementing his own innate sense of good order. In this respect snooker shared with cricket characteristics to which he was temperamentally attracted: the formal dress, the impeccable manners, the unblemished baize and sward, the restrained audience and the unobtrusive referee. Until his last self-neglectful years when the relentless claims on his time forced him to forsake the stable, structured framework that had proven to be so necessary for the effective channelling and articulation of his ambitions, Carwyn was always immaculately turned out; dapper and brylcreemed even on the training field, on tour as the *après*-match noisily wore on he remained conspicuous by his white shirt, blazer and tie, until he quietly withdrew, ready to crack the whip at a punishing coaching session the next day.

No boots were more highly polished, no jersey and shorts more spruce than those worn by the captain of the Welsh Secondary Schools

XV in 1948. For whatever his other accomplishments, in the study or the snooker hall, in the school choir or at the crease, it was Carwyn's exceptional rugby gifts that won him especial acclaim. The captain of the school fifteen (and head boy, of course) he won the first of his six schoolboy caps in 1947 under the captaincy of Clem Thomas of Brynaman and Blundells, who would also be his captain when he won his two senior Welsh caps in 1958. Hailed as 'a typical product of Welsh Secondary Schools' football, being elusive, neat, good at handling and blessed with an eye for the half-opening', the following year the pride of the Gwendraeth captained the Welsh schoolboys in every game.

Despite failing his Higher level geography (even a renaissance youth can miss a step) he took his predestined path to Aberystwyth, at that time the Mecca for all bright south Wales university aspirants, and to someone already seduced by the two diminutive giants of twentieth-century Welsh literature, Gwenallt and T. H. Parry-Williams, no other possibility was considered than the department in which they taught. When, later, Carwyn came to apply for a lecturing post he was supported by references from his two eminent former tutors at Aberystwyth, the equivalent, if he were applying for a job as a piano teacher, of having the backing of Horowitz and Artur Rubinstein. Yet neither the poets nor the pianists could get him elected onto the Welsh Rugby Union.

His career at Aberystwyth between 1948 and 1952, culminating in an honours degree in Welsh and a postgraduate teaching certificate, developed through and around a serious commitment to the students' guild, 'Y Geltaidd' (the Welsh Society) and an immersion in party politics which involved him in 1951 in a protest against the setting-up of a military camp at Trawsfynydd. This cemented a lifelong commitment to the Welsh Nationalist Party, Plaid Cymru, which acquired its most public expression when he stood as the Party's candidate at Llanelli in the 1970 General Election and captured a respectable 16.8 per cent of the poll with 8,637 votes, about the size of the average crowd at Stradey Park.

His rugby career did not immediately continue its inexorable progress at 'Aber', for the man in possession at outside-half for the College was John ('Alfie') Brace of Gowerton who shared many of his brother Onllwyn's exceptional rugby skills. Briefly Carwyn was consigned to the second team, and to a handful of games with the newly founded town club, but it was not long before the college magazine was acclaiming 'a born footballer whom one does not hesitate to put in the line of classic Welsh half-backs . . . pivot of the attack and tactician-in-chief'. In between he was exposed to the uncompromising hard knocks of west Wales league rugby as several clubs vied for his services, like the legation from Amman United who descended on 'Rose Villa' to persuade him to join 'the best and richest team in Wales'. If the broader political lesson was that what oiled the wheels of Welsh rugby was the knocking on doors, the evening visit, the active pursuit of a desired objective as opposed to passive expectation of its attainment, it was one to which Carwyn would always be resistant. His former headmaster was naturally anxious to recruit the golden boy on to the teaching staff of his old school, confident that if Carwyn were to canvass the support of one or two councillors, the post was safely his. It was an expectation that was not met; that slightly superior detachment prevailed, then and later. Carwyn would not canvass and that was that.

His comfortable survival of two years' national service in the Royal Navy with its obligatory spit, polish and punctuality, still induces sheer disbelief among those who came to know Carwyn in a later period of rumpled, nicotined disorderliness. In 1954, however, the Senior Service had its attractions for Coder (Special) James D/MX 918946. It instilled an attention to detail, encouraged a fastidious concern for personal appearance and reinforced his belief in discipline as a necessary precondition for achieving anything worthwhile. Fortunately for world peace, he was never allowed close to a gun let alone a warship, but his time was well spent perfecting his rugby skills and becoming fluent in Russian, an asset quickly utilized by Swansea when they invited Coder James to join them on their path-breaking visit behind the Iron Curtain to Romania in August 1954, though one which Llanelli were less inclined to advertise when he accompanied them to an increasingly paranoid Moscow in 1957.

After national service he taught briefly at Queen Elizabeth Grammar School, Carmarthen, just missing the young Gerald Davies who arrived there in 1957. He was now in a position to play regularly for Llanelli, whose supporters included the same young Gerald who would later remember Carwyn 'teasing opponents, almost daring them to tackle him, persuading them to go one way when he had made up his mind to go the other'. He was partnered at scrum-half, occasionally, by the equally willowy Onllwyn Brace, who recalls Carwyn as a prodigious drop-goal artist and tactical kicker with a penchant for the now obsolete grubber-kick whose unreliability was no bar to its becoming a fetish with many Welsh post-war fly-halves, but which Carwyn elevated to a fine art along with, in Onllwyn's words, 'a pass of unerring accuracy and timing'. It was with Wynne Evans at scrum-half, however, that Carwyn won the first of his two senior caps, against Australia in January 1958. Injury to Cliff Morgan – whose career ran parallel and whose more durable frame was better suited to the increasingly attritional, defensively minded international matches of the 1950s when fast-breaking, predatory wing-forwards increasingly called the tune – allowed Carwyn to drop a smartly taken goal in Wales's 9–3 victory. Carwyn identified the difference between their styles of play, the one unruffled and symmetrical, the other intuitive and undisciplined, as that between the classical and the romantic: 'I had to think carefully about what I did on the field. Cliff was different. He did everything naturally and quickly, instinctively and expertly. He was a much better player than I was . . .'.

Morgan returned for the Five Nations, but the selectors were unable to resist the all-round football skills and potent attacking threat posed by Carwyn James, and chose him at centre. The hope was to rekindle some of the fireworks seen earlier at an unofficial international (no caps awarded) in aid of the 1958 Empire Games at Cardiff when Cliff and Carwyn indulged in some bewildering interchanges of position. It was France who caused the bewilderment in March that year when Carwyn, winning the second of his two caps, was unable to make any impression on a French side winning at Cardiff for the first time. What were miracles to men from Lourdes, of whom there were seven on the field that day? 'We were outplayed', admitted Carwyn, adding prophetically 'and we all knew . . . that there was much, much more to come. It was a bad day for Wales but a great day for rugby football.'

By now he was a housemaster at Llandovery where the twelve years between 1957 and 1969 were probably the happiest of his life. It provided him with a hearth, a home and a community where his commitment to teaching Welsh literature, rugby and, in summer, cricket could attain full flowering. Things were done for him, while the hierarchical structure of the public school system and its 'houses' struck an emotional and intellectual chord. So did its amateur ethos with which he was sufficiently imbued to turn down, later, £20,000 to coach a world professional team. Had he, earlier, accepted the offer he received from Oldham Rugby League, it would have been a loss to both rugby codes. The thirteen-a-side game, whose ball-handling skills and angles of running he much admired, was hardly suited to his physique or his style; in any case, his older brother Dewi told him, the rugby league field was unworthy of an honours graduate.

Llandovery College was a different matter. There he shared, then inherited, the coaching mantle of the renowned T.P. ('Pope') Williams, master-in-charge of rugby since the early 1930s, who had exerted a decisive influence on the careers of such outstanding players as the legendary fly-half Cliff Jones and who, in the few years they overlapped, convinced Carwyn of the aesthetic as well as the practical benefits of the passing game. Whatever it owed to the inspired insubordination of William Webb Ellis (and historians are inclined to think, not much), what it did owe to older, less-organized forms of village football was its insistence on retaining possession of the ball, rather than kicking it towards the opposition. 'Pope' had been at Oxford in the 1920s when the Dark Blues' all-Scottish international back division of Wallace, Aitken, Macpherson and Ian Smith had been in their prime, and what impressed him had been the extra yard of space given the winger by the ball's fast transfer along the line. At Llandovery 'Pope's' emphatic encyclical was that it should reach the far wing 'like lightning', a doctrine which Carwyn took to heart, and which he further developed. He discouraged wingers from being tackled into touch with the ball; instead he insisted they keep it in play, which in turn meant speedy support by the flankers to recycle it, ensure continuity and switch the direction of attack. He demanded – and Carwyn the disciplinarian could demand – that all the school's teams adopted the same style, and he held coaching sessions so that the masters-in-charge of those teams got the message. 'I believe that rugby football is a dictatorship. I think there is only one man who can have the vision. Coaching can mean having a vision, seeing a pattern', he told a debriefing conference after the return of the 1971 Lions, whose success was built on the principles he expounded at Llandovery, since rugby 'is essentially a very simple game. It is a question of resolving the complexities into simplicities. This is the whole purpose of teaching'.

It requires by now as much a leap of the imagination as of the memory to call to mind how apparently impossible, and how staggering, was the achievement of the 1971 Lions. Previous Lions sides had abundant talent but indifferent management, little purposeful preparation and less idea how actually, in Colin Meads's phrase, to 'stop believing in fairy tales'. Hitherto Lions touring teams had announced on their arrival in New Zealand that they had 'come to learn', and clearly there was much *to* learn. As a result of the humiliating whitewash inflicted on the Lions by the 1966 All Blacks even the seasoned J. B. G. Thomas was 'prepared to forecast that no touring team will ever again win a Test series in New Zealand'. Carwyn, however, had been bitten early by the coaching bug: he was closely attuned to the coaching initiative taken by the Welsh Rugby Union since the South African *débâcle* of 1964. In 1967 he coached a West Wales selection captained by Clive Rowlands to a creditable performance against the Sixth All Blacks, and in 1969 he had succeeded Ieuan Evans as coach of Llanelli, the year he moved from Llandovery to a lectureship at Trinity College, Carmarthen, not only to facilitate this development but to be in a position also to bid for the post of coach to the British Lions. From the point of view of the greater freedom it allowed him, the move to the ecclesiastical foundation of Trinity College was a beneficial translation.

Many factors contributed to the Lions' record of two victories, a draw and a defeat in the Test series and an unbeaten provincial record, from the cool captaincy of John Dawes and the galactic talent at his disposal, to specific New Zealand weaknesses (early identified by Carwyn) and the mild winter which helped to camouflage the Lions' vulnerability at forward while releasing their outstanding backs. But the essential ingredient was the Lions' coach and what the *Guardian*'s David Frost called his 'percipient intellect and his tireless exuberance'. As part of his meticulous pre-tour preparation he set about compiling a dossier containing all he could find out about New Zealand patterns of play. He obtained copies of their almanacs of the previous four years to identify the strength of the various provinces, he sought the advice of recent visitors there like Don Rutherford and Ray Williams whose rugby judgement he valued, and his voracious reading included the classic account of the 1905 All Blacks tour by Dave Gallaher and W. J. Stead, who had been on it. What he gleaned above all else was the fundamental conservatism of the New Zealand game, whose fulcrum was still the Otago speciality, the ruck. Given the All Blacks' historic lack of penetration behind, the purpose of the ruck was to commit so many defenders it eventually cleared the midfield. Carwyn's approach was not to try to emulate New Zealand but to exploit the skills of his own players to stretch defences and encourage them to create *their* gaps. To counter the ruck, therefore, he concentrated on the scrum – 'Pope' too had been a great believer in strong props – to prevent the All Blacks from wheeling it so that when they eventually worked the ball out and the inside-centre took the tackle, the pack would be much nearer to support him and to set up yet another of their beloved rucks. He worked on the scrummaging of his front row and consulted the cerebral Irishman Ray McLoughlin on the intricacies of foot-placings, body positions, and the angle and timing of the shove.

Carwyn spotted from film he had watched even before the tour that New Zealand scrummaging was not as powerful as it was; it was too loose. So his main forward idea was of two scrummaging props and two flankers who were prepared to push. Ever flexible, he changed his tactics after the Second Test when, although the All Blacks were pushed back eight yards by a ferocious Lions drive, the surly Sid Going at scrum-half was still able to break the defence because the Lions back row stayed down. Since the momentum of the shove could be maintained by six forwards, for the vital Third Test Carwyn taught his flankers to disengage: the bulky and physically robust Derek Quinnell was detailed to guard the blind side, and Going's threat was neutralized. The Lions won the game 13–3, and with it the series.

Behind the scrum he sought a pattern of play that would stretch defences by the Llandovery gospel of the quick transference of the ball to the wings. This, like the execution of multiple scissors movements – dummy scissors, double scissors, six scissors! – depended for success on fluent midfield players who could give and take a pass (as Dawes and Gibson could) and on Carwyn's clinical honing of individual talent through unit skills: conventional units like the half-backs, but also unconventional ones like, for instance, the wings and full-back. 'Any player', according to one Lion, 'considered it a privilege to spend the afternoon at one of Carwyn's clinics.' This culminated in the kind of perfect team performance – glimpsed but rarely attained within the constraints of the amateur game – that was seen at its most complete in the nine-try 47–9 demolition of Wellington, a richly choreographed revelation of the imaginative possibilities of rugby as the ballet of the common man, with Carwyn as its Diaghilev, and the peerless Michael Gibson his Nijinsky.

'Every time we passed the ball down the line in practice,' wrote Barry John later, 'he would follow behind us, harrassing us, shouting "Think! Think! Think!"' This perfectly illustrates Carwyn's dual approach; the self-effacing ('As a coach my job is to get players doing the basics well') allied to the analytical ('The most important aspect of rugby football is the psychological side of it.'). It was his mastery of artful persuasion that underlay his empathy with Barry John, who as a youngster in Cefneithin had acted as ball-boy when Carwyn came out for an evening's practice. In the appalling Canterbury match in which the two first-choice Lions props McLoughlin and Carmichael were punched out of the tour, Carwyn's philosophy regarding the development of coaching people beyond the level of the conscious (that is, to a complete mastery of the skills) to the unconscious (of natural spontaneity) acquired a new meaning. He had wisely rested Barry John for that game; after twenty minutes of watching the petulant Kiwi full-back Fergie McCormick, a potential matchwinner already selected for the following week's First Test struggle to field awkward balls, Carwyn turned to Barry John and merely said 'Diddorol' ('interesting'). During a game of snooker on the eve of the Test, Carwyn casually remarked to his outside-half that he 'did not want to see Fergie again after tomorrow'. The next day Barry duly obliged by cruelly pulling the full-back from one side of the field to the other with a remarkable exhibition of diagonal line-kicking. It was the last the Lions saw of Fergie, and with him went the All Blacks' hopes of winning the series.

Carwyn's shrewd motivation of the 1971 Lions won him recognition as the world's leading rugby coach. His seduction of the media, his individual clinics and innovative training methods, his readiness to pick the brains of anybody whose brains were worth picking (unusually for a communicator, he was also an intent listener), his attention to detail as famously instanced by his phone call to the local meteorological office on the morning of the Third Test to get the wind forecast for the afternoon, his injunction to 'get your retaliation in first' (the compressing of the line-out as all eight forwards move across in concert, a physical ploy to wear down the opposition mentally) – all these became the stuff of legend.

Asked what training programme he had adopted at Eastbourne prior to departure, there was more than mischief in Carwyn's reply that 'We were very fortunate that the Four Home Unions Committee had provided us with very smart red track suits'. For Carwyn it was important that all the players were turned out in red not only for the engendered sense of well-ordered uniformity ('If the side looks good then it may well *be* good'); but because it was *red*. 'Carwyn did not just play for Wales', Barry John observed, 'he lived for it' at a level of intensity, perhaps, not felt even by 'the King' himself. Both were the products of a society and culture in which success at rugby was an entirely legitimate and socially acceptable aspiration, one which if realized brought with it acclaim and public esteem. For Carwyn, the Welsh jersey stirred an intense patriotism which was sufficiently deeply-felt and informed to exist independently of any superficial sporting success. But pursuit of that success was in no sense frivolous or somehow unworthy of either emotional or intellectual commitment. On the contrary, the game of rugby offered him the possibilities of fusing the aesthetic and the competitive which not even his love of Welsh literature could match. Alun Richards noted how, even in the late 1970s, Carwyn was invariably physically and emotionally drained after any game in which he was personally involved. If this was the case in Italy, then even more did it apply to his cherished Scarlets.

Carwyn had the measure of Ian Kirkpatrick's visiting All Blacks of 1972–3 as he had of their predecessors – their binding was too loose, he 'couldn't see the whites of their knuckles' he announced, knowingly, after their first game at Gloucester – and he applied the same techniques to defeating them once again. These were a strong front row, devices to contain them at the back of the line-out (as Mervyn Davies had done in 1971), an ability to ruck running backwards (also perfected in New Zealand the previous year), and to negate the All Blacks' favourite attacking ploy near the set-piece by instructing the last forward arriving at the ruck to stand out on the open side while the scrum-half sealed the blind; the arrival of Tom David from Pontypridd in the back row and Raymond 'Chico' Hopkins of Maesteg at number 9, both of whom relished a physical game, was central to the operation of this game-plan. The Scarlets' 9–3 victory is 'history', Macaulay's fusion of poetry and philosophy. Carwyn's Llanelli was well versed in both and even if the muse pulsed to a muscular metre that October afternoon, the careful thought behind it ('Think! Think!') was apparent to all. The All Blacks were out-thought and their confusion at an unexpectedly reduced line-out yielded the penalty that led to Roy Bergiers's try. The Llanelli midfield did not manufacture any fingertip passing that day, they made myth instead.

Carwyn thanked the Llanelli committee afterwards 'for leading Great Britain in the matter of selection by asking the coach to be chairman of the selectors and to be responsible for picking his own committee'. It was on these terms alone that he was prepared to be considered for the position of coach to the Welsh national team when Clive Rowlands's successful term came to an end in 1974. But having already been defeated in an election to one of the WRU's vice-presidencies, just as an earlier attempt to become a district representative had also failed, he could hardly have expected success this time. His essential shyness and reserve which were sometimes mistaken for unclubbability and intellect-ual arrogance were not well suited to touting for votes. It was a wilful innocence of the ways of the world, a studied *naïveté*, on the part of one who had already travelled many of them and for whom globe-trotting was to become a way of life, and death, to think he could ruck alone against a union whose own knuckles were prone to turn white with anxiety whenever he hove into view, and who, collectively, were unimpressed by his public stance against South Africa's apartheid regime, his rejection of an OBE, his linguistic zeal and his nationalist politics. It would be another sixteen years before the WRU got around to adopting the structure Carwyn suggested to them in 1974, but he would not live to see it, and by then the self-destruct mechanism of Welsh rugby as a world, even European, force was already in fast-forward mode. He did, though, see the shape of things to come in the two ominous home defeats of Wales by New Zealand (23–3) in 1980 and Scotland (34–18) in 1982.

In 1974, aware that as a coach he was unlikely ever to recapture the high plateau of the early 1970s and that, realistically, a fulfilling academic career was by now beyond him, he quit the safe haven of Trinity College for the open seas of free-lance journalism and broadcasting. He was now condemned to live constantly at the mercy of the buffeting winds of tight deadlines and inconsiderate schedules. There was to be no escape from 'the world of rugby', the title of a book he co-authored with John Reason based on a successful television series, while his laser-beam 'focus on rugby', the title of a coaching manual posthumously published to accompany yet another series, was to be directed with enhanced detachment but no loss of clarity from the press-box and studio couch.

His incisive match analyses and more reflective pieces, usually laced with literary allusion – how the disciplined Welsh style of play and the unfettered French expression of the late 1970s could be seen in contrasting terms of *cynghanedd* and *vers libre*, or how the distant sight of J.P.R., 'long hair flying in the wind, may remind us of Pwyll, prince of Dyfed, riding majestic and mysterious in the mists of the Mabinogi' – were avidly devoured in clubs, canteens and common-rooms everywhere. His standing within the game, his constantly sought-after opinion and his inability to refuse any request increasingly compromised his natural reserve. He was a private man who yearned to escape the glare of publicity. Even the two years (1977–9) during which, having earlier laid the foundations of Llanelli's five-year domination of the Welsh Challenge Cup, his unfailing Midas touch transformed Rovigo into Italian champions, were only a temporary station on his personal *via dolorosa*. Without any steadying influence and institutional framework to regulate and order his activities, his life-style became more disordered, even bohemian, aggravating an incurable skin complaint for which the only relief came from a bottle and several daily cigarette-packs. His vulnerability incited the tireless loyalty of colleagues and the devoted attention of several women friends. Like many who have poured all their energies and emotions into the male domain of rugby football and its affairs, he never married. But the struggle to contain his frustrations, anxieties and tormented sensibilities was exacting a heavy personal toll. When Alun Richards saw him in Italy in 1977 he found 'a man almost at the end of his tether'.

Time and the tether ran out for Carwyn James less than six years later. In a remarkable radio talk in 1960 he had described how as a small boy in Cefneithin he had watched through respectful curtains the mile-long men-only funeral *cortège* of a young neighbour killed underground, and how, for an instant, he had seen himself at his own funeral, 'the focal point of the emotions of the assembled multitude'. The unsettling dream became a final reality when he was found dead of a heart attack in the Kras Nabolsky hotel in Amsterdam in January 1983. By that time this most gentle, cultivated and complicated of 'rugby men' had become tired of the celebrity status, tired of the travelling, tired of the demands and the pressures, tired of his painful skin infection; tired of life. 'If you can't make the Welsh Fifteen', wrote Professor Gwyn Jones, 'translate the Mabinogion.' Carwyn James could have managed both.

BILLY BOSTON

Phil Melling

Of all those hundreds, if not thousands, of rugby players who went from Wales to the north of England and were born again in the revivalist atmosphere of rugby league, the two finest left home when they were teenagers. Both came from Cardiff yet neither played rugby union for his country. Both had Irish backgrounds and settled in a town with a history of Irish immigration stretching back to the industrial revolution. Neither player returned to live in Wales and both chose to marry and raise their families within the 'ancient and loyal' boundaries of the North. Either could have gone to another sport – Arsenal Football Club or Glamorgan County Cricket Club, or perhaps enjoyed a career in golf – and when they went to rugby league their signing caused an uproar in the press.

Billy Boston first came to the attention of the Wigan Rugby League club board through an article which Vivian Jenkins wrote for *The News of the World* in December 1952, in which he warned the Welsh Rugby Union not to repeat the mistake of thirty years earlier when it had lost Jim Sullivan to rugby league. In the sporting imagination of critics like Jenkins, Boston was destined for a place more remote than Outer Mongolia; a frozen wasteland populated by cultural Neanderthals who played a game more akin to formation mugging than one which pretended an affiliation with rugby.

Jenkins's view of rugby league is pure caricature and the kitchen-sink myths he chose to employ are hardly appropriate when discussing the careers of its finest players or its finest teams. In the 1920s and 1950s the Wigan club was one of those teams, culturally diverse and inter-nationally renowned. As early as the First World War it had sought to create a racially integrated team and its cosmopolitan style of rugby would become a continuous feature of its history, from the signing of the great All Black and Maori forward, Charlie Seeling, in 1910 to that delightful adventure with the Australian Aborigine, John Ferguson, more than seventy years later.

Northern suspicion meant little to Jim Sullivan the day he signed for Wigan in 1921 at the age of eighteen, nor did it have any measurable impact on the career of Billy Boston when he left Tiger Bay in 1953. In spite of the odd fallout – such as Boston's infamous suspension in 1956 after a disastrous cup match against Halifax – the relationship which both players had with the north of England was rock solid. Throughout their careers Boston and Sullivan were revered by Wiganers. The townsfolk named streets and buildings after them, paid homage at their pubs, and honoured and embraced them like long-lost relatives from overseas.

In the 1920s and 1930s, says rugby league historian Robert Gate, Jim Sullivan was 'the pre-eminent player of his era', a colossus who 'landed close on three thousand goals and topped six thousand points in an orgy of record-making and breaking', a record that lasted for twenty-five years. Sullivan still holds the rugby league record for goals kicked in a match – twenty-two against Flimby in 1925 – and in every season between 1921 and 1239 he kicked at least a hundred goals, 'a feat not remotely paralleled before or since'. In 1922–3 he established a league record of 161 goals and 349 points, which he extended in 1933–4 to 193 goals and 404 points. His sixty appearances in international and Test matches also remain a record as do the 160 goals and 329 points that he claimed in them. In a total of 921 first-class games he made three tours of Australasia (1924, 1928 and 1932) and was captain of Wigan in the Challenge Cup in the first Wembley Final in 1929, scoring the first points with a penalty kick. In Gate's view Sullivan was much more than a phenomenal goal kicker. 'As a full-back he was a paragon, possessing in superabundance all the skills necessary in terms of catching, kicking, tackling, positioning and bolstering the attack. He was always a model of sportsmanship and developed into one of League's finest and most demanding captains at both club and international level. When his playing days were over he proved himself one of the most successful coaches the game has seen.' At both Wigan, where he put together what Geoffrey Moorhouse regards as the finest of all rugby league sides – the Wigan team of 1947–50 – and at St Helens, where he nurtured the budding genius of Alex Murphy and Vince Karalius, Jim Sullivan was held in unparalleled respect.

If Sullivan was both hard man and family man, Billy Boston was a lyrical and charismatic genius. As a running-back Boston had the timing of a Gary Sobers, a Muhammad Ali, a Pelé, a Tiger Woods. As a rugby player he was beyond comparison in the post-war era, and in any World

XIII of the last fifty years his would be one of the first names on the team sheet. He was one of the few players from rugby union to make the game look easy and he did it by reinventing himself in a league career that lasted more than seventeen years. 'When he first came into the game', says his biographer Jack Winstanley, 'Boston was 13 stone with a nine-foot sidestep. When he left it, he was 15 stone with a nine-inch sidestep. Whatever his size it was impossible to read him. He mesmerised his opponents.' 'Fullbacks', says Winstanley, 'watched in astonishment.'

When he arrived in Wigan, Billy Boston was as fast as Martin Offiah and he had a knack of unbalancing a player and putting him on one leg. John Stopford, the ex-Great Britain and Swinton wing of the 1960s, makes the point graphically. 'He preyed on your mind', says Stopford. 'He kept you awake the night before a game, so when it came to kick off you were bog-eyed with worry.' At nineteen, Billy Boston had blinding pace, a great swerve, an ability to sidestep off either foot, an astute footballing brain and a big heart. Ten years later he still retained a tremendous turn of speed and was quick on his feet but he had also gained a fearsome hand-off and a huge muscular bulk – something he used to good effect when crash tackling his opposing centre the moment he received the ball. Boston's size made him very intimidating and, as John Stopford testifies, almost impossible to bring down (except by gang tackling) once he got into his stride. In attack and defence the effect on the crowd was electrifying. Jim Williams, who travelled each week from Manchester to Wigan, puts it succinctly: 'Billy lit up the town of Wigan in the 1950s. You have to remember what it was like. There were still coal fires, smogs, coal mines, the recovery from the Second World War, you could even pick up the tail end of the Victorian era. It was a great joy to be able to put that away on Saturday afternoon and watch this genius of a player ply his craft.'

During his career 'Billy B' scored 572 tries, a figure yet to be surpassed by any other British player and second only to the Australian winger, Brian Bevan. Boston scored 478 tries for Wigan, breaking Johnny Ring's club record by more than 100. Boston topped the league try-scoring list with sixty tries in 1956–7 and he scored more than fifty in 1958–9 and 1961–2 when again he headed the list. Billy won representative honours for Wales and toured Down Under with Great

Britain in 1954 (selected after he had played only six games for Wigan) and in 1962. On the 1954 tour he scored a record thirty-six tries, including two on his Test debut at Brisbane, and in his third Test match against New Zealand at Auckland in 1954 he ran in four tries, a figure not surpassed to date. In thirty-four internationals, including thirty-one Tests Boston scored thirty tries, a figure bettered only by Mick Sullivan, including ten against Australia, still a record.

Signed from the Royal Signals after a junior career with the Welsh 'feeder' club, Cardiff Internationals (CIACS), a crowd of some 8,000 turned out to watch his debut in the 'A' team at Wigan in 1953. In a fifteen-year career at Wigan, Boston owned the right-wing position. Eric Ashton, an immaculate centre to Boston for club and country, around whom the second, great post-war Wigan team was built, says that Boston was the complete footballer. 'No other player', he claims, 'could move so effortlessly from one position to another with no obvious loss of ability.' Whereas Boston's contemporaries, the Australian Brian Bevan and the Springbok Tom Van Vollenhoven, were great wingers, they were limited by their position. But Boston could play anywhere in the backs. He appeared at left-centre in the Challenge Cup Final of 1958 when Wigan beat Workington, and scored two tries from right-centre in the Championship Final of 1960 when Wakefield Trinity were hammered 27–3 before a crowd of over 82,000 at Odsal Stadium. When Wigan beat Oldham 8–3 in the Lancashire Cup Final in 1957 he played at stand-off. And during that year he scored twelve tries in four games from the number-6 position.

Few growing up in Wigan in the 1950s were able to escape the influence of Boston. The impact he had on the town's imagination bore testimony to its love affair with Wales, a relationship which stretched back to the time of Johnny Thomas, Tommy Howley, Sid Jerram and 'Dodger' Owens and which, in the case of my father, achieved its first romantic expression with the arrival of Danny Hurcombe from Mountain Ash. Behind everyone there was Sullivan, a sporting legend who spent thirty-one years at Central Park as player and coach.

The house in which I grew up put me on a private collision course with Wales, and Boston and Sullivan in particular. Number 120 Dicconson Street was an eyrie on the world, from where I could glimpse for the briefest of moments the private life of these two great men. I remember my brother-in-law Graham Thomas coming to the house and telling us how Jim Sullivan was looking after him. I remember his stories of how Sullivan took him to training at St Helens where he used these strips of silver paper and clean handkerchiefs to work on Alex Murphy's speed, throwing the contents of his pocket into the air, with Alex, who was no closer than ten yards away, expected to catch them before they hit the deck. It was the first time in my life I had heard anyone explain that the secret of success in rugby league was to train with cigarette papers and your Auntie Maud's Christmas present.

I wish that I had had the confidence to ask Billy Boston if the story was true when I met him in 1955, but I was eight years of age at the time and Sullivan's methods were far too complicated for a backstreet kid to put into words. Dicconson Street lies behind Wigan park and when Billy first came to Wigan he lived for a few weeks in a flat in Bridgeman Terrace with his brother, Herbert. There were 'backs' between Dicconson Street and Bridgeman Terrace, and on early summer evenings it was there that we would play cricket on the cinder path before it was paved. There were a lot of us – the Prestons, George Young, Malcolm Farrimond, Freddy Gardiner, the Aspeys and, sometimes, Billy and Herbert would join us. Billy bowled and Herbert batted. They stayed around for a week or two and then moved away. Herbert, I think, went back to Cardiff. And the word went out that Billy had 'shifted' to a place in Poolstock.

I never batted against Billy and it would be twenty-five years before I spoke to him again. At that time I was on a visit to Wigan from Swansea and an old friend, Derek Birchall, and the former British Lions wing, Johnny Stopford, invited me to the rugby league Lions Testimonial dinner at The Willows, Salford. Billy was coming as well, they said. We met at Stopford's pub and then travelled by minibus to Salford. At the dinner I sat opposite 'nasty' Jack Arkwright, a loveable old gent with a shock of silver hair; Jack had gone on the 1936 tour to Australia and had the reputation – as I later learned from Dai Davies in Garnant – as the dirtiest player in rugby league history. On the way home we stopped off at Westhoughton dog-track for a pint, and I phoned my wife who was more than eight months pregnant. By now, I was frothing at the mouth with excitement and I pleaded with her to come and meet Billy. She did and so I have a picture of Sue sitting on Billy Boston's knee with his hand on her stomach – a shot taken by Stopford who lay on the floor to get the right angle.

On that night I found Billy to be a person of great warmth and sensitivity, and I was reminded of this when I met Johnny Stopford while I was doing some research for this chapter. Johnny is one of Billy's closest friends and so I was anxious to speak to him. Unfortunately, Johnny had been diagnosed as suffering from lung cancer and he was due to undergo chemotherapy treatment the following day. Yet he did not hesitate when I told him I wanted to have a chat about Billy. 'Now we're talking', he said, and he was upstairs in a flash moving beds and wardrobe doors, banging about in the search for his programmes and Aussie souvenirs. Johnny was in a positive mood that day, all grins and bristling energy, and full of what it is to be a Wiganer. A Wiganer was something, he said, that Billy had become (a fact I was constantly reminded of by the people I interviewed over the next few weeks). I wondered what it meant to be called a Wiganer. I was one myself but had been badly corrupted by too much travelling and years of soft living in faraway places like Keele, Swansea and Baton Rouge. Johnny gave me his answer with a couple of stories.

In his view, Billy had become a Wiganer when he realized that no one in the town cared about his colour. 'I'd gone to Central Park after a spell in amateur rugby league. I played with Billy in the 'A' team before I did my national service. After I left the army I was transferred to Swinton on a "free". Cliff Evans was the coach. The first time I played against Boston was an away game. I walked to Central Park on my own and went straight into a pub near the Drill Hall and ordered two rum and blacks. I shouldn't have done it, and I never did it again, but I was scared stiff that day. It was what he was going to do to me; how much he was going to hurt me. It got no better when I got stripped off: the trainer had forgotten my ankle strap. I went looking for Maurice Hughes, the Wigan physio, to see if I could borrow one. The door of the Wigan dressing-room was open and Billy had his feet on a bench reading a comic. It was Superman. He just nodded and smiled. How I got through that match I'll never know. Billy scored a try on me but he didn't show me up. He congratulated me afterwards and we had a drink. We became good pals but it was obvious, even then, that Billy was conscious about his colour and he wanted to know what I thought of it. "I'll tell you something", I said. "Your colour doesn't bother me. I slept with two coloured lads in the army. And me in the middle. They were boxing champions." Billy asked me who were they. "Joey Jacobs from Manchester", I said, "and 'Joey' Sango from Wales." "Redfers Sango?" said Billy. "Aye", I replied. "Him who got murdered in a doorway in Cardiff." "Well, bloody hell," said Billy, "I went to school with him . . ." Then he looked at me and I could tell he knew his skin didn't bother me. I remind him of that every time I see him. "You don't look so good mate, I say?" "How's that", says Billy? "You look a bad colour", I say . . . He laughs and takes it.'

According to Jack Winstanley, Boston had an inkling he would never play for Wales because he was black. It is quite possible Boston was wrong about this and that he seriously misjudged the opportunities available to him in rugby union in the 1950s. Yet it remains a fact that until fairly recently players of colour, and black players especially, have not been willing or able to play international rugby union nor have they achieved very much.

Rugby league, though, had a different outlook on colour and Billy was aware of its history of signing coloured players: George Bennett, Alec Givvens, Roy Francis, Cec Thompson (whose autobiography, *Born on the Wrong Side*, is the finest book written about the sport). Billy's predecessors had distinguished careers in the game, yet nothing they had achieved for club or country – not even the skills of Roy Francis, who was an international wing at Wigan, Barrow and Hull – could remotely prepare the rugby league public for the explosive genius of the 19-year-old Boston. In the 1950s Boston was the Oscar Peterson of rugby league. He was the supreme entertainer. At Central Park he could play 'The Maidens of Cadiz' in a drizzle and reduce his opponents – wings, full-backs – to enthralled spectators. Yet Billy's colour was never an issue with the fans. All that mattered was his virtuoso style. Just occasionally he was called The Brown Bomber, but more often than not he was simply Billy B or Bouncing Bill.

Cec Mountford once summed it up when he described Boston as the 'blank cheque' player. Jack Winstanley agrees. 'If he came on the market today', says Winstanley, 'you'd have to pay well in excess of a million – probably two million – pounds.' 'Wigan', he says, 'made the most effort of any signing they ever made to get Boston's signature.' According to

Martin Ryan, the ex-Wigan full-back, they would have paid whatever it took, and he also notes that Wigan were ready to pay half a million to bring Wendell Sailor over from Brisbane. 'And all he does is run into people', says Ryan smiling. 'Billy ran round them. He had the feet.'

Be it Wendell Sailor today, Adrian Van Heerden in the 1920s, Green Vigo in the 1970s or Billy Boston in the 1950s, Wiganers have had a long affair with overseas wingers. They have loved their style: Springbok, Aboriginal, African, Welsh. A scan of the team lists of the 1950s and 1960s is most revealing with almost every continent, bar Asia, represented in rugby league. This seemed to suit Boston's personality and made him feel at home. It reminded him, perhaps, of the world he had left behind, the ethnic communities he had mixed with in Tiger Bay, the interracial atmosphere that drew him as a youth to the Cardiff International Athletic Club.

In the 1950s the CIACS were a cosmopolitan side formed in the heart of Cardiff's dockland with a huge range of players from many backgrounds: Greeks, Italians, Maltese, Arabs. According to Billy, they were a motley crew in coloured shirts but they helped break down ethnic barriers and gave him some of his happiest moments on a rugby field. Many of the CIACS players, like Johnny Freeman and Colin Dixon, also went North and had glittering careers at Halifax and Salford. While these players were not entirely free of prejudice in rugby league, the prejudice they did encounter tended to come from overseas; occasionally from New Zealand, and more especially in South Africa, where, on the 1957 tour, Boston was the victim of a colour bar.

If the streets of Wigan were uniformly white in the 1950s its rugby fields were not. Yet in its own way Wigan replicated the close-knit community of Tiger Bay and the raucous warmth of its streets, where Bill had been friendly with Joe Erskine and Shirley Bassey. In Ince, Wallgate, Whelley and Scholes, Billy could enter once again a tight, labyrinthine world of back-to-backs, Irish communities and rugby lovers in their pubs and in clubs like Wigan St Patricks. Martin Ryan, second only to Sullivan as Wigan's greatest full-back, is convinced that the protective, communal environment of a place like Wigan, with its extended family structure, was an ideal breeding ground for the hard school of rugby. 'It bred loyalty,' says Ryan, 'and whatever the drawbacks and the deprivation, it gave you the character to play a physical contact sport.' 'The team I played in after the war was just like a family', he adds. 'We relied on each other; shared our grief as well as our grub.' Ted Ward who played with Ryan, also made the same point when I met him in Garnant in the late 1970s. 'Our trainer was a farmer, Frank Barton. After the war rationing was still on and Frank used to give us a side of pig to share out after training.' Billy and Ted Ward felt at home in Wigan. The CIACS motto: UNIS ET IDEM, one and the same, went North with them.

There is something else in Wigan which made Billy feel at home. A mistrust of the demonstrative. Wiganers are not comfortable in the presence of exhibitionists, which is probably why they never really approved of Martin Offiah. Toughness and sentimentality are under-scored by humour: understated self-mocking, its job to deflate high-mindedness and pretension. Wiganers retain a quiet self-confidence. Not only do they know how to make the best pies, they also know how to make the best players (and in the case of Frank Collier they fed them pies). But not all players are pie-eaters and it is important that those who come to Wigan behave themselves and know what is expected of them. Green Vigo did not so he had to go. More recently Barrie McDermott suffered the same fate. So did Sean Long.

In a town where lifestyles and art styles tend to interact Billy Boston was rarely, if ever, reprimanded for his behaviour. Here was a man who lived the way he played, with humility. And Wiganers loved him for that. Billy was a showman without showing off. 'He scored his tries and there was no bloody fuss', says Jack Winstanley. He was a naturally diffident man who achieved what he did on a rugby field without undergoing a change of personality. In writing this piece I asked many of those who played with and knew Boston to rate him alongside Ellery Hanley, a player who was recently voted, by *Open Rugby* magazine, the greatest rugby league player of the last quarter century. Generally speaking, there were two reactions to my question and a subtle, if crucial, difference separates them.

The least popular view, and the one taken by Jack Winstanley, editor of *The Wigan Observer* and Boston's biographer, is that Hanley and Boston had separate, if equally compelling, skills. For him, Boston was a natural rugby player, while Hanley's genius was that of an athlete whose skills were manufactured and whose lack of natural talent was compensated by phenomenal strength, weights-room skills, and aerobic conditioning. But in Winstanley's view, Boston lacked Hanley's killer instinct and could have scored more tries had he been more ruthless. 'Boston's weakness, if he had one,' argues Winstanley, 'was that he picked his games; Hanley didn't. Every game for Hanley was a cup final in which he played as if his life depended on him breaking a record. Boston never took the game as seriously as Hanley. He didn't train as well. He didn't have the same grim determination; the same gangster seriousness. He didn't look as mean.' Joe Egan, who describes Boston 'as the most perfect rugby player', agrees with Winstanley. He insists that with a little more effort Boston could have broken the most tries in a season record, and that personal records were of little interest to him. Hanley was different. In Winstanley's opinion, Hanley was the best finisher of all time because he wanted to score tries every time he touched the ball. 'Boston, when he was against weak opposition, wasn't interested.' 'He once told me,' says Winstanley, 'I don't like hurting little lads who are not as good as me. Hanley would never have said that. Billy didn't need to tell anyone how good he was. Hanley had to. Hanley was a clean player, but he enjoyed giving little lads a drubbing.'

The more popular response I got to my question came from ex-players like Martin Ryan and John Stopford, both of whom claimed that Boston's lack of ball hunger was a myth. Instead, they stress Hanley's limitations and argue that Hanley was not a rugby player at all. According to Stopford, he was a fit athlete who could not pass a ball. Hence the reason for the 'crab-like' style and the long arcing runs to the line. Hanley was a receiver not a passer, a terminal player not a creative one. This is the reason, so it is said, why Graham Lowe, Hanley's coach, moved him to loose-forward. The emphasis that Stopford and Ryan place on Hanley's style might seem churlish, given Hanley's contribution to the success of Wigan during its golden period: his try-scoring achievements, indestructability, coolness under pressure, leadership qualities, will to win. Who cared if he ran sideways if he could score forty and fifty tries a season, which he did with some regularity, at both stand-off and loose-forward? Or if he could top the tackle count? So what if he was unorthodox? Isn't that what Wiganers claim to look for? The impromptu wit of a Henderson Gill, the mercurial brilliance of a John Ferguson.

The real problem for those who stress Hanley's limitations has nothing to do with his nonconformity on the field, and the people who are critical of him know this as well as anyone. The real problem with Hanley, is that, unlike Boston, he did not play like a Wiganer nor did he act like one. Hanley was considered by some to be anti-social and ill-mannered, his behaviour a kind of implied critique of the relationship that Billy accepted between player and fan. To them, he was too self-regarding, which is why he had to leave Wigan, or wanted to leave Wigan, before his time was up. Billy became part of the family, while Hanley was a loner with an iron will. You could see it, say his critics, in the way Hanley followed play around . . . in the way he took the last pass.

Whether or not it was a weakness, Billy Boston managed to resist the last pass; he could leave it alone. He did what was needed, and he was more than willing to share his tries with his centre partner, Eric Ashton. Hanley appeared to snub Wigan; he seemed unwilling to let the town love him, when all it wanted was to box him up and stroke him like a pet. Hanley was too cool for all that. He was an 80s man. He had Thatcherite values whereas Billy was old Labour – game for an outing on the St Pat's 'away' coach. Ellery Hanley played for Wigan. Billy Boston became Wigan. Boston brings to mind Garrison Keillor's Lake Wobegon's code from his novel *Wobegon Boy*: 'Do your job, don't tell lies, don't imagine you're exceptional even if you are, be glad for what you have done, don't feel sorry for yourself.' Once in Australia, in 1954, Billy let rip: 'I wish Australians wouldn't make such a damned fuss of me', he said. 'I've been lucky. I've got a long way to go. I've got the tries. But they were laid on for me by better players than I am. I hope the Australians will drop this attitude of wanting a spectacular show from me every time I play.' Jack Winstanley, Billy's biographer, makes the point clearly: 'Billy had a nice smile. He liked kids. He had a great degree of humility about him. That's why he was asked to open church bazaars and crown rose queens. Wiganers took to Billy Boston as a person, they didn't take to Ellery Hanley, because Hanley wasn't like-able. It's as simple as that. He wasn't friendly. We hardly ever saw him. Boston stayed on his doorstep, whereas after a game Hanley took off.'

In 1996 a joy-rider hit Billy Boston outside his home in Poolstock. Billy suffered serious leg injuries. Sentencing the young offender the magistrate placed him under a curfew order. 'I'm doing this for your own good', he said. 'There are people out there who are very unhappy with what you've done. If there's one person you don't knock down in Wigan, it's Mr Boston.' Billy, who was inundated with flowers and get-well cards, was in hospital for a few weeks. The car was a write-off.

I am grateful to all the people in Wigan with whom I discussed these matters, and especially Jim Williams, Martin Ryan and John Stopford (who died in August 1998) with whom I recorded interviews. Absolutely indispensable was Jack Winstanley's *The Billy Boston Story* published in 1963 by *The Wigan Observer*.

DAVID WATKINS

Chris Williams

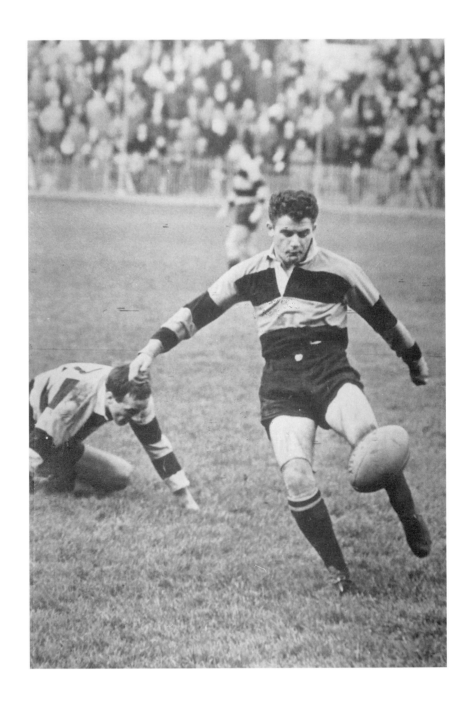

Passing, kicking, running and handling, tackling and speed of thought and action are all vital to the successful outside half. The one man who has all these attributes and who must surely be the best fly-half the world has known is David Watkins, of Newport.

Richard Sharp

It is 5 February 1966. At Cardiff Arms Park, Wales are playing Scotland in windy conditions and on a muddy pitch speckled with pools of surface water that, according to one journalist, looks like the recently photographed surface of the moon. At half-time Wales hold a slender 3–0 lead, but in the second half they face into a stiff, gusting wind. Twenty minutes from time, Wales win a scrum a dozen yards from the Scots' line at the Taff end, and five yards in from touch on the right-hand side of the pitch. The ball rattles back through the feet of the Welsh forwards and Allan Lewis, diving from the base of the scrum, rifles a pass to outside-half David Watkins, who is already moving on a forward diagonal towards the Scottish posts. Watkins takes first the ball, and next, two steps, directly at his opposite number Jock Turner. Then, seemingly without regard for the treacherous surface, he accelerates, scampering on a slight arc to the left and drawing his body away from his would-be tackler's grasp, at the same time cutting behind the Scottish centres, and leaving the covering back row trailing in his wake. With this furious burst Watkins has torn open the Scottish defence. Hinshelwood, the Scottish right-wing races across to tackle him in a desperate attempt to smother the attack, but just before he arrives to knock the Welshman to the ground, Watkins slips a pass out to his centre Ken Jones who, with two Welsh backs on hand in support, needs neither as he dives across left of the Scottish posts. The try converted, Wales go on to win the game 8–3.

'DAZZLING DAVID WATKINS SHATTERS SCOTS' HEARTS' ran Monday's headline in the *Western Mail*. Bryn Thomas lauded Watkins as 'the hero' of the side, 'the dominating personality behind the scrum

. . . the general who controlled affairs to ensure that the valiant work of an outstanding pack was never wasted'. Others praised his ability to skid and skate over the wet surface 'as if powered with an outboard motor', and to perform manoeuvres that reminded observers of, variously, a duck, a water-skier, and a telemark. The greatest accolade was that he was 'the equal of Cliff Morgan in the same mood and in the same conditions'. Playing what was probably his best game in a Welsh jersey, David Watkins had joined the ranks of the immortals.

David Watkins was born on 5 March 1942, the first child of Doreen and Jack, at Blaina in the valley of the Ebbw Fach, Monmouthshire. Blaina's origins, a century earlier, had been in the iron industry, like those of its northerly neighbour Nant-y-glo, but by the 1880s iron was in decline and had been superseded by coal. Immediately following the end of the Great War, at the height of the coal industry's prosperity, more than three-quarters of working men in the Nant-y-glo and Blaina area (total population 17,000) had jobs in mines such as the Griffin (employing around 1,800 men), Henwaun and Lower Deep (employing 1,400), and the Rose Heyworth (employing 2,700) where Jack Watkins worked for thirty years. In the two industrial counties of Glamorgan and Monmouthshire, Nant-y-glo and Blaina Urban District's employment structure was at that time the one most heavily dominated by coal. It was also one where men formed nine-tenths of the work-force, and where very few married women indeed went out to work. It was predominantly working class in social composition, English in language, Labour in politics, and Nonconformist in religion, and in many other respects was a typical coal-mining community.

The 1920s and 1930s had been extremely difficult decades for Blaina. Following the industrial dispute of 1921 seven out of the nine local collieries had closed down, throwing thousands of men out of work. With no other industries to take up the slack, unemployment rose to horrifying levels (44 per cent in 1937), at least 5,000 people left the area altogether, and Blaina took its place in 'a melancholy line of semi-derelict communities' along the Heads of the Valleys road between Merthyr Tydfil and Abergavenny. By the 1930s it was being regularly visited by journalists, politicians, and medical specialists all keen to witness the impact of depression on a once-vibrant mining settlement. Aiming to survey Blaina 'as truthfully and penetratingly as if [he] had been inspecting an African village', Philip Massey arrived in 1937 and repeated the observation of the local Medical Officer of Health that, to the eye at least, it was 'a dreary scattered wilderness of colliery tips and broken-down dilapidated over-crowded gloomy hovels'. This notwithstanding, the majority of local people were felt to have 'a very strong attachment to the district, and a strong sense of community'. Whatever its economic circumstances, Massey left Blaina proclaiming its citizens to be 'intelligent, friendly, and comradely', and noted in passing that although local sports clubs had suffered through the impact of unemployment and out-migration, a large proportion of local people remained enthusiastic followers of rugby football.

By March 1942, when David Watkins was born, Blaina was enjoying a measure of economic recovery after the misery of the 1930s, and the Mass Observation organization sent a researcher, Mollie Tarrant, to document the changes it had experienced. War work, in the construction and munitions industries, in the factories and in a small improvement in the mines, along with the demands of the armed forces, had swept away almost all the local male unemployment (falling from 1,176 in 1937 to 16 in 1942), and provided work for many women, married and unmarried. The 'purposeless air' that Massey had noted had been replaced with a busy and workmanlike atmosphere, with workers' buses toing and froing. There remained great uncertainty about what the future might hold – some feared that the end of the war would see a slump similar to that which had followed the First World War – but community feeling remained 'extraordinarily strong'. Tarrant, after conducting a close study of the hopes, tastes and enthusiasms of the youth of the area, could feel optimistic that their potential would be 'a counter-balancing factor against the drag of the pre-war years'. The chairman of the local council agreed: singling out the three international rugby players produced by Blaina in the 1920s for particular note, he proclaimed that 'the best of Blaina, is like a bright water-lily rising from the dark mud'.

The Watkins family was much like any other of its era and of this background. It was a mining family, with roots locally and in the Rhondda valleys to the west. David was to be the eldest of three boys, who lived with their parents in a standard terraced house (complete with outside toilet) in Club Row, Cwmcelyn. This was a 'sub-town' to the east of the Blaina to Nant-y-glo road with its own shops and school, a pond that was appropriated for bathing, and a patch of open ground that regularly featured as the local boys' field of dreams, the Wembley or Cardiff Arms Park of the juvenile imagination. David's father Jack, when he was not working in the mine (toil that progressively wrecked his health), earned extra money with a newspaper and a milk round. Mother Doreen was the constant presence and 'the brains of the family', and made her own contribution to the household income by working in the accounts department of the local Co-operative stores. Deeply committed to the local Calvinistic Methodist chapel she enforced her sons' regular attendance at the Sunday school. An equally important influence on the young Watkins was his maternal grandfather, Sempronius Bridgeman, who had played on the wing for Newbridge and who, after more than sixty years as a miner, had taken a post as steward at the local Miners' Institute with its reading-room, library and snooker hall. He retained a great enthusiasm for sport, if rather more for soccer than rugby by the 1950s, and Saturdays would be taken up with trips to see Cardiff City play at Ninian Park or Newport County at Somerton Park, accompanied by his eldest grandson.

Soccer certainly had its appeal for the young David Watkins. He was nimble, fast, and intelligent on the ball; he had inherited a fierce competitive urge from his father; and one of his most treasured possessions was an old Aston Villa shirt in which he made regular appearances on the aforementioned patch of waste ground that doubled as a sports pitch. But it was to be rugby, suffusing the local sporting culture, that eventually claimed him. Once at Glanyrafon Secondary Modern School he fell under the wing of teacher Russell Cooper, a former flanker with London Welsh, and began to play, first at scrum-half and then at outside-half, for the school XV. He listened to matches on the radio, enlivened by the commentaries of G. V. Wynne-Jones, revered the international stars of the time, such as Cliff Morgan, and of yesteryear, such as Haydn Tanner, and slowly realized that his talents could open up opportunities and horizons usually denied to fellow victims of the eleven-plus. His speed was sufficiently impressive to win him a Welsh AAA relay vest, his co-ordination honed over the summer months by playing cricket. Right-footed, he nevertheless utilized the nearby bulk and gradient of a local tip to develop proficiency with his left foot, incessantly kicking the ball up the slope and awaiting its re-arrival at the bottom. Although slightly built (he eventually reached five feet six inches, wore size five-and-a-half boots and, for most of his union career, stood at ten stones four pounds) he lacked nothing in either courage or resilience, and his elusive running, with sidesteps off either foot, enabled him to escape or ride the heavier tackles. He became dedicated to achieving and maintaining a high level of fitness (he abstained from alcohol throughout his union career), and his physical durability, allied to a passion for playing, allowed him to withstand and overcome minor injuries. Leaving school at sixteen he was welcomed into the renowned Cwmcelyn Youth side and immediately became its first-choice outside-half.

Leaving school at sixteen also led David Watkins into employment at Richard, Thomas and Baldwin's steelworks at Ebbw Vale in the neigh-bouring valley. His parents, like most others in Blaina and across the coalfield, had been adamant that their sons would not go underground, and the steel industry, although paying its new recruits less well than the National Coal Board, offered a much cleaner and safer working environment than the mines, and constituted a major success story in the reconstruction of the Welsh economy following the Second World War. The R.T.B. works had been built in the late 1930s on the cleared site of the old Ebbw Vale Steel Company, and was brought into full production in 1939. By 1947 it had three continuous strip mills and Britain's first electrolytic tinning plant, and was a key component in making south Wales the leading steel-making district in post-war Britain. David Watkins joined the work-force as a junior management trainee on a development programme, and continued his education with City and Guilds courses as well as studying the historical development of the iron and steel industry in south Wales. Upon completing his training he worked in production control, and made an even more distinctive contribution by turning out for works rugby teams.

By the end of the 1950s it was clear that David Watkins was destined for considerable success in his chosen sport. He graduated to, first, the Monmouthshire Youth side, and then the Welsh Youth team, winning six caps in the course of two seasons. After guesting for, and being tempted by, a number of local first-class clubs, he was advised by local policeman, and ex-Newport, Wales and British Lions back-row forward Bob Evans to write to Newport asking for a trial. Weeks later, in September 1961, David Watkins was making his first-team debut for Newport in the opening game of the season against Penarth.

Newport was already a club with a very fine history when it welcomed its young recruit from Blaina. It had been home to the great winger Ken Jones, the then record Welsh cap-holder, in the 1950s, and captaining it from the front in 1961 was the formidable Bryn Meredith, whose career included thirty-four caps for Wales (four as captain) and three tours with the British Lions. In the back row were the Welsh internationals Geoff Whitson, Brian Cresswell, and Glyn Davidge (also a British Lion in 1962). Locks Ian Ford and Brian Price forged an international partnership in the engine-room, and other players who had been capped or who were to go on to represent Wales included Billy Watkins, Des Greenslade, Gordon Britton, Brian Jones, and Peter Rees. Recent outside-halves to pull on the black-and-amber jersey included the fabulous Roy Burnett and the highly accomplished and versatile Malcolm Thomas.

If David Watkins was intimidated by either the renown of his team-mates or the achievements of his predecessors he did not show it, giving an excellent debut performance that had the crowd apparently 'hopping with joy' and the press acclaiming him as 'a natural footballer' who belied his apparent frailty, revealing himself instead as 'a tough steelworker built on Burnett lines'. In a crowd-winning flash of inspiration, at one point he had whipped the ball out of the grasp of a Penarth player, raced for the corner, dodged tackler after tackler, and then leapt over a despairing opponent for a try.

No repetition of the 34–6 scoreline was to be seen in any of Newport's other games in the 1961–2 season, but Watkins's ability to streak through seemingly infinitesimal gaps in opposing defences, to switch direction at high speed, and to bewilder chasing back-row forwards and other markers rapidly won him the enthusiastic support of the Newport crowd and the praise of the rugby press. It was felt that his original approach, and his refreshing readiness to launch scintillating running attacks, allied to a not inconsiderable ability with the boot (both in punting and in landing drop goals), had the potential to revolutionize Newport's forward-oriented style. Within six weeks of making his debut, his mercurial talents were inviting both serious comparison with Roy Burnett and the attention of the Welsh selectors. At the beginning of November he played in the first trial match, and went on to appear in the second a month later. Although more experienced fly-halves Alan Rees of Maesteg and Cliff Ashton of Aberavon displaced him for the final trial, Watkins's astonishing rise testified to his brilliant rugby brain and his dazzling running skills. In the course of the season, throughout most of which he was partnered by scrum-half Bob Prosser, he played thirty-nine times for Newport, scoring four tries and three drop goals, helping them to win the Welsh club championship, and also being selected to appear for the prestigious Barbarians. In the end-of-season free-flowing jamboree of the Snelling Sevens, he scored a superb try following an eighty-yard sprint as Newport overwhelmed Neath 19–3. Before long Newport had eased the problems he was having in adjusting his shifts at the steelworks to meet the demands of training and playing by finding him a job as the manager of a tyre depot in Cardiff for the legendary Ken Jones's company.

The 1962–3 season was, after the excitement of its predecessors, much more difficult for the young outside-half. Opposing defences had learned to expect his breaks, and worked hard to contain him. Before Christmas a frustrated Watkins struggled to find his best form, and yet, if only by virtue of the fact that other, more mature candidates for the berth had retired or gone North, he was selected as one of six new caps to appear against England in January 1963.

In neither that game (a 6–13 defeat at Cardiff) nor in the subsequent 6–0 victory over Scotland at Murrayfield did David Watkins get many opportunities to display his attacking potential. Clive Rowlands, his captain and partner at scrum-half, favoured a canny game of tactical kicking, and rarely did the ball reach Watkins in such a position that he could run on to it at speed. At club level he continued to impress, dropping a goal to snatch a great away victory over Cardiff at the beginning of March, and working non-stop in covering and counter-attacking. There was no doubting his innate ability, but Bryn Thomas thought his instinctive running resembled too much the scurrying of a 'startled hare', and felt that he needed to acquire greater shrewdness to play to his full capacity at international level. Often the criticism was made in the early stages of Watkins's international career that he was too much of an individualist, that he tried to beat men on his own and, due both to his scorching pace and unpredictability, isolated himself from his centres and supporting players.

Watkins opened his scoring account for his country with a drop goal late on in the home defeat by Ireland in March, and the international season ended with the wooden spoon following a narrow defeat away in Paris. A month later Watkins again starred as Newport retained the Snelling Sevens, scoring a magnificent try against Bridgend after rocketing through a gap between three defenders, leaving one raising his hands to the skies in a gesture of combined disbelief and exasperation. The highlight of the year 1963, however, for both David Watkins and Newport, arrived on a dull, damp Wednesday afternoon in late October when Wilson Whineray's All Blacks visited Rodney Parade to play before a capacity crowd of 25,000 spectators.

Seventeen minutes into the game and from a maul just beyond the ten-yard line on the Newport left the ball came back to Newport's scrum-half Bob Prosser. He immediately fed David Watkins, who spotted a gap in the All Black line and went on an electrifying diagonal thirty-yard run towards the right-hand corner. Holding the ball close to his chest he sprinted between the opposing centres and in crossing the twenty-five drew in the New Zealand left-wing before releasing a pass to Newport's right-wing Stuart Watkins, who promptly cross-kicked towards the New Zealand posts. At the ensuing ruck the Newport forwards won the ball and it arrived in the hands of Newport centre Dick Uzzell who kicked what turned out to be the decisive drop goal in a game that finished Newport 3 New Zealand 0. Of course it was a victory won overwhelmingly by the energy of the Newport eight, and by the discipline shown by all the home players. Apart from the crucial break, Watkins's running was carefully rationed: more telling were his long, intelligent, teasing kicks into the corners, which forced the veteran New Zealand full-back Don Clarke to turn and scuttle back to cover, and exposed his lack of pace. New Zealand's High Commissioner, present at the game, wondered whether Watkins would be interested in emigrating to his country! As it was, New Zealand would soon take considerable comfort from their first ever victory over Wales at Cardiff shortly before Christmas, when their pack dominated, and their back row closed Watkins down.

The 1964 international championship was an improvement for Wales and Watkins on that of the previous year. Two draws with England and France sandwiched two wins against Scotland and Ireland. In both of these latter games Watkins was able to demonstrate far greater attacking ability in a Welsh jersey than had been possible hitherto. Against Scotland he kicked intelligently, and worked a dummy scissors with Clive Rowlands that led to a try for centre Keith Bradshaw. At Lansdowne Road he played his finest game for Wales to date, with some beautifully balanced running, accurate kicking and dedicated covering. The highlight was a superb individual first-half try after a forty-yard arcing run from a standing start, with Watkins handing off Mike Gibson and sidestepping past defenders as he raced for the line.

Although as full of confidence as he was of running, Watkins's maturity was not yet complete. Against France, and in the heavy away defeat at the hands of South Africa in May, opposing back rows created channels into which they invited him to run, and then shut him down, isolating him from support. Back in Wales, and playing with the longer, smoother, swifter service of Allan Lewis in the spectacle of running rugby against Fiji in September, Watkins had a far more impressive all-round game, making frequent breaks with his tremendous acceleration over the first fifteen yards, drawing defenders, and then putting his centres into space. By this time he had taken over from Brian Price as captain of Newport, the youngest for forty years, and the responsibility of leading the club side enhanced Watkins's tactical nous and developed his awareness of the needs of the other players in his team. He was a great success as club captain, holding the position until he left rugby union in 1967, inspiring those around him, and bringing an impeccable poise and dignity to his duties off the field.

Whatever Allan Lewis's merits, Watkins remained teamed with the wily Clive Rowlands for the 1965 Triple-Crown-winning season. He operated largely as a link in the victory over England, albeit dropping a good goal, and although caught in possession rather too often against Scotland, managed to set up Stuart Watkins's try and invoke comparisons with Cliff Morgan with his dangerous, enchanting jinking. Against Ireland in the Triple Crown decider he scored an exciting try following a lengthy kick from inside his own half, which was tapped on by Stuart Watkins for his namesake and Newport club-mate to touch down. Unfortunately for Wales the Grand Slam proved elusive, as France whisked to a clear victory in Paris.

The year 1966 was a time of highs and lows for David Watkins. He opened his account with an imperious display for Newport as they took Bridgend's ground record, one that had stood for seventy games. Less than a fortnight later, playing outside the unobtrusive but highly effective Allan Lewis, he showed great control and experience in the defeat of England, when, finding himself closely marked, he handed on to his centres once he had created the initial spaces. In the game against Scotland he combined his natural attacking dynamism with this acquired tactical maturity to great effect, creating two tries for Ken Jones and, although the defeat in Dublin was a great disappointment, Wales won the championship for the second consecutive year when they came from behind to beat France at Cardiff. Watkins must have been an automatic choice for the British Lions tour to Australia and New Zealand that set out a few weeks later.

The five-month long tour, managed by Des O'Brien and led by Michael Campbell-Lamerton, was not a success, but David Watkins was one of the few Lions to emerge with an enhanced reputation. It started well, with the Lions winning five and drawing one of their games against provincial opposition in Australia, and winning both tests. Watkins made his first appearance against South Australia, as captain for the day, and was selected for the major games against Victoria and New South Wales before filling the fly-half spot for the First Test. It was as captain against Queensland, however, and then again in the Second Test, that Watkins blossomed as an attacking force, with crowd-pleasing jinks and darts, bursts of speed and magical weaving runs. In the last quarter of the Second Test the Lions cut loose, with an exuberant Watkins scoring one of the tries, to rattle up a total of thirty-one points without reply.

New Zealand was a different story altogether. By the time of the First Test against the All Blacks, the Lions had already lost three games and drawn one against provincial sides. Watkins played in the first defeat, against Southland, but otherwise had continued, on occasion, to display his inspirational running form, interspersed with a more restricted kicking game when conditions or opponents demanded. Watkins was again the obvious choice to face the All Blacks, with Mike Gibson outside him in the centre. The Lions went down to a heavy First Test defeat (20–3), and some serious soul-searching ensued. The major problems were up front, where the Lions continued to appear as a collection of talented individuals rather than as a forceful unit, but the inconsistency of the forward performances rendered it difficult for the backs to develop a singular style on the tour. Watkins played, again as captain, in a commanding tactical and kicking display, embracing two drop goals, in the defeat of Auckland, and, with both the tour captain Campbell-Lamerton and the Welsh captain Alun Pask out of form, he was picked to lead the Lions in the vital Second Test.

Even New Zealand journalists acknowledged the high quality of Watkins's steady leadership in this match, which the All Blacks won narrowly by sixteen points to twelve. Watkins was constantly under pressure from the New Zealand loose forwards, but kicked intelligently and the game was a much closer contest than the first encounter. Unfortunately, the direction of the tour was now in disarray, and, although Campbell-Lamerton returned to lead in the Third Test, that too was lost, even though the Lions ran the ball at every opportunity and scored two tries (one by Watkins). There was still time for one last mesmeric attacking performance by the first-choice outside-half, against Waikato, and another call to Test captaincy in the fourth and final clash with the All Blacks, but the series ended in a four–nil whitewash.

Despite the difficulties of playing in a losing side on the 1966 tour, David Watkins had confirmed his calibre as a world-class player. He had manufactured audacious displays of running rugby, perfected his drop-goal technique, and demonstrated that he could control a game with his line-kicking if required. His double selection as Test captain in New Zealand was ample recognition of his wholehearted commitment as a player and as a leader, and was sufficient proof to the miner's son from Blaina that he had no reason to doubt his capabilities either on or off the pitch. On returning from tour he decided that a new challenge was needed outside rugby and left the tyre world for a job with Forward Trust, a subsidiary of Midland Bank.

David Watkins needed all his self-confidence and strength of character when in November 1966 he was dropped in favour of Barry

John for Wales's forthcoming game against Australia. This was a great shock (the *South Wales Argus* termed it a 'bombshell'), not made any easier by the fact that three of the five selectors privately claimed to have voted for the Newport player. But whatever inner turmoil he experienced, Watkins acted gallantly in sending a telegram of congratulations to his rival. Before the end of the international season, however, he was back in the outside-half saddle, and this time as captain, playing against Ireland, France (both defeats) and then, in what was his final game for Wales, England. By 1967 his partner was the young Gareth Edwards, and outside him in the centre was Gerald Davies. The most instantly famous new recruit was, however, Keith Jarrett, who made such an amazing debut at full-back in Wales's 34–21 victory.

Nevertheless, in the autumn the old uncertainties returned. Expectations that he would captain Wales against New Zealand were not confirmed by the Big Five, who delayed either making or announcing their decision. David Watkins was twenty-five, and seemingly at the top of his game in the union code, yet his future as an international player seemed to him to be jeopardized by the inconsistency of the selectors. Via John Mantle, a former Newport and Wales colleague who had turned professional for St Helens and who had already been capped by Great Britain, negotiations were opened with Salford Rugby League Football Club. Northern clubs had sought David Watkins's services before, but the timing of Salford's offer, in combination with its magnitude (amounting in total to £16,000: then a record fee for a union player going North) was irresistible. On 19 October 1967 David Watkins signed for Salford.

David Watkins had played more than two hundred times for Newport, scoring thirty-two tries and fifty-five drop goals. It is probably true to say that the gap he left at club level has never, despite the undoubted talents of many of his successors, been completely filled. At international level he was capped twenty-one times, and had dominated the position for nearly five years. He was to be succeeded by players, in Barry John and Phil Bennett, with equally strong claims to greatness in terms of their personal talents, who were both fortunate enough to play in Welsh and Lions teams that enjoyed more substantial success than those of the 1960s. For the insatiable Welsh public, the attitude was very much 'The King is dead. Long live the King!' The Welsh Rugby Union, however, did have the graciousness to write thanking Watkins for his 'tremendous contribution to Welsh Rugby in recent years', remarking that he had been 'a great credit to Wales both on and off the field', and observing that his 'energy, enthusiasm and dedication' would be sorely missed.

Watkins set out to capture the hearts of the rugby league public of Salford in much the way he had done at Newport. In his first game, against Oldham on 20 October, a day after signing forms, he scored a brilliant interception try, scampering seventy-five yards in the process, and kicked two drop goals. Although it took him rather longer to adapt fully to the different code, and to win the respect of fellow players, David Watkins forged a career in rugby league every bit as successful as the one he had enjoyed in union. He played thirteen seasons for Salford, initially as an outside-half, later as a centre, and finally as a full-back, clocking up a total of 405 games and 2,907 points. Developing place-kicking skills that had lain dormant in union, he continues to hold world records for kicking 221 goals in one season (1972–3), and for scoring in ninety-two consecutive games. As captain he took Salford to the Challenge Cup final in 1969, and to championship titles in 1974 and 1976. Watkins was the nucleus of a glamorous side including his old Newport scrum-half Bob Prosser, Welshmen Colin Dixon and Maurice Richards, English rugby union converts Keith Fielding and Mike Coulman, and home-grown talents Paul Charlton, Ken Gill and Chris Hesketh. He played sixteen times for the Welsh rugby league team, and won six caps for Great Britain, touring with them both in 1974, and as player-coach for the World Cup of 1977. His final season, 1979–80, was spent with Swinton before his final retirement from the field of play.

Retirement from the game of rugby is, at the time of writing, still to arrive for David Watkins. He managed an attempt (in the form of the Cardiff Blue Dragons) to introduce rugby league to south Wales in the early 1980s and, from the early 1990s, returned to involvement with Newport RFC. A superb ambassador for sporting endeavour in all its forms, for his services to rugby he was awarded the MBE in 1985.

David Watkins's personal and sporting career, particularly in rugby union, may be held to symbolize a Wales in the grip of momentous economic, social and cultural changes. From a coal-mining community he had progressed, in his working life, through the modernizing steel industry into white-collar work and the financial services sector of the economy. On the rugby pitch there was a confidence about his identity and a pride about his play that encapsulated the recovery that Wales had enjoyed since the 1930s, and the escape that ordinary working-class people had found, through full employment, improved living standards, and the welfare state, from the 'twin psychoses of poverty and dread'. There was also a swagger and a self-expression about his demeanour at outside-half that excited crowds and eroded the social inhibitions of a culture not quite sure whether it should share in the personal liberations of the 1960s. But whatever his extrovert playing persona, off the pitch David Watkins was (and has remained) modest, respected, perceptive and accessible: truly a product of the 'intelligent, friendly, and comradely' culture of the close mining community of Blaina into which he was born.

I would like to acknowledge the help given to me in researching this chapter by the School of History and Archaeology at the University of Wales, Cardiff, by the Tom Harrisson Mass-Observation Archive at the University of Sussex, by the Resources and Archives Department of BBC Wales, and particularly by David Watkins himself, who gave very generously of his time and thoughts. Most importantly, I would like to thank my father Peter Williams who reared me on a diet of stories about David Watkins and the Newport side of the 1960s and who has ensured that, wherever I have lived, Rodney Parade has remained the centre of my universe.

GARETH EDWARDS

David Parry-Jones

I played rugby keenly until the close of the 1966–7 season. Having enjoyed a last fling with Cardiff High School Old Boys, I hung up my boots and (as a journalist already) decided to get involved with media coverage of the game. This timing meant that it was October 1967 before I first saw Gareth Edwards in action, at the start of his second season with Cardiff RFC. A memorial match was staged at the Arms Park for the international prop Cliff Davies who had died the previous January, and the 20-year-old Edwards was to appear against a British Isles XV. His opposite number would be Roger Young, a holder of eleven Irish caps, while the visitors' back row included mean opponents like Dai Hayward and Mick Hipwell. Though he had already been capped twice by Wales at scrum-half, first in a losing side at Stade Colombes, Gareth's status in the Wales XV of the day was still that of tyro. He next figured in the high-scoring win of 1967 over England, but failed to attract the limelight which that day illuminated Keith Jarrett, Gerald Davies and David Watkins. Now, in the autumn of 1967 there were three older rivals perfectly well qualified to wear the Wales number-9 jersey, in the shape of Allan Lewis from Abertillery, Cardiff's Billy Hullin and Glyn Turner of Ebbw Vale. Seated in the press box waiting for the kick-off I wondered idly if this 'G. Edwards' was a flash in the pan. After forty minutes of rugby in weather not calculated to promote running and handling, the answer was breathtakingly clear; and my match report for *The Times* reminds me why. 'Edwards made the first try for Samuel with a square break from behind the line-out followed by an inside flip. Soon a dummy and side-step by him sent Gerald Davies in at the corner . . . Edwards ended the first half by wriggling through for an individual try after a quickly-taken penalty.' Very well: there was little at stake. But, even in charity games, international forwards do not wave you through. Edwards had given a match-winning display.

My scrapbook reveals, too, that about this time I invited my friend Onllwyn Brace, himself one of the century's cleverest scrum-halves, to comment on the youngster's calibre. His response came without hesitation: 'He has the greatest potential of any scrum half I have seen since Haydn Tanner.' It is thus a privilege to essay a portrayal and evaluation of that potential's realization.

The bronze statue is a little larger-than-life, able to dominate the bustling St David's shopping precinct in central Cardiff. Many will agree that it is not a particularly good facial likeness of Gareth Owen Edwards. However, it certainly imitates the action of this tiger who represented his city, as well as his country, through one of those golden rugby eras which allow small nations to throw out their chests two or three times in a century. There were other big cats in the jungle who hunted with him; but it is in order to describe him as a first among equals.

The statue speaks volumes. Positioned at the heart of the capital city, it instates Edwards among Wales's favourite sons, recognizing how he had consistently provided his compatriots with the self-respect they needed, and the heroics they craved. Further, it epitomizes the degree to which their capital city, its common people, its businessmen, and its city fathers took this outsider to their hearts, for conferring fresh distinction upon its rugby club.

Outsider, yes: Gareth's roots, like those of so many other great Blue and Blacks, lie to the west, in the bleak upland village of Gwaun-caegurwen. This is where his ears were boxed for kicking balls into neighbours' gardens; where he began scoring winning tries for Wales on asphalt pavements; above all, where he knew the pressure-cooker valley upbringing on which many Welshmen have built so successfully in later life. Glan, his father, and grandfather Jacob were miners. In bygone days such men lived a horizontal existence, toiling endlessly in cramped and claustrophobic coal seams before twisting and contorting black-dusted biceps and torsos in order to load their six trams a day. If you ever marvelled at the dynamic built into Gareth Edwards's 5'-8" frame, ponder no further: the genes explain it.

The next, crucial, influence upon a budding career was the PE master at Pontardawe Technical College, a certain Bill Samuel. This was the first man to perceive the extraordinary talent, and promise, of the child who reported to his gymnasium in 1959 at the age of twelve. Through several years Samuel was to manipulate Gareth's ambitions, towards field sports as well as the two football codes. He smiled approvingly at the forbidding assault-course that the young Edwards conceived for himself: the 196 steps cut into the hillside above Pontardawe Technical School, up and down which he stormed five times during each lunch break.

On the whole Gareth seems to have accepted this regime. It finally nosed him away from Association Football (which he enjoyed a lot) towards the handling code. 'You will become a scrum-half', said the master to the stripling. Stripling? Certainly. Eleven stones and nine pounds were all Gareth would take into his first senior international match at the age of nineteen. A fellow school pupil destined to become Mrs Edwards, Maureen, told her pals sniffily, 'He's skinny.' Always she declined to be bowled over by her young beau. When he told her that he was leaving Pontardawe Tech for an English public school called Millfield she was unimpressed. 'Will you write to me?' he begged. 'We'll see,' she told him.

Bill Samuel 'sold' Gareth to Millfield, an institution that was years ahead of its time as a forcing-house and finishing-school for pupils who could demonstrate a reasonable academic record plus outstanding prospects in a sporting context. It taught and tutored the children of the rich; it seasoned its annual intake, and thereby broadened its base, by awarding scholarships to brilliant but less affluent teenagers who would add lustre to its name. Headmaster R. J. O. Meyer was advised by Samuel that a 16-year-old called G. O. Edwards had long-jumped 21 feet 6 inches, was a champion hurdler, threw discus, pole-vaulted and, by the way, played rugby and soccer too. Though taking care not to appear influenced by the hype, Meyer was far-sighted enough to admit the boy from the Swansea Valley.

The astronomic fees charged by the academy across the Severn were well known. Hence, although it was conceded that Glan Edwards and his wife Annie Mary would be contributing what they could afford to their son's sixth-form education, it was clear that a miner could scarcely foot more than a fraction of the bills involved. Hence there emerged a rumour, enthusiastically fuelled by the media, that a fairy godfather was backing the boy. It flared up again when Gareth returned for a another year among the millionaires' offspring. This second spell was to yield him individual trophies for athletics and gymnastics in addition to high success in team games, notably seven-a-side rugby tournaments. Gareth has consistently acknowledged help and helpers, a trait which lends credence to his playing down of the 'admiring benefactor' theory: the alleged shadowy figure who signed big cheques but otherwise preferred to remain anonymous, even to his protegé. He believes more simply that Meyer, wishing to hold on to him, made finance available from the school's contingency funds.

The two years at Millfield represented an experience for the Welsh teenager whose value defies computation. The nonchalance exuded by the comfortably-off, with whom he was not numbered, and the athletically outstanding, among whom he was, cannot but have enhanced his in-born assurance. When the time came to perform for and communicate with the watching world, from grander stages, he initially masked the big confidence that is part of a competitive sportsman's make-up; but it was always there. Cliff Morgan surely helped when he wrote in the press after seeing the scrum-half in a Welsh Trial that he would win 'dozens of caps'.

Now, in middle age, he is a speech-maker who can do thirty minutes before an important audience without a note. At the microphone, for television or radio, he is assured and has plenty to say (sometimes too much for the time constraints; but I have pulled his leg about this before and will do so no more). He and I have sat down to map out books on the game; insight and comment pour from him in an analytical torrent.

Rather like Millfield, or Manchester United and, it should be added, a select number of other rugby clubs in Wales such as Llanelli and Swansea, Cardiff RFC is an elite establishment. It does not have to defer to greatness, present or prospective; but it is not slow to identify high promise. Via the grapevine (perhaps the one-time Blue-and-Black Bill Samuel was still an active persuader) it would have known that a student of allegedly supranormal abilities had arrived in the city as a freshman at Cardiff Training College. Furthermore, two perceptive lecturers on its campus, Roy Bish (soon to become Cardiff's first-ever coach) and Leighton Davies, felt that his quality was such that he should be taken on at the Arms Park without delay – today, the fashionable phrase is 'fast-tracked'. The reputations of these two men, along with that of the College's PE department, depended to a large extent on the success of its rugby team, so that to put the interests of young Edwards first was an act of considerable unselfishness. As a result Gareth was enabled to make the move up-market; he reciprocated by turning out in College colours when it was feasible.

Like innumerable illustrious recruits before him he was obliged to observe tradition and open his Cardiff career by appearing in the club's second, or Athletic, XV. A first-team debut came on 17 September 1966, when Cardiff beat the then formidable Coventry RFC by 24 points to 6. Veterans on the Cardiff committee lifted their glasses and confided, 'Hello, we've got something here!' The club's historian, the late Danny Davies, had seen and often played alongside Blue-and-Black scrum-halves of the twentieth century including Wick Powell, Maurice Turnbull, Haydn Tanner, Rex Willis and Lloyd Williams. In his classic work, *Cardiff Rugby Club: The Greatest*, he wrote in 1976, 'I rate Gareth as the best of them all.' Had he lived to see Terry Holmes in his prime my guess is that he would have held, albeit narrowly, to that verdict.

For his part Gareth had already calculated that Cardiff RFC would be the springboard which catapulted him into representative rugby. It helped that Barry John was soon to make the move east from Llanelli and, once David Watkins had left for Salford and the professional game, would be installed as the Wales number 10. National selectors set store by club partnerships. This instinct was right: players selected in key positions by Cardiff arrive within reach of international honours simply through association with a club which has taken on and beaten the world's great rugby nations. Gareth acknowledges the debt; eternally Cardiff will be his club. The way the Blue-and-Blacks see him is personified in the dramatic portrait of the scrum-half from Gwauncaegurwen which graces their clubhouse.

So: he was now in the big time where harsh lessons lay in wait. The autumn of 1967 brought him a third cap at scrum-half against Brian Lochore's All Blacks, who defeated Wales 13–6 at Cardiff. For most, including the victors, this was a forgettable Test match. Not for the young number 9. 'I am the deliverer of the ball to the backs', he reflected. 'The New Zealand game demands that attacks are killed at source. So, at scrums and line-outs, the scrum-half is a constant target.'

Privately he recalled, 'Kel Tremain came through a loose maul and "accidentally" trod on my hand. It felt as if a ton of coal had landed on it.'

In 1968 he scored his first international try (only the second by a Welsh scrum-half since the war) during a drawn game against England, and was credited with a dropped goal in Dublin which most onlookers thought passed outside a post. But Wales's only victory in the Five Nations tournament was an uninspired one, over Scotland at Cardiff. Despite being given the captaincy Gareth did not find it within his powers to motivate the team. 'I wasn't ready for it,' the youngest player ever to captain his country later admitted. 'The truth is that with a number of old stalwarts creaking at the joints, the Welsh selectors needed a straw to clutch.' They clutched at him again two games later, to no avail; the French completed their first-ever Grand Slam in Cardiff at his team's expense.

However, summer 1968 did see him selected to tour with the British Isles in South Africa. His learning curve was now steep, and in eight appearances he went over for six tries before tearing a hamstring in the match with Boland. This injury sidelined him for the last three weeks of the tour, keeping him out of the Third and Fourth Tests. The Lions' historian Clem Thomas still felt able to describe the overall experience as 'a finishing school . . . the scrum-half's skills were soon to be unleashed on the European scene'.

That now came to pass. And as the Five Nations Championship of 1969 got under way other talents with huge potential were also to become available for Wales in key positions. The two young London Welshmen J. P. R. Williams and Mervyn Davies were blooded in Scotland, where Wales were comfortable winners. Dai Morris of Neath (Gareth's 'shadow') and John Taylor combined well in back-row defence and in support of the backs; there were big, aggressive tight forwards whose presence promised a front five that could rarely be subdued. Gerald Davies and Barry John were already ever-present team-mates. In a game like rugby football the company of such top-flight men is massively supportive. Should one player feel off-colour, or prove fallible on the day, the others run the show.

Gareth scored two tries in the campaign, one of them in Paris against a French side which denied Wales a Grand Slam; and deputized for injured skipper Brian Price in the Cardiff victory over England which secured a Triple Crown. Seven points from the Five Nations seemed a good enough launch-pad from which to leave on a seven-match Australasian tour. Alas: this was to be the true 'finishing school', not just for their scrum-half but for all the Welshmen.

The two defeats suffered by the tourists, under Brian Price, were in the Tests against New Zealand, by 19–0 and 33–12. Under the points-scoring system of the day these were catastrophic reverses. Three decades later the fatal inferiority complex about the All Blacks dating from those two Tests has yet to be exorcized from Welsh minds. Carwyn James would later speak of the hubris to which he believed successful rugby teams might fall victim; Wales's scrum-half felt a different, simpler emotion: extreme frustration, that he had been unable to show New Zealand how he could play.

Gareth reassumed captaincy of the national XV for the Test against South Africa early in 1970. He placed a penalty and squelched in for the try which gave his country a 6–6 draw, her best-ever result against the Springboks. In the Five Nations Championship Wales revealed fallibility at Lansdowne Road, but finished the season level with France on six points.

The apprenticeship had now been served. Before long Gareth would be acknowledged by the rugby world as a scrum-half without peer. In his own country he was to become a cult figure: one of that select few who are known by their Christian name alone.

By January 1971 he held nineteen caps and had appeared twice for the British Isles. His body-weight was up to twelve stones four pounds which, packaged in a low-slung frame, enabled him to blast through all but the firmest tackles. This had made him a lethal opponent close to the try-line from where he had gone in for four international tries. But his erstwhile PE master Bill Samuel was not yet satisfied. He teased his protegé: 'To me, you're not a finished product until you start scoring from 70 or 80 metres.' Whether Gareth was truly influenced, and fired up, by this challenge is anyone's guess. The fact is, however, that in the next two years he was to cross for three tries, each from very long range, which have immortalized him on video-tape.

Gareth's eyes now twinkled more than he had allowed them to in earlier years. An in-born sense of mischief, allied to relative seniority (in those days nine caps, let alone nineteen, were a sackful) encouraged him to outspokenness almost unheard of in the days of Welsh rugby's feudal system. 'After a particularly good win,' recalls Maureen Edwards, 'he was the one player who could chivvy the WRU's formidable Secretary Bill Clement into authorizing extra champagne.' Now came the next decisive influence upon his fortunes. In and out of Welsh XVs since the mid-1960s, John Dawes had ousted Gareth from the national captaincy in April 1970, to begin what would be a short reign but one bejewelled with triumphs. As the new year opened he was put in charge for the Five Nations campaign. 'John was not only a great playmaker; as a leader he exercised a huge steadying influence on the tearaways around him', his scrum-half has written generously.

My own surmise is that although Gareth enjoyed the glitz of captaincy he was less enamoured of its responsibilities. Occasionally in the future he would shoulder it again, as a caretaker; but the fact is that to play at scrum-half demands total, unending concentration on your task and circumstances, without having to de-focus for adjustments to tactics or the assessment of others' performances. Gareth, surely, was happy to wave the job goodbye. Perhaps, therefore, it is no coincidence that this was the juncture at which he began giving his most spectacular performances. These do not include the head bang accidentally administered to J.P.R. (which necessitated minor surgery on the full-back's cranium) as they both got below a high ball during the Arms Park victory over England. Gareth scored, however, in the pulsating 19–18 win over Scotland before crossing twice in the Triple Crown defeat of Ireland. In that match, watchers may recall his slamming the ball down unusually hard over the Irish goal line. It was eleven years before he revealed in *The Golden Years of Welsh Rugby* his frustration at what he considered an ungenerous press over the previous twelve months. 'But, if the media seem unfair, the best place to hit back is on the field', he philosophized. 'That's how you make them eat their words.'

A Five Nations title waited to be clinched at Stade Colombes on 27 March. Gareth plus ten of his team-mates crossed the Channel emboldened by their selection for the British Isles party to tour New

Zealand under John Dawes. The Welsh won a great victory to clinch their Grand Slam, and Gareth was to go in for one of the three greatest tries, if not the very best, of his career.

Unimpressed by anything that had happened in Cardiff or Edinburgh, France had posted a 5–0 lead through a Dauga try converted by Villepreux, and kept Wales on the defensive. Barry John was hurt in a tackle, but made a brave return. The Welsh needed a score. Gareth may not have carried the ball for eighty metres, but his try this day was truly the first of the long-range scores that Bill Samuel had demanded. In the Welsh twenty-five, J. P. R. Williams intercepted an inside pass from France's right-wing Bourgarel and set off speedily and determinedly up the left touch-line. At half way, prop Denzil Williams was still in touch, but losing ground rapidly, and two defenders were closing on the fugitive full-back in red. 'Suddenly,' J.P.R. wrote later, 'I glimpsed Gareth behind me and to the left. I checked the two coverers with an inside jink and fed my team-mate, who just reached the corner. How he got into the right place at the right time I will never know.' A handsome acknowledgement from one not noted for paying gratuitous compliments.

Thus, from seeing defensive chinks that he himself could exploit without assistance five or ten metres out from the line, Gareth was progressing to being able to sense, and support, thrusts by team-mates which could profit from his devastating finishing powers. The thought-process leading to that Paris try had started at the split-second when the counter-attack began, the athletic power which executed it reached back to the colossal stamina stowed away within the frame of a one-time crack hurdler. A Grand Slam became reality, and Barry John's superb try later on merely celebrated it.

But the Welshmen who flew into Auckland with the Lions a month later in May 1971 were wary. Top-dogs in Europe two years before, they remembered only too vividly how New Zealand had dismembered them. Some of the black destroyers were still active: 'Pine Tree' Meads, for example, McCormick and Going. This time, however, the Brits had the unflappable Dawes at the helm. Pugnacious Doug Smith was their manager: 'We'll win the Test series two–one with one match drawn.'

There was, too, Carwyn James, probably the best British coach of the twentieth century, certainly in the world's top three. Finally, their Welsh scrum-half was near the height of his powers: bursting to show New Zealand his true calibre.

The tourists took ten scalps in New Zealand on their way to Carisbrook Park, Dunedin, for the first of four Tests on 26 June. Gareth owns up to few crises in his career; but of these the greatest undoubtedly took place exactly forty-eight hours before that game. It led to rumours that the Welshman had been in tears; that he had been in a shouting match with the management; that he stood in danger of being sent home. Now, three decades on, the scrum-half smiles wryly as he recalls those days, and sets the record straight.

'I had been feeling good in training. Really, really good. As we were whistled towards the changing rooms I decided on one last "winder" the length of the pitch. I was accelerating into the final 25 yards when my boot went into a small pot-hole and, Oh hell! A tweak high up inside the hamstring. Oh, no. Oh, no. Please. Let it be my imagination.' But memories of the same trouble in South Africa, which had caused him to miss eight of the 1968 tour games, flooded into the Welshman's mind. And he knew that it was not his imagination. When he confided in management, there were two contradictory responses. James's simple attitude was that the injury must be kept a secret. For morale reasons, he wanted Gareth to start the game at Carisbrook in two days' time, even if he had to be substituted before the interval by the reserve scrum-half, Ray Hopkins of Maesteg. With an eye to the medium and long term, however, Doug Smith wanted definitive, difficult-to-give answers: how bad did Gareth really think the injury was? Could he play on the Saturday? If so, would he last for eighty minutes? If not, when would he be fit again? Was his plight so sore that the management should ask for a replacement and send him home?

Such exchanges, two days before one of the most vital games of his career, unsettled and upset the scrum-half. To his enormous relief a compromise was reached on the Friday evening. Accordingly, he took the field the next afternoon to play a full part in the Lions' resistance to New Zealand's supercharged start. After fifteen minutes the opening siege was lifted and, following a thrust when he actually came near to scoring, Gareth lifted an arm for Hopkins to race on in his stead. The medics on duty had been warned that the substitution might be necessary, and so gave consent without delay. An hour later the Lions had won.

Gareth was now just days short of his 24th birthday, and growing assurance can be detected in the interview he subsequently gave, quoted by Terry McLean in *Lions Rampant* 'Maybe I could have played on for a few minutes. But if I had, I might have . . . been out of the tour, and out of rugby forever.' And the *coup de grâce*: 'Everybody who has had anything to do with rugby or athletics knows how tender a hamstring is.' Sudden collapse of hard-bitten Kiwi hacks who knew about cauliflower ears and missing molars but not muscles behind thighs.

Carwyn James had brought his men to concert pitch for Dunedin. A fortnight later in Christchurch Gareth nursed his leg through the Second Test; he and other Lions tend to concede that their less-committed approach permitted New Zealand to square the series. No wonder, then, that on 31 July a three-deep queue stretched half a mile down the road from Athletic Park, Wellington, as the hemispheres braced themselves for the third impact. The opening quarter settled the outcome; and may well rank as the best twenty minutes ever played by the tourists' fit-again scrum-half. After Barry John's dropped goal which opened the scoring the Lions stormed back to New Zealand's 25-yard area. Here, when Gareth was given good ball and began moving menacingly right, every All Black defender girded his loins for the number 9 to strike. Hadn't he been doing that regularly for four years behind Welsh packs? But this time their bluff was called. After two strides by the scrum-half, which caused hesitation in the All Blacks ranks that was fractional but fatal, the lurking Gerald Davies was given a short, lightning-quick pass off which he eeled in at the flag. John kicked the goal.

At last, freed from fitness worries, this was the Edwards that Europe had come to know and fear. Snapping at the heels of his pack, booming great passes out to the midfield, walking tall, strutting his stuff. A one-man cause for alarm. Soon he struck a punt that climbed the sky and allowed his side to pressurize New Zealand's line yet again. The Lions called their 'Willie away' move and Gareth was sent into space guarded only by the luckless Bob Burgess. He fell victim to a stupefying hand-off before Barry John went under the crossbar, the second recipient of a scoring pass from the scrum-half.

Thirteen points to nil after twenty minutes: the match, and the series, were safe. Their 14–14 draw at Auckland made these Lions the first, and only, Brits of the twentieth century to win a Test series in New Zealand. Gareth and the rest returned home to heroes' welcomes, riding in open-topped limousines with proud wives and girl friends, waving to adoring fans. Rugby's Everest had been scaled.

There were numerous other Himalayan challenges still to be met. The state of Irish politics, however, dissuaded the Welsh from playing in Dublin during 1972. There could be no Grand Slam, but Gareth contributed to hard-won victories over England and France, and scored two tries in the defeat of Scotland at Cardiff. He rates the first of them as the more important, since it swung the match in Wales's favour. But he has named the second as the most pleasurable of his twenty international tries. No wonder. It was from long range; it was characterized by stamina, a supremely high skill level, broad vision, and finely-tuned decision-making. It was, simply, wondrous.

Essentially, it covered seventy-five yards. It started at the Wales 25-line, where Scotland's back row were suddenly missing persons. It continued as Gareth realized that his own support players were also absent. Two superb pieces of football followed, a chip ahead from the hand and a full-blooded hack to the corner. There remained the final, breathless sprint to hurl himself on the ball. The marl-smeared face on the walk back to half way is one of Welsh sport's twentieth-century icons.

The retirement from international rugby of first John Dawes and soon after Barry John meant that Wales now faltered a little. Selectorial uncertainty was revealed as the search began for a new captain; and likewise, though Phil Bennett picked up ten caps in a row, disagreement about his suitability as the new partner for Edwards rumbled like distant thunder. Hence for a while peaks were scaled by Gareth in other colours, notably those of the Barbarians. In 1973 Dawes came back to the big time as captain of their invitation XV against Ian Kirkpatrick's saturnine but successful All Blacks in the traditional end-of-tour game. Many of his 1971 Lions turned out, including their Test scrum-half.

Gareth chose the occasion to score the third of his great long-range tries – the one which holds an unofficial record for being the most-played on television. Once more, the opportunity is coldly computed by the scrum-half a substantial period before touch down. As Bennett, Pullin, Dawes and Tom David counter-attack Gareth is scarcely in the frame. Only when left-wing John Bevan slows fractionally, adjusting to Quinnell's pace as the flanker prepares to give him the ball, does Gareth surge into the attack, stride lengthening, left hand ready for the pass. The ball is then squeezed beneath his right shoulder; defender Joe Karam is out of range for the tackle; Edwards dives; on BBC TV Cliff Morgan gasps, 'What a score!'

Whatever reservations Wales might have harboured about Bennett in 1974, the Lions' selectors chose him as their first stand-off half for South Africa, where he stole much limelight. Gareth played in the four Tests (three wins and the draw which robbed the tourists of a 100 per cent record), dropping a goal at Cape Town but subsequently leaving the scoring to Bennett and other brilliant runners like J. J. Williams and Andy Irvine. He seemed to enjoy this laid-back status as the Lions' principal strategist; his tactical kicking reached new heights of excellence. Clem Thomas wrote that his running from behind dominant forwards was a constant threat, 'and this tour provided some of the finest hours of his illustrious career'. Endorsement of this verdict came with an MBE given him in 1975.

Now, John Dawes stepped up to coach Wales, choosing Mervyn Davies as his on-field captain. Gerald Davies, J.P.R. and J. J. Williams were at the height of their powers. Pontypool's grim threesome were Wales's front-line troops, Geoff Wheel and Terry Cobner raged at the heart of the action. For Gareth, ensconced behind such strong forwards, the long, golden afternoon of his career could unfold.

Records fell to him and the teams in which he played. Three consecutive Triple Crowns came Wales's way between 1976 and 1978, a fourth following after his retirement. He was in the two Grand Slam sides of 1976 and 1978. At Cardiff in March 1976 he passed Ken Jones's record of forty-four appearances for Wales, lifting his total to fifty-three, made consecutively, when bowing out against the French on 18 March 1978. By that time he had notched a record twenty tries for his country (later equalled by Gerald Davies); though he chose to sign off with a soaring dropped goal from thirty metres, his third for Wales. These were halcyon days; but, beyond doubt, every one of them had been well-earned.

So rugby mirrors life. Youth is tempestuous, volatile, ambitious, greedy for success, frightened of failure. With maturity comes the sheer pleasure of practising skills honed through many seasons, in the certainty that they will not fail you. By now the fans who screeched a decade ago that you could not pass the ball want to kiss your hand, or at least beg an autograph.

Gareth's judgement remained sound in his choice of the right time to finish. 'Why would I want to go on doing this?' he asked himself and Maureen as the summer of 1978 gave way to colder days. The new-mown grass smelt tempting. An enticing odour of liniment still hovered around his tracksuit. But, thanks, but no thanks, he reasoned: 'There's been success and satisfaction. But remember the pain of rugby at summit level. You can do without that at your age.' He was thirty-one.

The rivers, and the prey they concealed, had waited patiently to claim him back. As a small boy, he used to go fishing above Gwauncaegurwen with a bamboo stick and dangling string. Now he was happy to get his legs rusty again: had rods, would travel. To Taupo, with Andy Haden. To Scandinavia, Russia, South Africa with television crews, and often, to nearby Llandysul on the Teifi, whose local club made him an honorary member in 1971. Over at Llandegfedd in Gwent he landed a 45lb-6oz pike to set a British record.

This love of angling derives from the peace it affords his still hyperactive heart and soul. He continues to encounter turbulence: as a director of vehicle sales and rental firms in Wales, as chairman of Hyder's leisure subsidiary Hamdden, and as a consultant who travels the world for property giant TBI. Then, missions accomplished, he retreats to favourite stretches of water where, often at night, he fishes alone. There he will muse and dream. Seldom about rugby, more often about friendships: 'I look up at all those billions of stars, and I imagine that it would be nice if a few pals were to turn up and we could have a little party, maybe with some bottles of champagne.' Then come the sudden swirl and the bubbles that re-rivet concentration on the river. His good friend Clive Gammon, with whom he has fished for television and for fun in many parts of the world, believes that the call of the rivers also reveals something of the inner make-up which sets Gareth apart: 'He moves and manoeuvres further than the rest of us; the moon comes up but he won't leave the riverbank. There is a hunger for the sport . . . A hunger.'

It was another appetite, for supremacy in the mimic strife that is the handling code, which meant that he will undoubtedly be judged as the greatest of the century's rugby-playing athletes. 'In action, I always placed total trust in my ability. I truly felt there was nothing that I could not do.'

As it happens, there were two things which he did not accomplish. It would have been nice to win the Cup with Cardiff, instead of being a losing finalist twice. Also, to be captain of the club; but his team-mates never chose him. On the evening when he was standing for election Maureen waited expectantly for his return home. He came in quietly and tossed his kit bag into a corner. 'Well,' he said. 'They voted for Gerald.' Maybe he had spent too little time with the troops. Close-season tours meant that he restarted training later than the others. Some thought that he picked his games. Whatever lay behind it, this was a failure, a disappointment. But not one that you lost sleep over. That night he went to bed and slept the clock around.

Now, he readily admits to contentment amid advancing years. The teenage love affair with Maureen that became a marriage endures and matures. The couple are proud of their sons Rhys and Owen (who also attended Millfield). The residence beside the sea at Porthcawl is confidently Welsh in language, culture and attitudes. Even his physique, despite years in a collision sport, remains relatively unscathed: 'My luck held. I never broke a bone, nor even had a stitch in. Only now do I need new knees. But, then, so did my dad – when he touched eighty.'

Heart and soul? For Wales? It is a kind of impudence even to insert the question-marks. Gareth Edwards, it seems to me, has been a supreme lifter of spirits and morale; a vital component of the feel-good factor that is slowly but surely making itself apparent in the Welsh nation's persona, and its politics.

Do not mistake me. Chauvinism does not come into it. Like all great men in situations of challenge, Gareth sought first to meet his own demanding standards, not those of onlookers. That is, playing to his maximum effect was the imperative which motivated every stride or flex of muscle. Moreover he was bonded with men alongside whom he loved to play and who, it went without saying, should not be let down. Perhaps, now and then, team-mates failed to keep up with him on one of the dynamic sorties that brought great tries. But, as he returned to the half-way line, the agreeable tumult ringing in his ears would have assured him that a whole nation had been at his elbow.

BARRY JOHN

Hywel Teifi Edwards

Born the son of a ship's carpenter in a Cardiganshire seaside village, I was brought up on tales of voyages to distant places and later, gagging in incredulity and horror, I devoured the diary account of a fellow Cardi's pursuit of Klondike gold. To follow John Davies from somnolent Penrhiw-llan to Sgagway and on over the Chilkoot Pass to Alaska in 1898 is to traverse the hinterland of hell and I cannot even conceive of undertaking any such journey. But in the late afternoon of 26 April 1972 I did pack my family into our Ford Cortina and make for Cardiff Arms Park, some sixty miles from our home near Llanelli where rumour had it, accurately as it transpired, that Barry John was appearing for the last time on our 'National' field. His XV was to take on Carwyn James's XV in a match celebrating the jubilee of Urdd Gobaith Cymru (the Welsh League of Youth) and many of the triumphant 1971 Lions together with the 1971 Welsh 'Grand Slammers', were again flocking to the standards of Cefneithin rugby. In my own way I was also embarking on a madding journey for a final glimpse of gold.

Cardiff lay the other side of Port Talbot, a 'Slough of Despond' for travellers before the opening of the M4 by-pass in 1966. On that April day in 1972, however, it offered no relief; on the contrary, it bore comparison with the Chilkoot Pass as a place calculated to induce homicidal and suicidal thoughts in all who sought to move on – especially puce, bug-eyed, Barry John idolators who meshed in futile fury with homebound workers. Apoplexy belched from a thousand quivering exhausts. By the time we reached the Arms Park the first half was in its dying moments, our seats had been taken by similarly traumatized west Walians who would not be moved and we resigned ourselves to watching the last act of the passing of 'King John' seated on the concrete steps of the North Stand. And to be told at half-time that a regal try had long since opened the scoring simply deepened one's Calvinistic sense of having been singled out that day for retribution.

But, like some inspired Victorian sunbeam dispelling a poor sinner's gloom, 'King John' crossed again before our very eyes as the game neared its end. As he had done so often on so many fields, he suddenly materialized from somewhere with menacing ease, left a couple of forwards floundering, apparently doubled the width of the field with a feint or two and was over the try-line as if by divine right. He was subsequently to praise the intelligent play of his centre, Billy Raybould, whose running in support kept the thundering Llanelli wing, Roy Mathias, from getting at him, but noteworthy as was Raybould's contribution the abiding memory is of 'The King' moving through and away from his steaming would-be tacklers with the kind of movement that brought to mind Thompson's 'Hound of Heaven' – 'Deliberate speed, majestic instancy'. Barry John's last try on our 'National' field in 1972 was converted by Gareth Edwards with a kingmaker's sense of occasion. 'The King', after scoring fourteen points in his team's victory by 32 points to 28, disappeared into the changing-room from where he would emerge as one of our 'necessary figures' to act as a whetstone for our perennial great expectations. Another, cast in the same Arthurian mould, would surely come!

I had plenty of time under duress in Port Talbot to question the sanity of a long-confirmed soccerite who would willingly take his family on a hell-ride to see a game of rugby. Soccer won my allegiance when I was a boy in the 1940s and the memory of the post-war years when our communal fears were exuberantly volleyed to oblivion in town and village will never fade. For three intoxicating years my village, Llanddewi Aber-arth, its 'boys' having returned from active service, actually fielded a side in the second division of the North Cardiganshire League. Our first game was a 'friendly' against a team of PoWs in nearby Llan-non who had been kicking a ball around for the better part of five years. We lost 13–1 and my *mam-gu* developed an immediate interest in the Nuremberg Trials. It did not help that my father had been a prisoner near Bremen for the better part of three years.

On 21 October 1950, Aber-arth AFC went to Cardiff to see Wales play Scotland at Ninian Park. It was a trip worthy of Dylan Thomas's word-spinning. I had only once before been to Cardiff and that had been a Sunday school outing. The trip to Ninian Park would be a venture of a different kind. Perched on the parapet of the bridge we listened like so many ravenous nestlings to one of our stalwart merchant mariners as he warned us in unbiblical Welsh about the predators who preyed upon innocents abroad in big cities:

'Bloody hell, watch out for the women in Cardiff! Hell's bells, be prepared!'

'What do you mean, Rhys?'

'What do I mean? Listen boi bach, there are women in Cardiff who can play with your cock and take your ticket at the same time!'

Dear God! In the darker recesses of one's anticipation something stirred only to be instantly neutered by the terror of a lost ticket.

'Don't tell your lies Rhys'.

'Lies, be damned! Listen boi bach, the last time I went to a match one old sow tried it out on me, but nothing doing boi bach. This one of mine has been round the world!'

On our way home to an early bed we debated the veracity of our counsellor's anatomical evidence and decided that we would be well advised to disembark in Cardiff wearing a bathing costume over our underpants. And we made it to Ninian Park, giving females of all ages a wide berth and attracting compassionate looks as we crabbed along pavements, left hand thrust deep in trouser pocket, right hand clamped to right breast. There was a crowd of 50,000 to see the match and it was my first palpitating experience of being part of a nation exhorting its team to victory. I will never forget it. We lost, 3-1, but the boys from Aber-arth had actually seen their heroes for the first time – Barnes, Sherwood, Tommy Jones, Burgess, Paul and Ford – Trevor Ford! We would re-enact their roles on the village schoolyard until the following October.

I did not see the inside of the Arms Park until 26 January 1952 when I took another bus trip with my schoolfellows to watch Hennie Muller's fearsome Springboks reduce the Barbarians to kindergarten stature as they defeated them, 17–3. A heavy snowfall in west Wales saw a few of us make the journey to Cardiff in Wellington boots, only to be met with bright city sunshine without a snowflake in sight. We trudged, ruefully rustic, to the stadium but quickly felt at ease as the Barbarians, with the exception of Bleddyn Williams, played as if they, too, were wearing Wellingtons. I relished it as another initiative experience but to my mind it could not begin to compare with the fervour of Ninian Park. In the years ahead I would be disabused of that idea.

Aberaeron Grammar School was a soccer school but the post-war appointment to its staff of some highly charged rugbyites saw the gradual introduction of their game. (By 1951 I was sufficiently interested in the fortunes of the Welsh XV to be cast down when I heard that Scotland had trounced us, 19–0, at Murrayfield. The fact that Aber-arth AFC had also lost 7–1 that same February Saturday deepened my grievance against God.) Rugby football's attraction, its visceral excitement, was quickly felt by many boys, including those like myself who knew that it would never supplant soccer in their affections and resented the fascist hyping of 'rugger' as 'a man's game'.

The school soccer team, almost to a man, played rugby during its allotted term time and many years later I rejoiced on learning that Barry John, Gareth Edwards and Phil Bennett were talented soccer enthusiasts as well as great rugby players. It showed, of course, in their kicking; all three were magnificent tactical kickers, John and Bennett having also mastered the art of unfussy, fluent, accurate place-kicking which saw them breaking Welsh records. John's place-kicking is so easily recalled – a quick collier's squat behind the ball which was then briefly addressed before being sent, more often than not, between the posts. He returned from the famed Lions tour of New Zealand in 1971 with 191 points, thirty of them out of a total of forty-eight scored in the four Tests, and his haul in seventeen games included seven tries, thirty-one conversions, twenty-eight penalties and eight drop-goals. Little wonder that Carwyn James encouraged him to keep sharp when the tedium of training got to him by practising his soccer skills with Mike Gibson.

What his tactical kicking did to Fergie McCormick's positional play in the First Test has gone down in rugby history. Poor McCormick's tendency to lumber had been noted by James, long practised as a back-pew Cefneithin deacon in focusing on failings from afar, and he had on his very doorstep in John a hitman to destroy one redoubtable adversary with as deadly a demonstration of 'putting the boot in' as the game has known. One can picture James squinting orientally through a fug of cigarette smoke as he smoothly told John how he wanted his victim disposed of, certain in the knowledge that it would be done. John's purposeful kicking was masterly; he place-kicked with the sweet rhythm of Mike Summerbee taking a corner and angled his diagonals as perceptively as the splendid Ivor Allchurch did his through-balls. And like them he was unruffled, unhurried and seldom not in tune with his game.

My first teaching appointment in 1959 took me to the Garw Grammar School in Pontycymer, a fine school with a proud tradition of producing first-class rugby players, none better than John Lloyd and Jeff Young, a pair of sixth-form Titans when I arrived, and who were later to excel for Wales as senior internationals alongside Barry John. Married to a girl from the Garw Valley, we made our home on the outskirts of Bridgend at a time when Bridgend RFC was building an exciting team around Roddy Evans, Gary Protheroe, Ken Richards, Keith Bradshaw and Ron Evans. I was well and truly bitten by the rugby bug and having decided not to play 'my game' while I settled in as a teacher, I was free to watch top-class matches regularly for the first time in my life. I recall my Bridgend years with great pleasure.

I arrived too late in 'the South' to see Cliff Morgan for Cardiff scurrying as devastatingly as a soldier ant through the opposition. Of the outside-halves I saw I delighted in Bryan Richards's impish play for Swansea, Cliff Ashton's lancing runs for Aberavon, David Watkins's thoroughbred pace for Newport and Ken Richards's expansive kicking game for Bridgend. Richards, a fine soccer player for Swansea University College when I played for Aberystwyth, was the best two-footed kicking outside-half I have seen to date and his raking grubber-kicks to left and right set up attacks that destroyed the best defences. He place-kicked prodigious lengths, too, and was a mean runner when the mood took him.

As for David Watkins who was to yield his place in the Welsh XV to Barry John, I see him still as the demon of the Snelling Sevens when the Newport VII turned all their opponents' legs to water. In my view we never saw him at his incisive best for Wales, the rugby mind-set of that period caged him, but Watkins in the Snelling Sevens made you feel that he should be hobbled to make a fair game of it. I recall the satisfaction of hearing an enraged Cardiff supporter cursing 'that bloody gazelle from hell!' He excelled for the Lions in 1966 before going North in 1967 where his remarkable running, kicking and astute generalship were fully appreciated – and this was the player Barry John replaced in the Welsh team in 1966 when still a mere student in Trinity College, Carmarthen.

By 1965 we had moved to live in Llangennech, some four miles from Llanelli, which meant that we had landed in a rugby hotbed. The Scarlets were about to be transformed by the coming of Carwyn James, the Welsh XV was fast approaching a second 'Golden Era' and the name, Barry John, had already impinged itself on the awareness of rugby followers – not only in Llanelli where he had first played for the Scarlets against Moseley during Christmastime 1962, signalling his arrival with a try which he also converted.

In college between 1964 and 1967 he worked at his skills, perfecting his line-kicking and adding a lethal drop-goal to an armoury which his mentor, Carwyn James, might envy. Chosen to appear in a Welsh Trial at Aberavon in 1966, his faction's frequent exhortations, 'Drop goal, Barry, drop goal', soon had Watkins's followers shouting 'Drop dead, drop bloody dead!' Doubting the wisdom of remonstrating I remained silent but on Saturday, 28 November 1970, when he dropped four goals for Cardiff to defeat the Scarlets, I knew exactly how they felt.

In December 1966, he took David Watkins's place against Australia at the Arms Park and again in the following encounter with Scotland at Murrayfield. Both games were lost and he would have to partner Gareth Edwards in the Cardiff team and wait for Watkins to go North before reclaiming the Welsh jersey. Thereafter he would win another twenty-three caps, making himself 'a national necessity' before retiring, much too soon at twenty-seven years of age, from the fields of praise in 1972.

My work as an Adult Education tutor saw me teaching a Welsh literature class every winter for more than twenty years in Gwendraeth Grammar School, that rugby forcing-house which in turn sent out Carwyn James, Barry John, Gareth Davies and Jonathan Davies to quicken the Welsh pulse. I taught – and was taught by my students – within sight of the pitch on which their presence was imprinted in a myriad stud marks. I occasionally enlisted them as metaphors when our discussions focused on what inspired poets do with words. Their skills and the appreciation of literature could come together without any recourse to academic kitsch in that class which evinced the strengths – intellectual, moral and communal – that gave, and perchance will continue to give, the culture of the Gwendraeth Valley its vitality, creativity and resilience.

I taught what was at times 'a riotous assembly' of retired colliers, teachers and lecturers, ministers of religion, civil servants, housewives, the occasional farmer, the odd salesman etc – all of them Welsh to the core, deeply interested in their cultural inheritance and confident enough of its inherent worth to want to subject it to criticism. When the National Eisteddfod of Urdd Gobaith Cymru came to the Gwendraeth in 1989 a book, *Balchder Bro* (Gwendraeth Pride), was published in celebration of the event, to which Barry John fittingly contributed a valediction for Carwyn James. John has seen fit on more than one occasion to acknowledge his debt to Cefneithin and the upbringing which bred in him a sense of loyalty to family and community. He would have enjoyed participating in that class, which for me is to underline what was the bedrock of his excellence – a sharply critical awareness of what he was about, what he was capable of achieving and what faults needed correction when he fell short of the mark. Such an awareness bespeaks a confidence and resolve which has long stood Gwendraeth folk in good stead.

When Carwyn James died in 1983, Barry John expressed in Welsh and English with the kind of restraint that chimed with his style of play, his affection and admiration for the man who instilled in him early on a belief in the supremacy of 'the thinking game'. It is true that the Lions would not have triumphed in 1971 without a concerted will to win, brilliant individual skills and a readiness for physical confrontation which combined to produce performances of the same quality as the anthracite coal on which the Gwendraeth villages – Cross Hands, Cefneithin, Gors-las, Dre-fach, Pontyberem, Pont-iets, Pont-henri, and Trimsaran – were built. But to light and keep up an anthracite fire you have first to lay your coals precisely and then make judicious use of the poker as the need arises. Carwyn James laid the fire in 1971 and Barry John knew exactly how and when to use the poker. Their incendiary Cefneithin thinking illuminated the play which singed, and at times burnt to a crisp, New Zealand rugby.

Those were heady days for Welsh supporters. John partnered by Gareth Edwards, that incandescent piece of anthracite from Gwauncaegurwen whose prowess will glow as long as rugby has followers, exuded a confidence so all-embracing that miffed English correspondents were reduced to levelling charges of 'arrogance' against a nation usually so decently diffident. And there appeared to be no end to it. Starting with the Jarrett-detonated demolition of England by 34 points to 21 at the Arms Park on 15 April 1967, it went on throughout the 1970s, even gathering pace after John retired. I was there in 1967 when Keith Jarrett made his 'Boys' Own' debut, after which the Llangennech trips to Cardiff became Mecca occasions. I was there again on 12 April 1969 when England succumbed 30–9, indistinguishable at the end from the rubble of the old stadium which presaged the appearance of a grander temple. Maurice Richards, a wing who went for the line like an affronted zealot, scored four tries and Barry John, retrieving his own chip-ahead some thirty yards out, feinted and weaved through a phalanx of desperately clutching defenders to score his first try for Wales at the Arms Park. Lying prone near the posts after touching down, one of England's back-row forwards, understandably I thought, did his best to bury him, only to have his backside firmly booted by an exultant Richards. I like to think that he was the first to hail the coming of 'The King'.

By the time John embarked for New Zealand in 1971 his exploits in the Welsh teams since 1967 – teams which won the Triple Crown and the Five Nations Championship in 1968–9, shared the Championship with France in 1969–70 and achieved the Grand Slam a year later – had singled him out for obsessive attention. His tackling against France at Stade Colombes on 27 March 1971 as much as his try, which saw him slanting across and drifting through their cover defence, had increased the burden of expectations placed on him. John in harness with Edwards would do mighty deeds, and of course he did, leaving us to ponder what he would have accomplished for the Lions on the sunny fields of South Africa in 1968 had he not broken his collar bone in the First Test. If he had anything to prove in New Zealand, John more than proved it and was accorded legendary status on his return. What wonder, then, that thousands of us were prepared to take the Port Talbot trail in April 1972 to see this player grace the Arms Park for the last time.

In a post-1971 radio talk, Carwyn James remarked upon the melding of Celtic personalities that made the Edwards–John partnership as memorable as a classical *cywydd* couplet, a forging of strict-metre Welsh poetry seemingly as inevitable as it was unforgettable. Edwards explosively athletic, John the embodiment of calculating detachment. When his retirement brought their run of twenty-two successive games for Wales to an end, the Welsh, as has been our wont down the centuries, took comfort in the prospect of imminent disaster, only for

Phil Bennett, yet another Llanelli nuggett, to form a 25-game partnership with Edwards which ever since their retirement from the international arena in 1978 has triggered an endless debate about the respective merits of Edwards–John and Edwards–Bennett.

I content myself with the satisfaction of having been around to witness both partnerships in those years of elation. I saw much more of Bennett than I did of John and I rejoice in the memory of a glorious player. My first recollection of him goes back to a ferocious Youth International match against France at Llanelli in the late 1960s, eventually won by Wales after Bennett, his left eye closed as a result of French fraternity, lasered from a scrum on the half-way line, disorientating the full-back with a venomous sidestep off the right foot as he made for the posts. There would be many more such victims. He made a fitful start in the Welsh team, suffered the indignity of being dropped from the squad in 1975 after a sparkling tour of South Africa with the Lions in 1974, did not score his first international try until his twentieth game but retired as a distinguished Welsh team captain (who had also captained the Lions in 1977) with a record 166 points to his name after twenty-nine appearances. On his day he was as elusive as a fugitive snipe and as viciously penetrative as a gannet's beak. As a kicker he was as sublimely right-footed as Garrincha of Brazil. He was a small, dark, insurgent Celt and on 18 March 1978 when he scored two tries against France at the Arms Park to help clinch the Grand Slam, he was a Welsh Asterix. I see him still, ball tucked possessively under his left arm, eyeing the giant Bastiat as Welsby, the English referee, read the two captains the riot act.

I steer clear of arguments about the merits of John and Bennett. In Llangennech, the home of the illustrious R. T. Gabe, a Cardi soccerite's views on rugby are at best diverting. But when the argument rages I think of two scenes in one of my favourite Westerns, *Butch Cassidy and the Sundance Kid*. Early on in the film Cassidy's right to lead the gang is challenged by a 'grizzly' who wants the problem settled by sixgun or knife. On hearing that Cassidy does not want to shoot him he produces a buffalo-skinning knife. Cassidy promptly suggests that they should first settle the rules of combat, a proposition so outrageous as to disarm momentarily his would-be disemboweller. In that moment a crippling kick to the crotch drives his balls up into his flaring nostrils and a right to the jaw leaves him senseless. Such, so often, was the effect of Barry John's guile on the opposition. He weighed things up, saw a weakness and struck.

In the other scene, Sundance is playing cards in a dingy saloon and is on a winning streak. He is accused of cheating by a red-eyed gunslinger whose life is then spared when Cassidy, having let drop his partner's name, persuades him to apologize. As they make for the door the diminished 'baddie' asks, 'How good are you?', whereupon Sundance spins around, dropping on his knee, and in a cadenza of bullets removes his gunbelt and sends it flying into a corner. Rugby supporters asked the same question of Bennett after his early hangdog appearances for Wales, and on his return from South Africa in 1974 he gave his Sundance answer. From 1975 to 1978 he coruscated. You marvelled at John's artistry on realizing what he had done. You thrilled to Bennett's virtuosity even as he performed his feats. To express a preference is to choose between a pearl and a ruby.

After some twenty years of Welsh mediocrity at international level and a deepening impatience among followers with a 'professional' approach which to date has not been translated into rousing performances on the field of play, it is all too easy to find most of our post-1970s players sadly wanting when compared with their precursors. To yield to that temptation is to do the present cause of Welsh rugby a disservice. It is one thing to perpetuate the memory of the second 'Golden Era' as a source of inspiration; it is another thing entirely to fashion of it a distorting mirror wherein our current players should view themselves as Lilliputians.

Comparisons calculated to implant a sense of inadequacy are best not made. If not actually destructive, they will inevitably give rise to an over-fed anxiety to do the past proud which will manifest itself in furious effort – furious but seldom fruitful. Anxiety has been the undoing of our national teams for far too long and nothing better illustrates it than the fact that our coaches are now much exercised by a chronic disorder known as 'ball retention' which sees experienced, even professional players, frequently drop passes or lose possession of the ball when tackled. There have been games when players made one think of captured Welsh archers deprived of their thumbs by the enemy. In contrast, what most marked the rugby played during the Barry John years in the Welsh jersey, and throughout the 1970s, was a quality of perceptive control that engendered a sense of confidence even when the team was on the back foot, and it needs to be remembered how often it was on the back foot when confronted with teams fiercely intent on silencing talk of Welsh invincibility. But anxiety was never allowed to intrude to the extent that play became frantic in its want of vision and purpose, because in Barry John the Welsh had a thinker at outside-half for whom a game plan was not a thing immutable. The same was true of J. P. R. Williams, John Dawes, Gerald Davies, Gareth Edwards, Mervyn Davies and John Taylor, but the game of rugby demands that the outside-half orders the play in such a way as to spread confidence throughout the team and this Barry John did – as did Phil Bennett, too, when he found his international feet.

In everything he did John was perfectly co-ordinated and composed. I doubt that there has ever been a more composed outside-half. He knew full well what he was capable of and his self-confidence transmitted itself to his team-mates and to the supporters. Gareth Edwards has put on record the uplifting effect of that confidence on him when they met on the playing field at Trinity College, Carmarthen before their first appearance together in the Welsh team. The famous Edwards spin pass was still to be developed and he knew that his service could be a little wayward. John's assurance was immediate: 'You just throw it and I'll catch it.' And he did. Carwyn James contented himself with a nod in his direction before he went out to destroy McCormick in the First Test of the 1971 tour of New Zealand. He knew it was enough. When Hawke's Bay resorted to thuggery in a vain attempt to tame the Lions, John slowed to a walking pace the better to show his contempt – and remained unscathed. There is no gainsaying the debilitating effect of such composure on the opposition.

The Arms Park that I first entered on 26 January 1952 is no more. It has been demolished and much of it auctioned off both to profit the Welsh Rugby Union and satisfy the many aficionados who would possess a permanent 'piece of the action'. I cannot count myself among the latter but I can well understand their craving. My Arms Park, and I am sure that of countless others, remains intact, a theatre of high endeavour ever loud with the acclaim of great players acting out the drama of unremitting contests. I have committed my Arms Park to memory, its legends to be summoned at will and construed as the mood may be without fear of my assessments suffering the correction of more 'knowledgeable' observers. And on the turf of that inviolable Arms Park no presence better communicates to me the artistry of rugby football than that of the consummate number 10 from Cefneithin. When Barry John left the field of play we felt deprived of a luminous Celtic talent, a talisman, another 'Excalibur' in whom we reposed our faith. As long as John was around no foe was unbeatable. Welsh poets accorded him the age-old tribute due the people's warriors in praise poetry. Cefneithin boasted its very own folk poet in Dai Culpitt who attended 'the class' in Gwendraeth Grammar School and he was quick to salute his renowned fellow villagers – Carwyn and Barry – marking the latter's final game with a characteristically warm-hearted sonnet. Dic Jones, Gwilym R. Jones, and Rhydwen Williams – three celebrated National Eisteddfod poets – all saw in Barry the lineaments of 'y gwaredwr'(the saviour). 'Gwilym R.', a fervid Welsh Nationalist, in his eulogy insisted on seeing him as an iconic figure reflecting a politically inspired national revival, 'Ein draig yn y newydd drin . . .' (Our dragon in the current battle), whereas Rhydwen Williams exulted in his wizardry, 'cnawd ac esgyrn yn cynganeddu'n gerdd /o rithmau mawreddog . . .' (flesh and bone harmonizing in a poem / of majestic rhythms).

It was left to Dic Jones, however, to fix the popular image of the 1971 Grand Slam team in fifteen demotic *englynion* (strict-metre epi-grammatic verse) which were then sung to the tune of 'Sosban Fach' in traditional style with harp accompaniment – and recorded – by Parti Menlli from north Wales to crystallize in seven puckish Welsh syllables what the general view of the Cefneithin maestro was – and is. 'Boi ar jawl yw Barry John' by dint of *cynghanedd* transmuted 'Barry John is a hell of a boy' into an aphorism. It has lodged itself in the national memory, as crisp, exact and finished as a typical Barry John try, and if adopted as a mantra by today's chanting supporters I would not be surprised to see the Welsh XV winning Rugby's World Cup in 1999. Praise be!

JOHN TAYLOR

Peter Stead

The clearest image I have of the flanker John Taylor is of a Boxing Day game at Stradey Park. London Welsh had scored an early try and had silenced a crowd who all too quickly had lost their festive mood. Clearly the Scarlets were finding it difficult to shrug off seasonal excess whilst the visitors were rampant: a second try soon followed. The Exiles were playing like the home team, enjoying Christmas to the full, and nobody was relishing the freedom of Stradey more than John Taylor. He was everywhere, orchestrating the whole charge, his unruly hair and ragged beard making his head the most readily identifiable thing on the field of play, his distinctly military-like instructions and encouragement clearly audible to everyone in the mute crowd.

By this time we all knew who John Taylor was. That had not always been the case. As a virtual unknown he had made his debut for Wales in 1967 at a time when both the process of selection and the attitude of fans to selectors were changing perceptibly. We had all grown up in a rugby culture in which our fortunes as a nation were in the hands of the selection committee, a group of men universally referred to as 'the Big Five'. In this pre-devolution era 'the Big Five' constituted one of the Principality's most distinctive, identifiable and most frequently talked-of institutions. Its status can only be compared to the College of Cardinals or the Soviet Politburo. They were not public figures, for the most part they seemed to be shadowy figures who had emerged from a committee system that was the most obvious but least understood aspect of Welsh life. Individually they were nothing, but once closeted they became the arbiters of our fortunes. We brought them in to almost every conversation, we expected to see them cited in every cartoon, not least the wonderful 'Ponty and Pop' saga. We were in awe of their power, we waited anxiously for their every pronouncement, but ultimately we had little respect for them. They always made mistakes, they clearly had favourites, they were always biased in favour of the glamour clubs, they had almost certainly never been to Maesteg, Pontypridd and Newbridge. They were obviously afraid of real talent, and were undoubtedly in cahoots with J. B. G. Thomas and the *Western Mail*. When Wales lost or won unconvincingly we had no difficulty in allocating blame.

For some reason, and I remember this very clearly, our dissatisfaction with the Big Five and our feeling that the whole selection system was intolerably rotten began to be associated with the presence on the Big Five of somebody called H. M. Bowcott of London Welsh. At that stage of the 1960s we did not take London Welsh too seriously: they were a bunch of teachers from the Home Counties who rather like Devonport services, St Luke's College and Watsonians came to Wales at holiday times to fill-out fixture lists and more importantly to contribute to good sing-songs in the clubhouse. Suddenly H. M. Bowcott was in a position of power with what seemed to us the sole aim of ensuring that at least one teacher, student or medic, who had registered with London Welsh having failed to make much impact at grammar school in Wales, was included in every national team selected. We were convinced that he was bamboozling his colleagues, a case of the valley 'apparatchiki' being intimidated by metropolitan bluff. At the same time we saw his success in placing his men as clear proof of the trade-offs and quotas that we had always assumed to be the basis of natural selection.

Wales were always capable of losing one or two games a season and we felt our distrust justified. But things were changing, although we had every reason for not realizing that historic forces were at work. Over a year or two an era of mystifying choices and of compensatory caps to old favourites (usually against France) gave way to a new pattern in which surprise selections paid off and virtual unknowns either immediately or quite quickly played like men marked by destiny. In time, we came to realize that our notions of the selectors as constituting a typically dull and all-too-fallible committee had been replaced by a conviction that the team line-up was being handed down on a tablet of stone. The transitional season was that quite remarkable one of 1966–7. In December, Wales lost to Australia at the Arms Park but had given new caps to Gerald Davies, Barry John and Delme Thomas. The new year began with defeat at Murrayfield, a game in which John Taylor had made his debut. In March Ireland came to Cardiff, scored an early try and won 3–0, a bleak occasion which those of us who experienced it can never forget and a score-line which later generations had difficulty in believing. With three defeats it was inevitably 'one-cap wonder' time and on April Fool's Day at Stade Colombes we were not surprised to see two 'nouvel international' asterisks in the Welsh line-up, one of which was against the name of a scrum-half called Edwards who was not given an initial. A tannoy announcement indicated that at number 8 our beloved Alun Pask would be replaced by another 'nouvel' player, D. Morris of Neath. Wales lost 20–14 and so the scene was set for the game against England on 15 April. England came to Cardiff seeking the Triple Crown, the first time in history that this particular fixture would determine that honour. The whitewash was on, but the selectors had an ace card to play. Out of nowhere they conjured up Keith Jarrett who obliged by playing out of position at full-back and scoring nineteen points and Wales won 34–21. I recall my disbelief as standing in the North Enclosure I watched this 'unknown' pass me on his way to scoring a try that he alone had known was on from the moment he fielded the ball. We could not wait for the next season to start.

It was a remarkable story and it was not over yet. The most golden of eras was in the making and selectorial 'chutzpah' was the hallmark of the process, not least the 1969 blooding of two more London Welsh discoveries, J. P. R. Williams and Mervyn Davies. We now took it for granted that the whole force of history was on our side and that the committee in their blazers and slacks were as inspired as the team itself. In this new art of Welsh alchemy perhaps the most dramatic discovery of a nugget had come in the form of John Taylor who in the incredulous words of the official programme had come into national consideration 'on the strength of only four games'. As a newcomer to the London Welsh side Taylor had a good Christmas tour in Wales and on that evidence alone was 'plunged into the trial'. What a hit-and-miss phenomenon those trials were, the air of unreality compounded by ruthless and confusing orders for players to swap jerseys and sides at half-time. But on this occasion, at least, the event was justified for Taylor went straight into the team that travelled to Murrayfield.

In every respect he was an outsider. Nobody knew him and his credentials were in every respect unconvincing. In those days place of birth told you almost everything you wanted to know in judging a player, school attended was also relevant, and the formal assessment came after only at least a couple of striking performances at Stradey, the Gnoll, and Rodney Parade. 'Born in Watford, educated at Watford Grammar School' did not cut much ice. Loughborough was better (Gerald had gone there), but a London Welsh Christmas tour was hardly first-class rugby. Furthermore the man did not look Welsh, it was an English head, and the width and cut of the jib seemed better suited for Sandhurst than the Arms Park. And it was not as if we were short of open-side wing forwards or, as we often called them, winging-forwards. Indeed this was perhaps one of the positions we cared about most, cared in a particularly personal and even idealistic way. For all their speed, bravery and dexterity backs were, for the most part, short men: the powerhouse meanwhile was made up of big men bred by nature to perform superhuman feats. Back-row forwards, however, tended to be perfectly built, often fast, fearless and clever but essentially cool and laid-back too. We noted their air of detachment at the back of line-outs, or as they deigned to join a scrum. When they went into action they did so with something of the precision, dash and romance of fighter-pilots. Most Welsh fans warmed especially to their own teams when success was spearheaded by an effective back-row unit, and no sight in rugby gave as much pleasure as the break-away taking the opposing stand-off, man and ball. Since 1958 Haydn Morgan of Abertillery had been one of the darlings of Welsh rugby, and voices would break with emotion as tales were told of how this red-haired former paratrooper had broken so quickly and tackled so ferociously. The newly selected John Taylor was made very aware that much was expected of him if he thought he was better than a predecessor who had won twenty-seven caps and gone on two Lions tours. The comments of other fans suggested that it might have been better if that treasured number-7 shirt had gone to Omri Jones of Aberavon or Dennis Hughes of Newbridge. Those few who took London Welsh more seriously pointed out the club's first-choice open-side was Tony Gray who, although a north Walian, was quicker to the tackle and to the ball than any other qualified player in that position.

The selectors had opted for John Taylor and their man was not to let them down. Strangely his career was in some respect a carbon-copy of that of his predecessor: twenty-six caps, one fewer than Morgan, and two Lion tours. But whereas Morgan had been a romantic figure in a hit-or-miss decade, Taylor was to play an integral role in what he later chose to celebrate in print as 'the Decade of the Dragon' when nine championships were won or shared, three Grand Slams and three Triple Crowns recorded, and with Wales contributing decisively in 1971 to the most important and memorable of all Lions tours. In that decade

Taylor's great moment of individual fame came at Murrayfield in 1971, when he revived Grand Slam aspirations by winning the game with a last minute touch-line conversion that seemed so improbable that it took many fans several moments of mental arithmetic to determine the significance as far as the score was concerned. The year 1971 was certainly what Americans would call his 'career season': he could do little wrong and four Lions Test caps rightly came his way. He was a star player, not least because of his increasingly individualistic appearance, the bushier hair and beard giving him a prominence that his rivals often envied. He was greatly valued as a player, increasingly treasured as a stand-out character with flair, but above all appreciated as a member of a back row that was as good as any that had every played for Wales, and a back row that was in every respect ideally suited to the kind of rugby both Wales and the Lions required at that time.

The future Wales and British Lions flanker had grown up at Abbots Langley near Watford and had so enjoyed his junior school days as a flying left-wing at soccer that he was reluctant to take up his place at rugby-playing Watford Grammar School. Of course, he had impeccable Welsh credentials: his mother was from Pontycymer in the Garw Valley where her north Walian father was known as 'Towyn Jones': even John's East Anglian father had some Welsh blood. There had been many holidays in south Wales, but it was a visit to Abbots Langley by Welsh relatives on their way to Twickenham that had first prompted young John to consider Welsh ambitions: an uncle's jest 'You will play for Wales' had done the trick. Initially a fly-half, his prowess as a sprinter took him first to the wing and then to centre where he could indulge his love of tackling. At Loughborough College he found himself in competition with an outstanding centre, Gerald Davies, and that forced a decision to transfer to the back-row. Because he had consciously opted for a new position, Taylor found himself having to think out what was involved; he did that with the help of John Robins, the former Birkenhead Park and Wales prop who had played in New Zealand and Australia with the 1950 Lions and who then became the first ever Lions coach in those same countries in 1966. Robins was the ideal man to instruct his Loughborough students in the increasingly complex nature of back-row play.

Loughborough won the Middlesex Sevens at Twickenham and, as it happens, spent the evening celebrating at the nearby London Welsh club house where 'a deal was done' that took several players to that club. The year 1966 was a marvellous time for a young player to be arriving at Old Deer Park where the Welsh had played since their move from Herne Hill in 1957. Dai Hayward, that incomparable writer of Cardiff programme notes had referred to the move as one from 'Hernia Hill' to 'Old Dear's Park'. But all the jokes had to be put aside now for the club had entered what was to be its greatest era. For eight years between 1965 and 1973 the prosperity and educational dynamic of Wales ensured a flow of talented Welsh people to London and the Home Counties, and the Old Deer Park club house superbly placed between Kew Gardens and the pubs of Richmond became the place to be seen whether you were a student, a teacher, an MP, an opera singer or just Richard Burton or Hywel Bennett. Here as much as anywhere one sensed that everything was flowing the Welsh way. This was a famous old club that in its first hundred years was to provide 170 international players, but they were never to be so thick on the ground as in this eight-year period when eleven of the team played for the national side. When John Taylor went to South Africa with the 1968 Lions he was the only London Welsh player selected: when he went to Australia and New Zealand in 1971 he was one of six. The captain of that Lions side was John Dawes, the centre whose appointment as captain of London Welsh in 1965 had been the vital step in their emergence as possibly the best club rugby side in the world. For Taylor, Dawes was the game's great thinker, the man who inspired the philosophy that lay behind success for his club, his country and the Lions, 'Possession is precious' was what Dawes taught, 'use the ball, run it: make it count.' The tutelage of Dawes was what rounded off John Taylor's rugby education. It was time now to enjoy himself alongside his great colleagues: first at Old Deer Park with Tony Gray and then a little later with Mervyn Davies, and for Wales in time with Dai Morris and again Mervyn Davies.

Many forces conspired to give Wales its great moment of rugby excellence. There were new cultural energies in the land and its young people were playing a game in which administrators and newly appointed coaches were willing players to respond to role changes by providing faster, more fluent and entertaining rugby. The game's new thinkers headed by Dawes at Old Deer Park and Ray Williams at the Welsh Rugby Union had a vision of fifteen-man rugby and then, somewhat to their amazement, a new emphasis on fitness and a greater seriousness of purpose had given them the fifteen men they required. Scrums became solid, line-outs and mauls were won: the basics were there as were a new breed of super-fit and intelligent backs. What was needed to bring the two parts together, and at the same time to lubricate the whole machine was a new kind of back-row. Certain fundamentals remained, the men with 6, 7 and 8 on their backs had to be tacklers and not afraid to do some grafting in rucks and mauls. But now there were new requirements, or at least possibilities. If it was a running game then back-rows had to be up with the pace, indeed even dictating it. Pace in itself was not enough: traditionally the flankers in particular had been, as Taylor himself explained, hunters and destroyers: now they could become creators too. If good possession was now the essence of the game then the vital link in the whole process of attack was the degree to which the back-row man knew how to win the ball and then to use it once he had arrived at or caused the breakdown. More than ever support play was vital too; whichever back was crossing the advantage line he wanted to know that a fast mobile, strong back-row man was there beside him. In short, number 8s and flankers were encouraged to become the very cutting-edge of the new game. Showing off and individual moments of athleticism, long the hallmarks of some prominent favourites were no longer enough, creativity and intelligence had to go hand in hand with even higher levels of fitness.

In truth nobody was to be as good at all of this as Tony Gray who had to settle for being the great hero at Old Deer Park: he gained only two Welsh caps although he later became national coach. Wales felt more comfortable with Mervyn Davies in the middle and Taylor and Morris on either side. Like Taylor, Davies had just suddenly appeared in the London Welsh team. He too was 'unknown' although this was surprising as he had grown up in Swansea and his father had been a 'victory' international. He was teaching in the London area and was recommended to Old Deer Park as 'a bit of a beanpole who will win some line-out ball but do nothing else'! He was certainly something of 'a stick', six feet and four-and-a-half inches with not much meat on him and a player whose whole manner, 'languorous' as Dai Smith and Gareth Williams recalled it, seemed more suited to the basketball court. There was always something unlikely about him, the affectionate 'Merv the Swerve' tag reminds us of that exaggerated almost slow-motion way he would bend in the middle; the headband and increasingly full moustache gave him an erotic quality; perhaps he really was a black player on loan from the New York Knicks. For five years or so John Taylor lived with this quiet, friendly giant and saw him grow in every way. He filled out, he talked about the game and he went on to become one of the greatest ever number 8s. He won enough line-out ball to allow his team to get away with shorter flankers, he tackled tirelessly and, more than any other player I ever saw, he had the ability to effortlessly cover the whole width of the field: he had a fuller sense of the breadth of the game than anybody. How he got there so quickly we never knew. He became one of the great captains too, robbed by misfortune of the chance to captain the 1977 Lions. Mervyn like John Taylor was twice to go on Lions tours, an honour that Dai Morris of Neath never achieved. The British selectors thought him too small (at more or less six foot he was a shade taller than John Taylor), too silent, and too poor a traveller: but in Wales nobody was more deeply loved. He was the support player *par excellence*, the shadow, the scrum-half's bodyguard, he rarely left Gareth Edwards's side. 'Suddenly there was Dai', we explained as we recounted another try.

This was the company with which most of us will always associate John Taylor, although others will recall him as captain of London Welsh, a frequent try-scorer at the Middlesex Sevens, or playing in the hoops of Surrey. Wherever he played there was always a great brio to his game, a confidence, a flair, a clear determination to be getting on with things. He always stood out: even at that first all-important Welsh trial some of Omri Jones's supporters claimed that it was the head bandage he wore after an incident involving Norman Gale that brought him to the selectors' attention. We could always see him, we could count his tackles, appreciate his support play and above all spot that decisive midfield injection of pace and touch of class that opened up the game. But more than that there was always his sheer individuality. We welcomed the fact that he was that little bit different from the rest of the boys. In time J.P.R.'s long hair and Gerald's moustache had something of the same effect, but initially it was John Taylor's whiff of metropolitan sophistication that gave the Welsh team something just a little extra. Barry John was always fascinated by his accent and dubbed him Lord Kew. John's claim was that in Watford everyone spoke like he did. But in truth there did appear to be just a little touch of arrogant swagger and we loved it. There was the upright stance as if the 5 ft-11½ in. (1967 programmes) or 5 ft-11 in. (1970 programmes) flanker was imagining commentator Bill Maclaren once again referring to him as 'wee John Taylor', the open-chested run, and the almost military bearing. John Taylor has always had the look of an army officer on secondment to an expedition about to go into the Himalayas. French fans saw him rather differently, to them he was 'Le Hippy', one of the symbols of 1960s rugby. Whatever the tag he was his own man as is apparent in so many photographs of that time. Just to look at those action photos of him is to be reminded of how Welsh rugby in those days, however carefree it might have seemed, always rested on a sense of dynamic urgency.

That John Taylor was his own man and somebody with a slightly wider frame of reference than most Welsh rugby supporters was shown by the stand he took in 1969 over the issue of South Africa. Following his experience of South Africa with the 1968 Lions he informed the selectors that he did not want to be considered for the Welsh side to play the Springboks in Cardiff early in the new year. The official historians of the Welsh Rugby Union take care to ensure that their readers do not make too much of this incident for indeed, after being left out of the side for five games, Taylor was back in favour for the end-of-season visit of France. But Taylor's stand was a brave one and a greatly encouraging one for those of us who were deeply ashamed of that tour and some of the incidents that it occasioned. It was wonderful to have one small indication that at least somebody in Welsh rugby was aware that there is life after the final whistle. The player himself took a bit of stick, more so in England than in Wales where he was accused of being 'too big for his boots', but he was greatly impressed by the tact with which Peter Hain and the Anti-Apartheid Movement used his protest, and enormously encouraged by the support he received from the south Wales miners and in particular their eisteddfod. Amongst reporters Frank Keating was very supportive.

In 1970 Taylor had been the outsider, but as we have seen in 1971 he moved to the heart of things. The sheer no-nonsense control that allowed him to take that conversion at Murrayfield, a kick taken with all the sang-froid of the left-footed soccer player taking a corner, ensured his own popularity just as it 'heralded' a golden era. In that year too he became a Lion again, and this time an ever-present Test player too. Mervyn Davies was probably the most effective member of a Lions pack whose main job was just to feed the great backs who scintillated on that tour. Taylor's best day came in the Third Test at Wellington, a match for which he had not been an original selection: Fergus Slattery's withdrawal had given him a chance and he responded with some devastating tackling and winning key line-outs which contributed to a 13–3 victory. He revelled in the new seriousness, with coach Carwyn James and skipper John Dawes now spending hours in careful preparation: the days of bombast and rhetoric were over. He noted the effectiveness of Carwyn's innovative individual clinics and loved the way this Welsh intellectual teased and baffled the New Zealanders as he plotted their undoing. One day the New Zealand press corps came to a training session hoping to discover valuable training secrets only to discover the squad playing soccer, a game at which so many of them, not least Barry John, excelled. The learning process of the tour itself was sustained by a subsequent London conference where individual Lions gave papers and answered questions. Taylor's contribution to that seminar and the subsequent published volume provides a classic analysis of 'Loose Forward Play' and indicates how well suited he was to becoming a pundit on the game.

His international career ended in 1973, but John Taylor went on playing for and captaining London Welsh until 1978. Inevitably his life became focused not on what he was to describe as 'the 55 miles by 30' of the south Wales rugby world but rather on London, where schoolteaching gave way to consultancy and then to journalism, commentating and business interests generally. His thoroughly metropolitan credentials were confirmed by his contribution to *Time Out*, that weekly guide indispensable for anyone wanting to know the London scene. At first he wrote for the magazine as John Thomas but only until John Thomas interviewed John Taylor: his cover was then rumbled. As a television commentator he developed wider interests: his expertise on gymnastics took him to four Olympics. A new age of rugby coverage in which the BBC lost out to ITV made him invaluable for Thames Television as the chief commentator and advisor and put him in the front line for World Cup games. Combined with his no-nonsense crystal clear analysis were further business opportunities which led to his very successful video of the 1997 Lions. He is regularly asked to provide programme notes which allows him to give full rein to nostalgia and to tell all the old stories. Meanwhile as a staff writer for *The Mail on Sunday* he can be as outspoken and hard-hitting as any observer of the Welsh game.

'Wales is a second rate rugby nation – repeat 110 times daily until you actually believe it and then perhaps we stand a chance of joining the first rank again.' This was his response to his nation's abysmal showing in the 1991 World Cup. 'There is no longer room for pussyfooting' he went on. 'The gloves are off and those who are not with us are against us. Somehow we are going to drag Welsh rugby kicking and screaming into the Nineties.' For him things had started to go wrong even in the glorious 1970s as the Welsh were seduced by power play. Perhaps the Pontypool front row was partly to blame for they encouraged Wales to believe that other packs could be mastered, that total control could be achieved, and vital points scored at will. The deliberate holding of the ball drained all the genius out of the Welsh game and neglected everything that John Dawes had preached. The ball that Wales won was so late it was largely useless and so in season after season talented backs, often the equal in skill to the earlier heroes, were made to look predictable. This was the fate of Terry Holmes, Gareth Davies and even Robert Jones. Intelligence had gone out of the window and with it went flair. In report after report *The Mail on Sunday*'s man urged Wales to stop making excuses and to go out and seek the help of the world.

There is no doubt that John Taylor's enterprise and urbanity have allowed him to adapt to the new world in which rugby finds itself a good deal more successfully than the Welsh Rugby Union itself has done. His home now is in deepest rural Kent where he and his wife Tricia, a former model of Hungarian-Mexican descent, have several acres to share with their dogs and cats. Rugby fixtures and dinners often take him back to Wales and he is in regular touch with his old colleagues. He calls in to see Dai Morris and his horses at Rhigos, and he has helped Mervyn Davies with advice about his business ventures. He is loyal too to his beloved London Welsh, a club whose identity he has fought to preserve over the years. He is now deeply involved in the company that is trying to restore the club's fixtures and he wonders why the Welsh are now so much less effective than the Scots at defending their interests, at organizing ventures that cut across class divides, and at using social links as the basis of getting things done. He has been invited to join the new SWS (Sexy, Welsh and Social) lobby but as yet has not found time. It is a full life for a middle-aged man who has lost much of his hair but who retains so many of the qualities that made him a great player. The eyes are warm and friendly but the jaw (that one so vividly remembers being wired up after one injury) is firm and the voice commanding. To me he still seems an army man, the dashing Lieutenant or Captain Taylor who took charge of his men, led by example, and made sure that on the day the job was done.

PROSSER'S PONTYPOOL

Edward Butler

There should be no mystery to Pontypool Rugby Football Club, no obscurity beyond the murkiness of its brutality, no depth beyond the single dimension of its rudimentary code. This was a rugby club that stripped itself bone-white clean of tactical complexity and romantic charm, and clove a path to the top. The ideology was nine-man fundamentalism, fanatical, disturbing, plain, simple, unloved, and unmourned when oblivion reclaimed their mauling mullahs. And yet, beneath the concrete surface there lies a labyrinth of contradiction, and the town at the mid-point of the Eastern Valley becomes an extension of the Bermuda Triangle, known as the Pontypool Paradox . . .

The most apparent contradiction is the setting and the style. In the fantasia landscape of Pontypool Park the town's leading rugby club chose to play a brand of the game better suited to an urban wasteland. Year after year through the 1970s and the early part of the 1980s, the glorious changes of hue in the trees above and all around the ground from September to April stood in stark contrast to the colour of the sport. The shirts were striking enough with their red, white and black thick horizontal stripes but the spirit of the style was dark grey: scrummage, box-kick, line-out, drive, penalty – scored by a full-back who each year broke a world record for points almost without ever touching the ball by hand – or pushover try scored by the one of the two last players in numerical ascendancy with licence to lay hand on leather, the number 8 or scrum-half at number 9. This was simple enough to explain. The Gwent valleys had always produced good forwards and Pontypool were merely developing the tradition, albeit by taking it to its extreme and then a few rolling mauls beyond that.

And yet, the first post-war success for Pontypool had been achieved by a different means. In the late 1950s the pack was apparently adequate but little more. The forwards served only to provide the ball so that scrum-half Colin Evans could dispatch it out of their reach to Benny Jones at outside-half, who might unveil some new trickery or release Malcolm Price in the centre or Fenton Coles on the wing. When it came to the development of tradition – legend even – it was that generation of Pontypool three-quarters who led the way, not the forwards.

At least, however, the tradition of success had been established. Without the habit of winning, no club could look forward to the increasingly competitive structures of future decades with any confidence. Or so it might be thought. Instead, Pontypool left the 1950s and slid away in the 1960s until they found themselves approaching the age of the Coach, the Cup and the general brilliance of the 1970s from the bottom of a grim pile-up. At the start of the golden decade they were adrift in that awful, lonely place known as Below Penarth. That is the moment when Ray Prosser was appointed coach. Now the age of legend could really begin. And here surely there was no room whatsoever for any ambiguity.

Pross was a single-minded monster, a rock in the second row who had been the one guaranteed supplier of possession for Benny and the three-quarter jets in the 1950s. At some stage of his upbringing somebody had inserted railway sleepers where his shoulders should have been. He had played on twenty-two occasions for Wales between 1956 and 1961, a lock converted to prop for international duty. He was hard and crude, skilled and analytical. He was an enforcer and a technician, but only, it seemed, with regard to eight-fifteenths of the side. He professed always to have a fearful mistrust of three-quarters.

He was above all a character. And if much of his colour came from his use of language – Anglo-Saxon at its most effluent, an invective that would draw crowds in their hundreds to the Park on training nights and which could cripple the feeble of spirit at fifty paces – much, too, came from his self-projection as the small-town simpleton. Pross could just about make it five miles up or down the valley, north to Blaenavon Forgeside where he would supervise Sunday morning gallops led by John Perkins high up on the tramways above Big Pit, or south to Cwmbran, but any further than these neighbouring towns in the Eastern Valley and he would fall victim to homesickness. In later years, after his career had progressed from driving a bulldozer to overseeing slag-reclamation at Panteg Steelworks, he would talk of his dislike for the weekly 30-mile round-trip to Cardiff to pick up the wages.

'Yes, it must be worrying, Pross, having the responsibility for all that money, and you not particularly fond of driving.'

'Bollocks to the money,' Pross would say. 'It's just that Cardiff is such a long way away.'

He hated flying even more than driving, he claimed. They once managed to strap him into an aircraft seat for a tour to Washington DC in 1977, but he swore that he would never go into the air again.

And yet . . . and yet. In summer months his great frame could sometimes be found lying flat out, creating a bow in the warm corrugated-iron roof of his little hut with its stove-pipe chimney among the mountains of slag at the far end of the steelworks. He would be staring straight up into the sky. High above him would be the vapour trails of the flight path to and from the New World, and at their head distant silver specks of flying machines. Pross would know not just every passing plane by its shape – 747, DC10, Concorde, Airbus – but also its specifications and, above all, its safety record. What he feared became the object of serious study.

And as for being a small-town simpleton, it was to some extent true that when he had toured New Zealand with the Lions of 1959, he had pined for home. But it was also true that he spent a large period of the tour in hospital, and that while he was there he dedicated himself once again to serious study, this time of the rugby of the New Zealanders and, in particular, their forwards.

In 1983 Jim Telfer of Scotland toured New Zealand as coach of a Lions team that would be whitewashed by the All Blacks. He learnt from the experience and will go down in history as the coach who absorbed his lessons – and especially the rucking techniques of the New Zealanders – conditioned them to suit the Scottish game and ended up with Grand Slams in 1984 and 1990. Ray Prosser preceded him by more than twenty years. He analysed the New Zealand game from his hospital bed, went home, played on, retired and stepped back for further contemplation. Pontypool went into decline and all the while the coach-to-be stayed away and formulated his coaching philosophy. No doubt, just as he would do with his jet planes, he investigated specifications and performance. Only this time he was not so concerned about the issue of safety. The giant of post-war rugby in Pontypool crossed his bridge from playing days to coaching career.

It was the start of the 1970s and Welsh rugby was embarking on something gloriously adventurous on the international stage; brilliance and self-confidence were to make the age glitter. Pontypool, typically, were at the rock bottom of the club ladder. Below everyone. Brilliance was for others. Pross started to climb by another route, up a more extreme col. The country was starting to gasp at the exploits of Edwards and John and Gerald and J.P.R. Pross however needed forwards and he needed backs who would be subservient to his forwards.

From Newport he garnered such backs as centre Ivor Taylor who would become his right-hand man later on the coaching front. But most important of all he welcomed home Terry Cobner after the latter concluded his teachers' training course at Madeley College near Stoke-on-Trent. Cobner of Blaenavon became the on-field inspiration from wing-forward and captain of the new Pontypool.

It seemed that Pross had not had to move outside his self-proclaimed five-mile exclusion zone, although perhaps he extended it to ten miles for that rarer commodity, a back in the county who fitted his bill. Once again, however, it is worth pointing out that while Pontypool truly developed a game that was exclusively theirs – a sort of evolutionary blip, as if they were up some deep-sided valley off-shoot where the sun never shone and that time had forgotten – the reality is that Pontypool never suffered from such acute introspection or even geographic isolation.

Travel north from Pontypool towards Abergavenny and to the left rise Mynydd Garnclochty and the Blorenge Mountain, high ridges over which lies Blaenavon, a town of coal and iron. But from right on top of the mountain, at the Keeper's Pond, a reservoir whose waters used to be piped down to the town and the water-balance tower at its forges, the view reveals that this is the first ridge of the industrial valleys of Wales. To the right of the Pontypool–Abergavenny road lies the rolling pasture-land of the Vale of Usk. Pontypool is not confined by twin steep sides. It has always enjoyed flat access to Monmouthshire and the Forest of Dean. There are even in the Eastern Valley accent certain similarities to the drawl of the Forest in terms of quirky grammar, like the use of 'be' for 'is'. The Pontypool voice is obviously Welsh but it is closer to the sounds of Coleford than to the nasal strains of Newport to the south.

It is more than accent. Strong rugby connections exist between the easternmost club in Wales and the clubs of the West Country of England. This story will reveal how relations between the Pooler and many, many clubs grew strained to breaking point, but Gloucester were always strong allies. There were wonderful nights at Kingsholm, of baying crowds and unfettered mischief, of huge confrontation and regular reductions to fourteen players per side. More recently, Bath have been stout supporters of Pontypool's latest drive, in 1998, to climb out of crisis. And closest of all were Berry Hill, from within the boundaries of the royal forest itself, who were like blood brothers, even on the day of the game against the Pontypool second XV, the Athletic, when play was stopped for a search to be conducted in the mud for half an ear. It was a day of brown and crimson hues in the Park.

For the moment, though, at the outset of the Prosser years, isolation referred only to Pontypool's position in the pecking order of Welsh clubs. They were adrift at the bottom. Cobner soon changed all that. Pontypool climbed to eighth in the unofficial championship. The next season they were champions.

There was local talent on tap. Graham Price was playing in the front row as a teenager, a slender, curly-blonde prop on orange squash, who would go home after each game shaking with exhaustion. Ron Floyd, Bill Evans – an outsider from as far away as Abergavenny – and soon John Perkins, another to make the short trip down from Blaenavon, filled the second row.

The message from Pross to his charges was straightforward: utter devotion to the collective cause. In the summer he flogged them up and down the Grotto, a gruelling run from the pitch up to the then ruined Folly Tower – a hilltop landmark rebuilt in recent years, having been destroyed by the army in 1940 to prevent enemy bombers using it as a beacon on their way to the munitions works at Glascoed – and in the winter the forwards themselves flogged other packs at the scrummage.

The anonymous efficiency of the Pontypool pack had its advantages and disadvantages. Ron Floyd was picked to play for Wales B against France B away, a just reward for the big lock's largely unseen contributions at club level. On the eve of the match, as the players of both sides stood awkwardly at some mayoral get-together in the local town-hall, one of the Welsh selectors approached the tall, swarthy man of Gwent and with great deliberation asked him, 'Bonsoir, do you speak English?'

Pontypool were operating at full power. The pack was awesome at the scrummage, fearsome at the line-out, destructive at the ruck. Full-back Robin Williams kicked goals from anywhere inside seventy yards from the opposition posts, equally adept and long-distanced with either left or right foot. Terry Cobner was immense on the charge, hugely strong and with a centre of gravity as low as his boot-laces. But perhaps the power would never have truly been galvanized without the arrival of two players in those rebuilding years of the early 1970s. Two-thirds of the Pontypool front row. They came from the town of Newport via the rugby club of Cross Keys. Yes, Pontypool was transformed for ever when Bobby Windsor and Tony 'Charlie' Faulkner turned up.

Graham Price in those early days was, as suggested, pushing uphill in the grown-up game. He was a local pup, a product of West Mon. school in the town, destined to become one of the Rolls-Royce players of his generation. He was to be a player way ahead of his time, a prop as fast as a back-row with handling skills to match, a tight-head who would win a record number of caps for his position – forty-one between his debut in 1975 at the age of twenty-two and 1983 – and who would play in twelve Lions tests, another record for a prop, on three tours between 1977 and 1983. But three years before his debut for Wales he needed help in the Pontypool front row. It came in the form of a double-act: 'The Duke' at hooker and 'Charlie' on the loose head. Pricey was the quiet one; the other two spiced things up.

They were not that big, although Bobby, when he came home from the Lions tour of 1974, was eighteen stone of world-class athletic venom. Charlie had a strange bottom half to his body, or maybe it just looked slightly spindly compared to his torso from the middle of his back upwards. He was fantastically strong around the shoulders and neck, and if Bobby had an utterly ruthless edge, Charlie had the martial arts of karate. To be fair, he never seemed to use them on the field to hurt people; he preferred to employ more straightforward arts when it came to dishing out pain. Charlie became well-known for his reply to the press when asked about the skills of scrummaging: 'Up, down, inside out – anywhere but backwards.' But he also had another phrase which he would shout out in the club if anyone asked him about his days in the Territorial Army. He would remember nocturnal patrols in Gibraltar: 'Alto. Arriba las manos o disparo'. (Stop. Put your hands up or I'll shoot).

They were certainly not angelic. When I first joined the club in 1976 there was a story going round that the pair of them had been taken in for questioning by the police over some minor misunderstanding. Nothing serious, but it was essential that they synchronized their stories. After the briefest time to prepare, they were led into different rooms and asked to give their accounts separately. Remarkably, every detail of two highly convoluted tales matched perfectly. Except for the moment when a cat had apparently run in front of their car. Bobby said it was black, Charlie said it was white. They were hauled back in for round 2. The colour of the cat was a serious stumbling point. Was it black or was it white? 'Ah, that,' said Charlie. 'Well, you have to remember, it was a very frosty night.'

On the field they could be lethal, although it must be said that they respected the conventions of the battlefield. I once played in a second team game alongside Bobby after we were well past our retirement date, a long time even after the day on tour in Canada in 1985 when he became a grandfather and a father on the same day.

Anyway, the Athletic were playing against Tredegar and Bobby simply could not resist giving their scrum-half a little belt. The scrum-half, suitably annoyed, waited and waited until the coast was clear and gave Bob his best shot in return. A neat punch, too. At that moment the referee blew his whistle for the end of the game, and Bob set off after the scrum-half, who not surprisingly had headed for the safety of the tunnel. Suddenly the Pontypool hooker with a trickle of blood coming from his nose was alongside him. The scrum-half turned to run again, but Bob reached out and grabbed him. 'Game's over, Ian,' he said. The scrum-half looked even more worried. 'No, I mean that's it. Whistle's gone, time for a pint, no hard feelings.'

Those hard feelings were reserved for the field of play. There was a time in the mid 1970s when the scrummage was nigh-on uncontrollable, so fast would the front five propel it forward. Oh, in big Cup games the opposition would raise their game and hold firm and Pontypool would be denied yet again a taste of the high life, but in the course of a season's bread-and-butter fixtures, the pack would generate a special quiver, just prior to the put-in by the other team's scrum-half, which meant that the timing of the drive was just right and that somebody had better watch out because rib cartilage was liable to pop. It was the elevation of a humdrum restart activity to some sort of Stalinist collectivist ideal whose goal is the pure joy of destruction.

Bobby Windsor was also the master of the rolling maul. It was said that Pontypool as a club were masters of taking the ball in, especially at the line-out, setting up a drive and churning their way downfield until Robin Williams or, after the first full-back took his bi-pedal skills to Brescia in Italy, his successor Peter Lewis, could step up to claim three points. But really, if Bobby wasn't playing, the co-ordination was never quite right and the rolling maul bumbled to a halt. The rolling maul was as reviled as the scrummage. The nation, it must not be forgotten, was on a high of Five Nations poetry. Price, Faulkner, Cobner and Windsor were all required to do their bit for Wales; but, please, may they keep their tedious, prosaic practices for their own dark patch of the land.

At the same time, the list was growing of clubs who felt legitimate forward power was slipping into mere brutality. Swansea, Llanelli and London Welsh all declared the working practices of the Viet-Gwent, as Pontypool were dubbed by the *Western Mail*, as unacceptable and fixtures were duly cancelled. Now, it has to be said that Pontypool could be a dirty side. Any front-row opponent who denied them their precious drive at the scrum by turning in or taking it down was liable to need medical attention. And Pontypool loved to ruck; it was one of the key elements of the game that Pross had brought home from New Zealand – Otago, in particular – all those years previously.

The Welsh, like most of Europe, preferred a mauling game with the ball kept above ground. It was a more measured way of retaining control after the tackle. When the ball-carrier went to ground, players scrambled over him to lift the ball back into the arms of the next wave of forwards. Pontypool, despite their association with the rolling maul – a ploy reserved for certain situations only – preferred in most other areas of broken play to leave the ball on the ground and simply clear space around it, presenting the scrum-half with quick, uncluttered access to the ball on the ground. It was this notion of 'clearing the ground' that created difficulties, for any scrabbling opponents were simply tumble-dried out of the way, the infamous single stud at the end of the Adidas boot that was all the rage then inflicting a fair amount of soft-tissue damage.

Pontypool, scrummagers, rolling maulers and mountaineer-ruckers were roundly booed wherever they went. When Gerald Davies ran in four tries from five touches of the ball in a Cup game in 1979, the world rejoiced that Pontypool could never hold sway against the proper Welsh way. A decade later, however, Wayne Shelford's All Blacks were pushing back the frontiers of the game with an all-scrummaging, driving, rucking game, while Wales were about to enter a period of emasculation from which they never recovered in the amateur era.

And so the 1970s turned into the 1980s. Charlie surrendered to the ravages of a bad knee and, who knew, perhaps even age. Bobby was never quite the same beast after he lost his international place, his back having been severely burned by a lime mixture used to mark the pitch one day. Changes in the front row apart, however, little else evolved, on the face of it. The forwards continued to dominate the Pooler game, culminating in the day at Murrayfield in 1983 when the club supplied five of the eight forwards for Wales to face Scotland: Staff Jones, Graham Price, John Perkins, Jeff Squire and myself. Mark Brown would be capped later that year on a somewhat less successful mission to Romania, while hooker Steve Jones would have been capped had he not been sent off in one of those gladiatorial nights at Kingsholm, Gloucester.

No, little seemed to change. Gloucester gave as good as they received, but the list of disgruntled opponents elsewhere continued to grow. Newbridge, Orrell and Leicester joined the fixture boycott as the decade unfurled. Business as normal.

But things were changing, within the club and without. First came the split between Terry Cobner and Ray Prosser, a superficial spat that became a rift never yet healed. The architects of the club's revival fell out with a bitterness that only father-son upheavals can generate, the circumstances rendered genuinely tragic by coinciding with the death of Ray's wife, Nancy. It all went to show that, for all the outside world's perception of massive solidarity, Pontypool could be as insecure as a ten-ton truck with the hand-brake off. And in typically perverse fashion – and just to prove further that all those preconceptions about insularity and blinkered thinking were false – the internal divide went hand in hand with an outward expansion on the recruitment front that heralded the start of the last and most successful period in the history of the club.

It was all to do with the backs. A pair of local stalwarts entered their personal golden age; Peter Lewis, on his way to becoming a consultant surgeon, at full-back, and Goff Davies, on his way to becoming a headmaster, on the wing. But suddenly all around them were players from afar: Mike Goldsworthy from Penarth at outside-half, Lyndon Faulkner from Newport in the centre alongside Lee Jones from Pontarddulais, a place so far to the west it might as well have been a sunset, and Bleddyn Taylor, assistant coach Ivor's cousin from Swansea.

On the other hand, perhaps it was not really so much to do with the backs. Or the forwards for that matter. It was all to do with a certain scrum-half. For this was the age of David Bishop. The Bish was in town. He came from Ebbw Vale with a track record as an amateur boxer, of having been thrown out of his home club Cardiff for generally being wild, of having been decorated for throwing himself into the Taff to save a drowning woman, and with a prison record for grievous bodily harm. In short, he was ideally suited to Pontypool.

He would sit, went the thinking, behind the pack and control the destiny of the club. The forwards, despite the presence of the great Jeff Squire in the back row, were never quite the heavyweight set-piece force of the 1970s, but they now had extra mobility, and there was a set of backs out there who not only had the best defensive system in the club game, but who could even be entrusted with a ration of possession. A limited ration, mind you; Pontypool could embrace the challenge of the Bish but to offer passing employment to the three-quarters was still beyond the pale.

The Bish would rule. He played his first game, a celebration affair to open the floodlights at Berry Hill (you see what the Forest notion of a romp is, and why they and Pontypool have certain things in common?), declared his new pack over-rated and ignored the three-quarters completely. He would have to sort things out himself. Five games later he was flat on his back in hospital with a broken neck. It happened at Aberavon away, a bogey ground whose influence Bobby had never really helped dispel over the years by declaring just before kick-off on each visit, 'Roll on half past four.'

By the time Pontypool went there in 1981, it had already come to the notice of his fellow players that the Bish was prone to collapsing in a heap whenever he needed a rest. The same players had decided that at such theatrical moments he was best ignored. And so it was that at the Talbot Athletic Ground, David Bishop went down in a heap, his neck broken, and the rest of his team walked on by.

A year later he was back. He marked his return by blasting Gloucester apart on his own. On one occasion he ran from beneath his own posts, went eighty yards and handed a try to Bleddyn Taylor. In the Cup semi-final of 1983, on the same Aberavon pitch where he had broken his neck, he defeated Bridgend with a try and a drop goal from forty-five metres to take the club to a final in Cardiff which they won – not with much adventure, obviously – with the Bish winning the Man of the Match award. He was sent off for fighting against Saracens, he was taken to court for punching Chris Jarman in a Newbridge game and nearly served a second gaol sentence, and he played just once for Wales, against Australia in 1984, a day when Wales lost and he scored a try.

As the second half of the 1980s unfolded Pontypool had a new coach as Bobby briefly took over from Pross. The success went on and this time Pontypool did branch out into an expansive game inspired by the Bish's new half-back partner, Mark Ring and another exile from Cardiff, Paul Rees at full-back. The Cup was never won again, but other trophies continued to flow in.

And then the Bish went to Hull Kingston Rovers and rugby league, and the 1980s turned into the 1990s, and rugby union began to travel inexorably towards professionalism. The Bish had gone North but other Pontypool players began to move south – centre Roger Bidgood and second-row Kevin Moseley to Newport – or west, like hooker Garin Jenkins to Swansea, either lured away by enlightened approaches elsewhere or driven away by disillusionment as it seemed that their old club would do nothing to embrace the shamateur spirit. Pontypool had survived years of assaults on their playing style and had come through years of condemnation of the club's propensity for violence. The honours board was the counter-balance to criticism. But money was a different matter, a threat that simply overwhelmed the club.

There had always been a feeling that if hard Pooler could be resisted, then they might crack. Hence all those failures in the Cup – bar 1983 – when other sides on the big day raised their game and withstood the single-minded battering up front. Hence defeat against touring sides. In 1982 a struggling Australian side were taunted as they limped around Wales, 'Wait till you get to the Pooler.' At the very first scrummage on the day they did come to a packed Park, English referee Roger Quittenton penalized Pontypool as the Wallabies were in retreat, and that was that. It was not the best decision made by a referee with whom the club never really saw eye to eye, but it should not have been a signal for instant capitulation. Pontypool heads dropped in a fatalistic acceptance that this was not to be their day after all, and Australia piled on the points. Sometimes opponents did not have to wait until the last quarter before Pontypool cracked.

But money and professionalism crushed them even faster than a first-minute blast from a ref in tight shorts. Not even the return of David Bishop in the late 1990s as player-coach and venerable institution has saved them from market forces that they do not understand. Not even flat access to the lands of the east and the riches of England has brought forth an investor who might single-handedly offer salvation to one of the grand old names of the game. For the moment Pontypool are trapped in a sunless, steep-sided valley as dark and as deep as the evolutionary trench where they – or Pross – formulated the original master-plan for revival. Nowadays, however, close-quarter, un-spectacular devotion to a collective cause, fully armed with brute force, is not an option. The game has gone open in all senses of the word.

The fate of Pontypool seems simple: a fallen force heading towards oblivion. Yet this is a town that remains a major nursery of talent, and nowadays in all positions, not just forwards. The surrounding Torfaen County Borough retains a potential for large-scale support and as long as the nights of floodlit throngs on the natural bank of Pontypool Park remain in the memory, there is a chance that they will return. Above all, this is a landscape of many shades, a club of hidden depths and many mysteries. Say that it is finished and it will surely rise again.

IEUAN EVANS

Gerald Davies

Ieuan Cenydd Evans achieved greatness, but it certainly did not come easily. This should not suggest that he won the accolade through grim and tireless determination, pursuing a course of single-minded persistence to get there. There was no sense of hard graft in him. Greatness, after all, goes hand in hand with an appearance, at least, of easy accomplishment, of a natural flair, even if not entirely of effortlessness. Rather, one felt that the tyrannical and capricious gods who rule sporting destinies had it in for him in a big way. They may have bestowed upon him those elusive and subtle virtues that determine a player's place in the pantheon – the speed, the guile and the instinctive wherewithal – but they redressed this generosity by sabotaging his advance with a series of untimely and hindering injuries. And, more crucially still, they ensured that it would be his misfortune to play during a period when Welsh rugby was largely impoverished of success. These are hardly auspicious circumstances for a winger, isolated at the best of times, to show off his gifts. Somehow, there seemed to be a tide against which he constantly had to strive, and yet Ieuan Evans managed to rise above all this to become one of the deadliest finishers in modern rugby, the possessor of a talent which would have added distinctive colour, movement and rhythm to any game of rugby at any time.

Aficionados of rugby often claim that it is the perfect team game, with its imaginative but often thick-edged harmony between the robust muscularity of the men who make up the scrum and the sinewy, sometimes elegant, athletes who count themselves numbered among the backs. This uneasy alliance between the beefy, bull-necked men of the forwards and the lithe wimpishness and will-o'-the-wisp mind of the backs, is one of the great game's abiding and appealing distinctions. A Pontypool front-row forward could happily feel at home with a Phil Bennett. For every pit-bull terrier like Brian Moore there is a silky Jeremy Guscott. For such aficionados an intricate balance exists between the feudal toils of the forwards close to the soil and the aristocratic lightness of touch among the half-backs and three-quarters. From the backs emerges a pedigree of players from whom the great are anointed with sovereign titles. Bleddyn Williams was the prince of centres, Barry John was crowned a king. The forwards, on the other hand and in their own earthy vernacular, are mere 'donkeys'; as beasts in the field they carry the yoke. Sometimes, because of their lack of lustre and title to fame, they carry resentment too, and now and again they need to be molly-coddled and their confidence bolstered. Yet for the game to flourish, each class of player must respect his colleagues' place in the team's construction, the one depends on the other; the whole more than the sum of its parts. A team's triumph is not, however, always forged just by the lop-sided symmetry between forwards and backs. There may be another, more unorthodox, way to success.

If rugby's aspirations are generally towards teamwork and the melding of various forces into serried ranks of cleaving equality of effort, there persists in Wales the much fonder attachment to the romantic image of the solitary player. Gifted and glorious in his sure-ness, a single player is perceived as making all the difference; the match-maker and matchwinner. He stands out above all the rest. In a land short of heroes, or whence they are allowed to depart unsung, Wales's rugby pitches have offered a space where such heroes can still be nurtured and praised. Ieuan Evans was such a player. He rose supremely above the mêlée. A great player is always part of the team but he is capable, at the same time, of not being entirely of it. His specialness forces him apart; his unique gifts adding another dimension to the way a team plays.

Evans is remembered above the rest. Even when he did nothing or had an unremarkable match, people still remarked upon him. 'Ieuan had a quiet game today', opines the man standing on Stradey Park's tanner bank, before trudging home all the more wearily for not having glimpsed one of Ieuan's effortless runs down the wing and for which he had paid a large portion of his entrance ticket to see. The idiosyncrasies of the modern game then get blamed for the way wingers are neglected, an accusation often unsubstantiated. In Llanelli's year of the double in 1993, when they notched up a record 136 tries in the Championship, Ieuan Evans scored thirty-five tries in thirty-two games. But is was not just for Llanelli that he excelled; he stood out in a British Lions team with a plethora of outstanding players around him. Even in a team of famous names he flourished.

The 1980s and 1990s have been for the most part an unbroken period of dismay and unprecedented failure for Welsh rugby. During these two decades Wales has won the Championship outright only once, in 1994. The national team shared the Championship with France in 1988, the year in which Wales last won the Triple Crown of victories against the other home countries. These spare successes along with other occasional victories gave intermittent hope of a resurgence in Wales's playing fortunes, but such promise has yet to be fulfilled. Wales has become accustomed to see the sun rise in hope one season, in one game, only for it soon to be clouded over in the darkest hues of disappointment. If the century began with thunderous success, with the 1905 victory against the All Blacks famously establishing rugby as the national game, it draws to an end with Wales seemingly intent on self-destruction. It is within this context that Ieuan Evans's career must be considered. In a sterile and frequently humiliating time for Welsh rugby, he emerged as a rare player of world-class quality, both resourceful and exuberant. If in 1987, his opening season for Wales, he was to experience the first of several defeats which would cause the record books to be rewritten, not at any stage did he himself falter nor be seen to be weighed down by his team's inferior performances. In the inaugural World Cup of that year, held in New Zealand and Australia, Wales lost by forty-nine points to the All Blacks in the semi-final in Brisbane, although the team later salvaged some self-respect with an unexpected victory over Australia in the match for third place.

Defeats of even greater magnitude were to be suffered by Wales in the next eleven years of Ieuan's career. It was a time when the Welsh team could no longer feel confident of beating anyone. Its grip on rugby reality was unstable, and the team's influence among the hierarchy of world rugby dwindled. In this period, Wales lost face and its reputation against teams hitherto classed only as emerging countries in the pecking order of world rugby. Western Samoa (in 1991 and 1994), Canada (1993) and Romania (1988) would all inflict unexpected defeats during Evans's tenure in the number-14 shirt. In fact, of the seventy-two times he appeared for his country, he was to be on the winning side on only thirty occasions. He was on the losing side forty-one times, with one drawn game. His career has to be judged in the context of these sad statistics.

This was hardly the germinal green belt in which a rugby wing, the most delicately exposed and vulnerable of all positions, could sprout and flourish. In such, circumstances, survival alone would be a major task. Yet, for all the depressing vicissitudes, the agonizing loss of standards and the prolonged inertia that enveloped Welsh rugby at this time, Ieuan's own reputation remained untarnished. Alongside Jonathan Davies, Bob Norster and Robert Jones, Ieuan Evans continued the vein, once so rich, of classy Welsh players but which now during the last decade had become so reduced. Nigel Walker was special, too, but the selectors appeared to mistrust him, unable to see beyond the track athlete to the fine footballer which he so clearly was, and Allan Bateman and Scott Gibbs, after they had returned from rugby league, should also be included among this select and diminishing band.

Born in 1964 in Pontarddulais, Ieuan Evans was nurtured in that corner of west Wales which has long boasted its part in the development of men who can play and run the ball with a sleight-of-hand and with tongue mischievously in cheek. Seldom did Evans seem to take the game too seriously except, perhaps, in his occasional penchant after scoring a try to stand upright and with an intense expression on his face, smack the ball firmly down to the earth as if to say . . . THERE!! BEAT THAT. Rugby is meant to be spontaneous; a sense of teasing fun and release. A profession it may be, but it is still a game where excitement and joy should be present, and Ieuan Evans always provided us with that sense.

From such a village, and there are quite a few which nestle only a drop-goal's distance from Stradey Park, Llanelli, has emerged as clearly and silently as spring water many a creative talent with a head full of wishful thinking and dreams of Wales. The character of rugby is perceived to be different here than it is, say, in the harder valleys of Blaenau Gwent. When Ieuan was six years old, the Evans family moved westwards towards Carmarthen, but this did not dilute the source of the spell which, in the main, seemed to beget outside-halves: Carwyn James, Phil Bennett. There have been centres, too. Albert Jenkins is still a legend in Llanelli, as is Ray Gravell. They have become part of the spirit of the place. Then there were others like Barry John and Gareth Davies at outside-half, or Cyril Davies and D. Ken Jones, in the centre, all of whom moved away and, to the town's dismay, played for other clubs. Each of these was an artist in his own right, and touched by greatness, but they committed tribal treachery by travelling to play beyond the Loughor Bridge and were not easily forgiven. A pardon might have been more easily come by had they gone North to play rugby league in those far-ago days. Ieuan, too, went North after a fashion, to Salford, but it was to the university, and after three years he was back at Stradey.

That Ieuan Evans played his final season (1997–8) with Bath, after his third tour with the Lions, is neither here nor there. Only the pedant and a stickler for the facts will remember that, for a few brief months, he graced the fields of a West Country town. He had played his fourteen most important and memorable years for Llanelli. Like Ray Williams in the 1950s and early 1960s and Andy Hill in the 1970s, Evans became the favourite wing of Stradey's tanner bank which is home to the perennial scoffer and the grumbling unbeliever. A player has truly to earn his spurs with them.

Evans – or should I say Ieuan by now for it was by his Christian name he came to be known – was well liked. This is no idle comment. Llanelli is not always protective of its sons nor approving; nor necessarily are other rugby clubs in Wales. The conferring of world-class status else-where is no guarantee of tolerance at home, nor of an endorsement; unless, that is, every sense of glamour is overwhelmed by modesty. Is he one of us? This is the echoing question upon which tanner-bank judgment ultimately rests. In such company, never sip a Chardonnay wine when the beer everyone drinks at the bar is made in the brewery down the road. Never act the *numero uno* part. Ieuan was always perceived to have his feet firmly rooted in Llanelli's earth although when he ran he seemed always to be gliding above it. His head, though, was never in the clouds.

There is another thing about Ieuan. There were other challenges he had to overcome: His first injury occurred when he broke his leg playing for Carmarthen Athletic at nineteen years of age. Later, as he was about to make his mark after playing for Wales 'A' in 1985 and scoring six tries in their victory against Spain, he twice had serious shoulder injuries which kept him out of the game for nine months. In 1988 he dislocated his shoulder, and then suffered the same injury in the Lions' last game on the tour to Australia in 1989. If this was not enough, no sooner had this weakness been corrected through surgery than he suffered an horrific leg injury on the first day of October 1994 when playing at the Arms Park against Cardiff. This had to be the end, it was gloomily predicted. But return he did.

This is the background. What of the player who was to become so famous? There is a part of the National Stadium which will always belong to Ieuan Evans. The south-east corner, which provided us with the Westgate Street-end try-line for a hundred years and more, underneath the South Stand, was home sweet home to the Welsh winger who became his country's most capped player. Against Italy in February 1998, he won the last of his seventy-two caps. But this was not the only record which he held; he captained Wales on twenty-eight occasions, the first against France in a celebratory match to open the floodlights at the National Stadium in 1991. This succeeded by ten a record previously held by Arthur Gould so long ago that it did not even belong in the twentieth century. There at the ground's only open end he carved for himself a substantial piece of Welsh rugby immortality. With Welsh familiarity, intimacy and sense of possession this could easily be remembered as Ieuan's corner. Drawn in flight like a homing pigeon he veered to this corner to score three of the most exciting and dramatic individual tries ever seen at a ground which has not been short of heroic deeds since 1905 when Wales defeated the unbeaten New Zealand team of that year. Each of the tries were different in their fashion.

The first of these was against Scotland in 1988 and was nudged further into rugby mythology by Bill Maclaren's strikingly apt words: 'Merlin the magician couldn't have done it better'. As Ieuan danced his way closer to the posts, the BBC's rugby commentator, who more than any one man in broadcasting helped to bring a more cosmopolitan audience to understand and indeed to embrace rugby, continued unabashed: 'Jink, jink, jink – . . . It was magic, magic all the way'. After some classic passing in midfield the winger was given the ball by a beautifully judged pass from Mark Ring, that intuitively talented Welsh centre. With a crowded cover defence converging desperately towards the deep south-east corner, Evans made a mockery of all their presumptions by changing the direction of his run. His first sidestep brought him inside. The defence attempted to reverse, by which time Evans had executed his second sidestep. It was all ends-up for Scotland's hapless defence by the time he performed his third. A dive avoided the outstretched arms of David Sole, Scotland's prop and captain, for a try of mercurial virtuosity.

In all our dreams we long for such a triumphal note, a singing moment. Magic, magic, all the way. Oh yes, indeed. This is the rugby player as entertainer; the show-off on the stage with the flourishing sleight-of-hand which leaves the audience agape. 'This is what I can do', he declares in that prima-donnish mode which, if they are honest enough to admit it, infuses the spirit of all the best competitors. Partisanship disintegrates, we are all of us left admiringly in his thrall.

Then there is Ieuan Evans as patriotic hero; courageous and bold, holding the dragon aloft on the besieged and beleaguered ramparts when around him all seems doomed to failure and defeat for Wales. All in all, taking a long and well-worn history into account, for better or for worse, such a gesture could only find its true cause against England. This spirit is as true, conversely, of England. Wales can be a cause for them, too, although we need not go as far as Evelyn Waugh when in his humorous novel *Decline and Fall* he wrote, 'We can trace all the disasters of English history to the influence of the Welsh', a sentiment reflected more seriously in the cant and campish conceits we, in Wales, have grown to expect from some of the preening London journalists at the end of the twentieth century. This sense of aggrieved sensibilities was illustrated in 1991 when the England coach Geoff Cooke and his captain, Will Carling, in what was widely seen as an ignoble and discourteous gesture, refused to turn up at a post-match press conference. This was on the occasion of the first English victory on Welsh soil in twenty-eight years. Despite their later protestations it was clear that something deep-rooted rankled. Two years later England returned to the National Stadium in an attempt to win an unparalleled triple Grand Slam. They received their come-uppance in the most dramatic fashion, and in a very 'in-your-face' sort of way. Ieuan Evans proved to be their nemesis.

England dominated the game. The Welsh team was assailed and tormented on all fronts. It hardly matters now whether the kick from Emyr Lewis, the Welsh flanker, was speculative or not. What matters is the manner in which Ieuan, 5 foot 10 inches and just over thirteen stones, went haring after the ball. With their opponents in control of the match, the whole of Wales understood that few if any chances were likely to come the Welsh team's way again. This was the one. The ball was loose, a kick and chase. First Evans had to outrun Rory Underwood, at the time believed to be the fastest player in rugby boots. Underwood's concentration seemed to lapse as the ball went over his shoulder. Evans raced away from him and his splayed feet now in overdrive he cruised past Jonathan Webb the England full-back to hurl himself on the ball as it rolled tantalizingly towards the dead-ball line.

Ieuan Evans had beautiful balance, and nothing can epitomize this better than his try against Ireland, also in 1993. Teetering in the narrowest corner on the touchline he maintained his balance for thirty metres before lunging away from three sets of despairing arms to score at his favourite end of the pitch. He did not score all his tries here, of course. The genuine athlete's pace he possessed was shown to good effect when he chased the ball to the north-west corner, avoiding Gavin Hastings on a soggy pitch, to get the touchdown in 1994.

Whenever Ieuan stepped on the field there was never any sense of antagonism towards him. He appeared to swagger, his feet splayed, posture erect and his arms swinging akimbo. This had the appearance of an arrogant strut. But it was merely his awkward gait. Curiously, there was never any sense of the latent energy which characterized other great wingers of the era as they waited for their rare moment of expression and exertion. As there was, say, in our awareness of the speed in Rory Underwood; or of power about to be unleashed in John Kirwan of New Zealand; or of the beguiling improvization of David Campese of Australia; or the ruthless cutting-edge applied by Patrice Lagisquet of France. Ieuan's mind seemed to be on other matters. He had a casual air, almost indifference, appearing alert only when in motion and called upon to run with the ball in his hands. At that very moment he was transformed into an athlete, combining pace with an economy of effort.

First and foremost a rugby player, he none the less rose above the perspiring crowd in another sense, too. It might be an old-fashioned idea in current sporting circles, but Ieuan's courtesy and good manners made him a wonderful ambassador for the sport especially when he took over the captaincy of his country after Wales had not only lost but behaved badly on the infamous tour of Australia in 1991. The following season in Paris he delivered his after-match speech entirely in French, a gesture which helped restore a semblance of dignity to Welsh rugby. With the wing assumed to be the most impractical position – indeed a position without any merit in some eyes – from which to lead the team, he demonstrated that strength of personality counts for a good deal. Such graciousness and humour were important to him and helped to make him a superb role model for the young aspiring rugby player.

As the master of deceptive flight on the field and with his honest smiling dignity off it Ieuan Evans represented the very best of Wales and the Welsh. He could have graced the Wales rugby team of any generation, though I hope that he might have had more severe competition in some periods than others. If you see what I mean!!

ROBERT JONES

Huw Richards

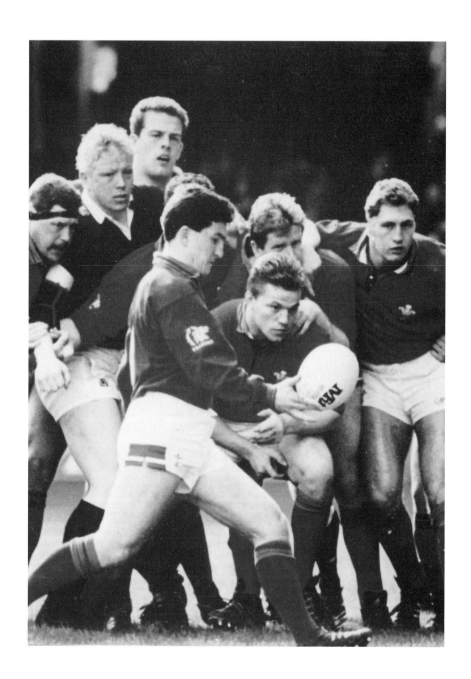

A few minutes into the France v. Wales match at the Parc des Princes in early 1995, the first line-out formed. Hooker Garin Jenkins threw in and Wales won possession of the sort that teams are often better without. A flapping hand pushed the ball down and in the very general direction of the Welsh scrum-half. Dark and diminutive – by some distance the smallest man on the field – he moved without apparent hurry as large French forwards converged and in a single fluid movement retrieved the ball and sent it rocketing towards Neil Jenkins at outside-half, creating time and space for him to clear. All too typical of the international career of Robert Jones, it at once made a nonsense of his exclusion from the team over the previous twenty-two months and went some way to explain it. It was a sublime demonstration of grace under pressure, speed of thought and execution disposing of a minor crisis created by the inadequacies of his forwards, of colossal natural gifts devoted by force of circumstance to damage limitation rather than creativity.

The rest of the world acknowledged him as a scrum-half of incomparable quality. South Africa, far from desperate for quality half-backs with Joost Van der Westhuizen already in Springbok colours, were sufficiently impressed first to offer Jones a contract to play in the Currie Cup for Western Province, then to make a serious attempt to persuade him to settle in the Republic and qualify to play for them. Joel Stransky, scorer of the decisive drop goal in South Africa's 1995 World Cup win, said on the basis of their half-back partnership for Western Province that Jones was 'the ideal scrum-half: he has a superb pass, kicks with both feet, defends well, has the eye for a break and reads a game perfectly'. Australia coach Bob Dwyer talked in similar terms after his World Champions had been outplayed by Swansea in 1992. New Zealanders recognized his quality the first time they saw him – at the 1987 World Cup – and the comment heard after the World Cup semi-final in 1987, the First Test of 1988 and the World Cup group match of 1995, all crushing defeats, was that Jones was the one Welshman who might have been selected for a combined Wales-New Zealand XV. Yet Wales dropped him six times in seven years.

Robert Jones was at once the most conspicuous and least deserving victim of the precipitous decline of Welsh rugby in the 1980s and 1990s. A public grown accustomed to success during the 1970s showed little patience with even comparative failure. Players were subjected to savage criticism with – as both Jones and Jonathan Davies discovered – the hugely gifted coming in for even greater barrages than the patently inadequate. Partial immunity was granted only to Ieuan Evans, whose position on the wing made it obvious to the dimmest critic why he was unable to repair the manifold limitations of his team-mates. His penance was instead – like Ken Jones and Gerald Davies in the latter halves of their careers – to fall victim to the Welsh version of unilateral disarmament, a devastatingly dangerous winger spending entire seasons waiting unavailingly for a pass in the opposition half. There was, inevitably, a local dimension to this. In adversity, Wales turned inward to look for explanations and scapegoats. Intense local rivalries and rugby's cultural importance, greater than in any other home country, are a strength and a source of good-humoured, if fierce, debate in good times. In the bad times they take on a bitter, rancorous and destructive edge. Jones, a Swansea Valley native who gave the Swansea club both class and commitment for thirteen seasons, invariably found support in the club, the city and local media although his quality ensured that he was much more than a local hero – his first and most consistent champion in the national press was Gerald Davies, a Cardiffian since the 1960s.

Two of the outstanding club sides of Jones's time at the top – Pontypool in the early to mid-1980s and Neath at the end of the decade – built their success in part on intense local loyalty and resentment of more obviously glamorous clubs (Pontypridd in the mid to late-1990s provide a further example, if rather more classic rugby). Highly effective in creating an intense collective club spirit, it proved deeply divisive nationally. Ron Waldron's attempt to transplant the Neath style, together with most of the team, to national level concluded in Neath v. The Rest factions and a shameful brawl during the 1991 Australian tour.

Jones, less than a year after being voted the outstanding European player at the first World Cup and just before contributing to the first Welsh Triple Crown in nine years, was furiously abused by the Pontypool crowd at a cup-tie in January 1988 while an east Wales newspaper campaigned to get Pontypool's dynamic scrum-half David

Bishop, the Randall MacMurphy of Welsh rugby, into the national XV at his expense. Jones acknowledged Bishop's brilliance, while saying that he would have distanced himself from any such campaign on his behalf, but it is unsurprising that the word 'parochial' recurred consistently in his published comments on the Welsh game when his international career appeared over after the 1995 World Cup.

The Bishop campaign also reflected the perennial debate about the role and requirements of scrum-half play. Two broad streams can be discerned – the classic quick-passing operator, often small, whose priority is to set his back division in motion and the extra flanker, larger, more powerful and as much an attacking threat himself as the catalyst of the backs. Wales had grown accustomed over the previous twenty years to having a physically imposing scrum-half. Gareth Edwards's unique combination of talents places him, like the most fearsome mountain ascents in the Tour de France, *hors categorie*, but his Cardiff and Wales successor Terry Holmes – who saw off the more 'traditional' challenges first of clubmate Brynmor Williams and then Bridgend's Gerald Williams – large, forceful and downright lethal at close range, represented the high point of the extra flanker breed in recent times, rivalled only by Scotland's ferociously combative Gary Armstrong.

At five foot seven inches and eleven stone when first selected for Wales in 1986 at the age of twenty, Jones represented a return to the classic ideal. His exemplar, he explained, was neither Edwards nor Holmes: 'I haven't got Terry Holmes' physique, so if I have modelled my game on anyone it is All Black Dave Loveridge, who is more my build. To me Loveridge is a marvellous player with all the scrum half attributes. With his pass he concentrates on speed, not length. That gives his backs as much time as possible to develop things and I prefer passing off the ground whenever possible.' He expounded the advantages of the classic scrum-half in conversation with Gerald Davies in 1995: 'I've never had any doubts that the classical scrum half will win always win that argument in the long run. An aggressive player will sometimes turn a bad option into a good one, but the player with vision will take the right option more often. I've always felt that the scrum half's first duty is to be the perfect link between forwards and backs. He has to move the ball quickly and to be able to kick accurately, both in defence and attack.'

If his immediate inspiration came from New Zealand, Jones nevertheless represented a distinctive Welsh tradition. Gwyn Nicholls, distilling his philosophy of the game in 1908, emphasized the importance of subordinating individual talents to team requirements and said that a half-back 'must act instinctively, in obedience to the dictates of some inner conscience'. In his memoirs Townsend Collins, as Dromio of the *South Wales Argus* and chronicler of the Welsh game from Arthur Gould to Bleddyn Williams, described Dickie Owen, Nicholls's contemporary and one of Jones's predecessors at scrum-half for both Swansea and Wales, in terms that are Jones to the life: 'He was little, but stout-hearted, plucky to the last degree, great in defence, but in attack more notable for what he enabled others to do than what he did for himself.' Where they differed was that Owen, and for that matter Edwards, played in Welsh teams whose forwards were good enough to guarantee them a decent supply of possession. Jones, for club and country, was fated to play behind underpowered packs. His experiences with Swansea drew the sympathy of an earlier Wales scrum-half, Onllwyn Brace: 'Almost every Saturday with Swansea, he is going backwards and still manages to make an impact and turn bad ball into usable ball.' The Swansea eight had outstanding individuals and some great days during Jones's career, but the description 'chameleon-like' applied to it by Paul Rees of the *Western Mail* in 1990 applied for most of this time. It was typical of his fortunes that leaving Swansea in 1996 – just as the All Whites showed serious signs of at last developing a consistently dominant pack – landed him behind a Bristol pack that, in an English club game increasingly dominated by the cheque-book, was not so much underpowered as underfunded.

Asked his opinion of All Black scrum-half and captain David Kirk after the 1987 World Cup, Jones responded that he had been impressive but had benefited enormously from the best pack in the competition: 'It is not easy to imagine what he would look like going backwards behind a beaten pack.' It was all too easy to find out what Robert Jones looked like going backwards behind a beaten pack – simply a matter of turning the television on for almost any of his forty-two international starts against International Board countries (or the matches against Western Samoa in 1991 and Romania in 1988) between 1986 and 1995.

While the causes of the decline of the 1980s and 1990s have

occasioned as much debate, and been as apparently intractable, as the longer-running failure of the British economy, the prime symptom has been unmistakable – a chronic loss of forward power. The most recent Welsh forward universally recognized as world class was lock Robert Norster, who played only three times after the 1987 World Cup and not at all after 1989. The Lions packs who contested the Test series in New Zealand in 1993 and South Africa in 1997 contained not a single Welshman, and the eight who dominated the final two Tests in Australia in 1989 included only one, prop David Young. Sixteen forwards played an entire Test series for the Lions between 1983 and 1997. Only two, Young in 1989 and Graham Price in 1983, were Welsh. Price did not play for Wales again and Young only once before going North.

The consequences for any scrum-half playing behind struggling packs were explained by Jones: 'I've got confidence in my ability to exploit any gaps but you don't see too many openings when you're trying to tidy up bad ball or receiving it with half the opposition pack breathing down your neck.' The battering he received was both physical and psychological and it was a natural, if unperceptive, reaction for many critics to want a larger, more obviously aggressive figure at the base of the scrum. Like the succession of wicket-keepers who have been dropped from the England team not for any deficiencies in their keeping, but because the specialist batsmen could not be trusted to score enough runs, Jones – a good enough cricketer to have played for Wales at under-15 and under-19 levels – paid for the failures of others.

In any debate on nature versus nurture, Robert Jones offers encouragement to both sides. His father Cliff had played outside-half for his home Swansea Valley village of Trebanos and occasionally for Neath, older brother Anthony had been scrum-half for Llanelli, Aberavon and Penarth, while younger brother Rhodri would eventually become his chief rival for the number-9 shirt at Swansea. Robert would also, in 1987, live up to the promise of the song by marrying a scrum-half's daughter. The scrum-half in this case was Clive Rowlands, yet another Swansea Valley trickster, all of whose fourteen Welsh caps in the 1960s were won as captain, infamous for a ruthless kicking game that led in the 1963 Wales v. Scotland match at Murrayfield to 111 lines-out, five touches for outside-half David Watkins and the sort of spectacle that led in 1969 to one of rugby's most liberating rule changes, the outlawing of the direct kick to touch outside the 25. An engaging mixture of shrewdness and volubility – players nicknamed him *Calon* for his frequent invocation of that quality, while historians Dai Smith and Gareth Williams saw in him the Welsh Sergeant Bilko – he would become national coach, selector, union president and Lions manager.

Trebanos already had one Welsh scrum-half controversy to its name. Few west Walians in the early 1950s doubted that the brilliantly individualistic Roy Sutton should be the Wales scrum-half, but the selectors, not unreasonably wanting to get the ball as often and as fast as possible to Cliff Morgan and Bleddyn Williams, opted for the steady service of their Cardiff clubmate Rex Willis. When Trebanos (population in 1986: 1,611) stopped mining coal it took up the production of international sportsmen. Three doors down from the Jones household in Swansea Road lived Glamorgan fast-bowler Gregory Thomas, who departed on England's tour of the West Indies in the very week in January 1986 when Robert was first capped. Around 100 yards away was the home of Bleddyn Bowen, who won his seventh cap at centre on the day of Robert's debut, would captain Wales to the Triple Crown two years later and form the other half of a short-lived all-Trebanos half-back pairing in 1989. Just to prove that this was not some genetic freak of the first half of the 1960s, Trebanos in 1986 was also home to an 11-year-old named Arwel Thomas whose outside-half performances for Wales a decade later would display some of the local characteristics – diminutive, instinctive, combative, controversial at home and admired abroad – in his case by French observers such as Serge Blanco and Pierre Villepreux.

Like Gareth Edwards with Bill Samuel, Robert found a teacher whose role as mentor would long outlast his schooldays. When out of form and favour in 1993 he turned to Goff Davies, the former Bridgend and Swansea centre who had first seen him when he arrived at Cwmtawe School as an 11-year-old: 'He was already such a smooth operator, with time under pressure, that the physical education staff at the school were aware that he was something very special,' said Davies, who as coach at Bridgend would also play an important part in the early development of Robert Howley. Jones won Welsh caps at under-15, 16 and 18 level, leading the under-18 team to a Grand Slam, and was still in the sixth form at Cwmtawe when he made his senior club debut.

On 23 November 1983, a week before his eighteenth birthday, he played for Swansea against South Wales Police. He enjoyed the benefit of a dominant pack, but otherwise the style described by Ron Griffiths of the *South Wales Evening Post* was the one that would become familiar over the next fifteen years: 'His pass, long, swift and flat, was the centrepiece of a performance that might some four or five years ahead be of some significance. While it is never easy to assess any player on the basis of one match it is clear that young Jones is rather special. His partner last night, the normally reticent Wales fly-half Malcolm Dacey, acknowledged that "It was a pleasure to play at the end of that pass. He's another player with a future".'

As a schoolboy he had contemplated a teaching career – hardly a novelty for outstanding Welsh backs. But earlier generations had not been required to balance their studies with the multiple squad sessions now routinely required by the 1970s and 1980s from youngsters playing representative rugby. Less remarked upon than the miners and steelworkers, the teachers who once formed as significant a component in Welsh playing strength disappeared almost as completely and quickly – Paul Rees pointed to Robert's Swansea team-mate Kevin Hopkins as the only teacher in the Welsh top flight in 1987. Robert married a teacher – his wife Megan was to teach at Trebanos Junior, his old primary school – but A-levels disrupted by training demands precipitated him into the finance industry jobs characteristic of rugby players in the immediate pre-professional period – first clerking for a Swansea firm, and once he was established as an international player by posts where his celebrity was of potential use. The OCS Group in Cardiff took him on as a group liaison officer handling both industrial and public relations within two months of his first cap, then he moved in 1987 to work for a finance company run by former Swansea and Wales centre, and soon to be Wales selector, David Richards.

Players in the last decade of ostensible amateurism had to combine ever-mounting demands on their time with the need to find another income. Sympathetic employers were essential – Robert's joking comment in 1990 that 'When I get the opportunity I'm in work' reflected real pressures which were partly relieved in 1994, when he accepted a post as a development officer with Western Province in South Africa. Those pressures also help explain, though not justify, the one occasion on which he seriously disappointed many admirers – joining the World XV which went, against Welsh Rugby Union advice but with the shameful connivance of some WRU officials to apartheid South Africa to celebrate the South African Rugby Union centenary in 1989.

His first Wales call-up came following Holmes's departure to rugby league in late 1985, and amid fears that the loss of this dominating figure presaged disaster. Robert's first three seasons were not seen as especially successful at the time – standards and expectations were still set by the 1970s and there were three massacres at the hands of the All Blacks – but by subsequent standards 1986–8 was a period of relative prosperity for Wales with a third place in the 1987 World Cup and a Triple Crown in 1988. Fifteen of Robert's first twenty internationals ended in victory and if Clive Rowlands's post-World Cup comment that Wales would simply 'go back to beating England every year' looked silly and parochial even in 1987, it was at least true until 1989. With Jonathan Davies, still in the first flush of youthful exuberance, thriving on the end of the Jones service and Bowen unobtrusively oiling the wheels at centre, Welsh back play was livelier than for years. That victory over England in 1989 displayed another facet of his developing skills, the ability to control a game through precise kicking. Bob Norster dominated the line-out, Jones tortured the English with controlled box-kicks and, not for the first or last time, England became enmeshed fatally in their own tactical inflexibility. Already a near-certainty for the Lions tour to Australia, that display ended any doubts.

The Lions tour finally answered the question of what Robert Jones might achieve with a competitive pack of forwards. Australia's Nick Farr-Jones, by general consent the best number 9 in the world, was eclipsed for the only time in his career. In the Second Test he displayed his box-kicking virtuosity at Australia's expense, and in the Third he unsettled brilliant wing David Campese, who was to give away the decisive try in the last few minutes, by artfully angled kicks. A Second Test brawl with Farr-Jones was a rare open display of aggression – possibly, given the punch Arwel Thomas landed on Philippe Carbonneau at Paris in 1997, the launch of another Trebanos tradition – reflecting the ferociously competitive attitude of the Lions.

Dean Richards, the Lions number 8, noted his tactical acuity and flexibility: 'If one method wasn't working he would quietly and calmly change the way things were done during matches.' Most spectacular of all was the evidence of what his service might do for an outside-half. England's Rob Andrew had underachieved since winning his first cap in 1984. His obvious gifts kept the selectors faithful to him, but while outstanding at club level his decision-making, a matter of split seconds at international level, let him down persistently for England. Excluded from the original Lions squad, he replaced the injured Irishman Paul Dean. Paired with Jones, he found 'I have never felt more comfortable, more quickly with any other scrum-half'. Centre Jeremy Guscott confirmed: 'Robert Jones was playing brilliantly at scrum-half and his quick pass had helped to transform Rob Andrew's game.' Andrew partnered Jones as the last two Tests were won and returned to England firmly established as a top-quality, if conservative, outside-half. It was far from the last time the Jones pass would have this effect. After he had led the Barbarians to victory over the 1994 South Africans – only months before they won the World Cup – Stephen Jones of the *Sunday Times* noted: 'Craig Chalmers, Mike Hall, Scott Hastings and Simon Geoghegan all had easily the best games I have seen them play all season. Coincidence? Far more likely that they were all thriving in that almost agoraphobic extra yard of space that lightning service from a scrum-half can provide.'

The 1989 Lions represent a dividing point. Until then, in spite of the Bishop campaign and the foretaste of the future provided on the 1988 tour of New Zealand when Wales were overwhelmed in the First Test and he was displaced by Jonathan Griffiths of Llanelli, best of his extra-flanker rivals, for the Second, Robert Jones had progressed steadily to become certainly the best scrum-half in Britain and arguably in the world.

The year 1990 brought the captaincy of Wales. He had always wanted the job and was the obvious man for it. There was no decline in his skills. But from here on he was engulfed in the calamitous decline of the Welsh game. Limited resources were dissipated by deplorable man-agement, starting with the sacking of the Triple-Crown-winning coaching team of Tony Gray and Derek Quinnell following the New Zealand tour of 1988 – against copious competition the worst decision made by the WRU during Robert's career. That incomparably stupid action epitomized Welsh rugby's loss of confidence from the late 1980s.

Tactics and selection oscillated wildly with changes of coach, but the constant factor was loss of faith in the traditional virtues of instinctive speed of thought and movement. Jones, exemplar of those virtues, was in and out of the side as more powerful but less skilled players were preferred. Stuart Barnes, outside-half for Bath and England but a Wales Schools cap and, as player and journalist, a firm believer in the primacy of wit over weight and skill over size, saw in Jones 'a throwback to Welsh greatness' and argued that: 'When Jonathan Davies headed north and Robert Jones was dropped, Welsh rugby lost its ambition.'

Significantly, Jones retained the support of his predecessors at scrum-half. Terry Holmes, quizzed about the alternatives in 1991, took the view that: 'Robert Jones is in a class of his own. I think there is a lot of rubbish talked about him lacking a physical presence. Today's game demands an all-rounder and if I were playing now I would have to adapt my style to survive.' Gareth Edwards, in 1995, hailing him as 'simply the best scrum half in the world', added: 'What makes it even better for Wales is that they could not have a better role model. During all the times he was left out of the side by different coaches, Robert never moaned or whinged about it.' He handled the droppings, the changes of coach, and incidents such as coach Ron Waldron crassly making it clear that he had been outvoted on his choice of scrum-half when Jones was restored to the side after missing the 1990 tour of Namibia with an injury, with the same calm composure he brought to tidying up poor possession.

He was barely on speaking terms with Waldron by the end of the 1991 tour of Australia and angered by Alec Evans's allegation that members of the 1995 World Cup squad had dissipated their chances by irresponsible drinking. But not until his sixth exclusion, when he found out from the press rather than the Wales management that he had been left out of the squad to play Fiji in late 1995, did he express his feelings, telling *Rugby World*: 'There has always been a communication problem with the Welsh Rugby Union and their man-management skills have been derisory.' This was not simple resentment at being left out. He retained mutual respect for Alan Davies, the coach who left him out for longest – an exclusion which at least offered the rugby world the Pythonesque spectacle of Rupert Henry St John Barker Moon at scrum-half for Wales, faced by Dewi Morris for England – defended him publicly in 1995, and chose to join him at Bristol in 1996. The physical and psychological battering he took undoubtedly affected him. In 1993 he admitted that criticism had affected his on-field judgement: 'Over the last couple of years I had started to try to play the way the critics said was the way I never could play – physically. Maybe I wasn't exactly charging through head down. But I was certainly taking on opposing players . . . and just to prove a point. It was the wrong way to go about it.'

In or out of the Welsh side, he remained a focus for local pride in Swansea – which suffered along with its industrial hinterland during the recession of the early 1980s, did not share in the benefits east Wales derived from the later 1980s from its position at the end of the M4 corridor and in the 1990s perceived itself as increasingly marginalized while public projects such as the Opera House and Millennium Stadium were planned for Cardiff. With Swansea City Football Club also in precipitous decline following the unprecedented success of the late 1970s and early 1980s, the city's sporting fortunes were firmly pinned to the All Whites. Jones's fruitful half-back partnership with Aled Williams, a modern continuation of Swansea traditions of diminutive deceptiveness established by the James brothers and the 'Dancing Dicks' Owen and Jones either side of 1900, helped ensure that they were always watchable and often successful – winning two championships and a Swalec Cup in the first half of the 1990s.

Scott Gibbs said the chance to play with Jones was one of his main reasons for moving from Neath to Swansea. Robert Howley, his first competitor of comparable quality and eventual successor – and whose experiences as Wales captain in 1998 have doubtless given him some insight into what Robert went through at the base of the Welsh eight – still carries memories of a master-class in scrum-half play handed out in a club match in 1993. There were also spectacular displays against tourists – in 1990 going down 37–22 to the All Blacks but with a dazzling display of running becoming the first Welsh side to score four tries against them, then outplaying the world champion Australians 21–6 in 1992. All of which, along with his role in the Barbarian defeat of South Africa, merely deepened international mystification at Wales's indifference to the one player envied by other nations.

That indifference was never mutual. Stuart Barnes, whose unstinting admiration of Jones survived having his head accidentally kicked open by his half-back partner during the 1993 Lions tour, was possibly exaggerating when he described him as having 'an insane degree of national fervour'. Yet while other ill-used stars took their frustrations to Widnes, Leeds or St Helens, Jones rejected the lucrative opportunities to forsake Wales offered first by Salford then by South Africa – always giving a desire to play again for Wales as his chief reason. When he finally did leave Swansea for Bristol in 1996, he said he hoped the fresh challenge might revive his chances of representative rugby – although he was later to complain that Swansea officials had made him promises that were not kept.

Fifty-three starts equalled Gareth Edwards's Welsh scrum-half record (his fifty-fourth cap was won as a replacement on the wing against Ireland in 1994). Yet still a sense of frustration attaches to Jones's career – one he clearly feels himself. In his last few years he became identified with Welsh failure – he played in thirty-one defeats, a figure since exceeded by Gareth Llewellyn and Ieuan Evans. It is a melancholy record, but one that says more about his circumstances than about Jones. The case for his exclusion rests entirely on the three consecutive matches won with Rupert Moon in scrum-half in 1994 – not an achievement to be dismissed lightly, but the only wins in the twelve matches against International Board countries between 1986 and 1995 where somebody other than Jones was scrum-half.

One distinguished observer of the Welsh game commented, 'People say Robert Jones is a world-class scrum half. But world-class players should win matches and how many matches has he won for Wales, apart from the 1989 game against England ?' An admissable question, but not a fair one. Nobody was winning many matches for Wales during Robert Jones's career. The greatest loser in Five Nations history, measured on matches lost, is Mike Gibson – the one player from elsewhere in Britain who would have won a place in the Welsh back divisions of the early 1970s.

It was said of American politician Adlai Stevenson – hugely respected in Europe, twice thrashed by Eisenhower for the US presidency – that he ran for president in the wrong continent. Robert Jones did not play in the wrong country – his talents were exactly those which have underpinned the Welsh game at its best since the days of Gwyn Nicholls – but he certainly played at the wrong time.

JONATHAN DAVIES

Siân Nicholas

In January 1989 Jonathan Davies became the most expensive rugby league signing ever in the British game, and yet he had played only four full seasons of first-class rugby union. He played for Wales in four Five Nations Championships, on two overseas tours and in the inaugural World Cup in 1987, captaining the team three times. He never played for the British Lions. Yet he was the most famous rugby player in the northern hemisphere, regarded by many as the most complete outside-half the game had ever seen. Six years later, after winning almost every prize in the league game, he made history again as the first player to switch back from the league to the union code, and went on to win four further international caps before his retirement from the game in August 1997.

Was he the greatest talent the Welsh game had seen in a generation – or simply the most unfulfilled? Certainly, his rugby career was one of the most unlikely, the contradictions in his career reflecting the character of the player. He was the inheritor of a glittering rugby pedigree that played little or no part in his rise to stardom, the pale slight figure originally passed over on account of his size who surprised opponents and spectators alike with his physicality in both attack and defence, the local boy who used rugby to travel the world, the 'cocky little bugger' who was physically sick with nerves before big games, the irrepressible mischief-maker whose career was marked by a succession of family tragedies.

But if the contradictions in Davies's career partly reflected his own mercurial temperament, they also painfully exposed the contradictions in the Welsh game itself in the uneasy period between the glorious seventies and the unhappy nineties. The traditions that had characterized Welsh rugby in the past did not sit easily with the demands and pressures of the modern game; the tensions between amateurism and professionalism in rugby union in the 1980s went well beyond Rule 18(iii)(c) to the very core of the game's administration and outlook. At a time when the credibility of the amateur ethos throughout world sport was under its most sustained attack, Davies, to whom many of these traditions were either irrelevant or frankly incomprehensible, revealed these contradictions to us all.

On one level, Jonathan Davies appeared fated to play for Wales. He was born in the village of Trimsaran, just outside Llanelli, in the heart of the west Wales 'outside-half factory', in 1962. His father had played centre for Swansea and Llanelli (and had turned down an offer of £2,000 to go North and play for Leigh). On passing his 11-plus, he went to Gwendraeth Grammar School, whose past pupils (as future commentators would never tire of reminding us) included Welsh outside-halves Carwyn James, Barry John and Gareth Davies. When he was only eleven, the great Carwyn himself predicted that he too would play for Wales one day.

Yet this illustrious rugby heritage appears to have played little part in the young Jonathan's rugby education. Trimsaran was a tight-knit community based around the village rugby team and it was for the village team, captained by his father, rather than the local giants Llanelli that Davies gathered balls on Saturdays. It was not at Gwendraeth but at Trimsaran Primary School, encouraged by his primary school teacher Meirion Davies, that Davies first made the number-10 jersey his own, outside-half the only possible position for a speedy and boisterous (though very small) boy with a natural ball-handling ability. His first-ever appearance at the National Stadium, for West Wales v. East Wales under-12s in 1974 in the curtain-raiser to Wales v. Tonga – a tiny red ant (his mother's description) on the giant pitch – might so easily have been his last: despite Gwendraeth's rugby tradition, larger schools had bigger players and greater sporting successes. The support (both emotional and financial) of Trimsaran Rugby Club during the long illness and finally the death of his father when Davies was fourteen served to strengthen local rather than school loyalties, and it was conflict between the two that brought Davies hard against the game's authorities for the first time and probably cost him his only chance of a Schools' cap. In 1980, shortly after being selected to attend the prestigious Welsh Schools Rugby Union residential course at Aberystwyth, and in part through an adminstrative confusion, Davies opted to play for Trimsaran Youth in the district cup final instead of East Dyfed under-17s in a county schools cup tie. The school reported this breach of priorities to the WSSRU; Davies's place at Aberystwyth was withdrawn and Trimsaran Youth were banned for a month. He left school soon after without having taken his A-levels (taking up a painting/decorating apprenticeship), and the blow of rejection in a trial for Llanelli appeared to close off the prospect of first-class rugby.

In 1982 a chance word from Phil Bennett attracted the attention of Neath, then struggling to find a first-team outside-half, to Trimsaran Firsts' energetic young number 10 (according to different sources Davies was either the eighth or the thirteenth tried out that season). He made an impressive debut (supported from the stand by half the village) against Pontypridd in a midweek game in February 1982, with a try early in the game and a late drop goal, and his 'polished performance' was singled out for praise by the *Western Mail*'s Malcolm Lewis. Bad luck intervened: a knee injury at the Snelling Sevens at the end of the season put him out of the game for the next season and a half. But when he finally restarted for Neath, dauntingly thrown into the team against Newport in the quarter-final of the 1984 Schweppes Welsh Cup, it was as if he had never left. This time it was J. B. G. Thomas himself who named Davies man of the match, impressed by his 'cheeky confidence' and a forty-yard dropped goal. A month later he was instrumental in Neath's comprehensive semi-final defeat of local rivals Aberavon. Although Neath went on to lose the Cup Final to Cardiff, Davies found himself, after just a handful of first-class appearances, in a team with the potential – and in veteran Neath and Wales forward Brian Thomas the coach – to reach the top flight of Welsh rugby, with a new job (paints' estimator for a Cardiff firm, working alongside Wales scrum-half Terry Holmes), a new wife (he married his longstanding girlfriend Karen in August 1984) and spoken of as a possible challenger for a national place 'in the years ahead'.

He was challenging for a place in a team where old certainties were crumbling. After the glory days of the 1970s, the Welsh team of the early 1980s was reeling from a succession of bad results, high-profile retirements and defections to rugby league. Although the problem of forward dominance on the field – and squad morale off it – lay at the heart of the trouble, argument centred above all on the outside-half position as the selectors prevaricated between the respective merits of Cardiff's Gareth Davies and Swansea's Malcolm Dacey, neither of whom seemed able to reproduce his club form consistently on the international field.

Jonathan Davies's rapid rise under Brian Thomas's encouragement saw him picked for Wales 'B' against France, and for the Wales squad for the Five Nations Championship in 1985, although it was another young Neath player in his first full season, Paul Thorburn, who won a first cap ahead of him. The weather played havoc, however, with the fixtures, and after lacklustre performances by Gareth Davies against Ireland and France, Jonathan's luck turned. When the Welsh selectors took the extraordinary step of releasing the team for the rescheduled England game with 'A. N. Other' pencilled in at number 10, Gareth Davies, who, despite his twenty-one caps had not even been informed by the selectors of the decision, made the only possible riposte by immediately announcing his retirement from the international game and comprehensively outplaying Dacey in Cardiff's game against Swansea the following Saturday. Jonathan, playing against Gloucester at Neath, did enough to secure the place. It had been his first game back after the sudden death of his father-in-law and there were emotional celebrations at Trimsaran Rugby Club.

Having waited so long for any chance, this one was not wasted. Typically, his debut was marked by both inspiration and good fortune. In a match which the England team threw away, presenting the Welsh for once with more than enough possession to dominate the game, Jonathan impressed onlookers not so much with his kicking, which was erratic, but with his sheer enterprise. His first try for his country (the first outside-half to score a try on his debut for fifty-four years) was suitably dramatic: an overkicked high ball, followed up at speed, which England full-back Chris Martin fumbled on his own line; he also kicked an inevitable drop goal. After a successful summer tour to Fiji, Davies became the automatic choice for the 1985–6 season, partnered by newcomer Robert Jones, in contrast to Davies a distinguished product of Welsh schools rugby. Terry Holmes had moved North, to Bradford Northern for a (then) record £80,000.

Over the next two seasons Jonathan Davies's career exposed the gulf in Wales between club and international rugby. The reputation of the new Wales half-back pair strengthened from game to game, and Davies's performances, especially against Scotland and Ireland in 1986, marked him out as one of the greatest rising talents in world rugby. However, weaknesses in the pack and a sad dearth of fast ball from the scrum offered little opportunity to the young back line, and Wales won only two games in the 1986 Five Nations Championship and only one in 1987. By contrast at the Gnoll, supported by a pack that could compete with any in Wales, backs who could set the ground alight, and a coach who made fitness, commitment and initiative the priority, Davies (still only twenty-two) captained the Neath machine to the double of Merit Table and Cup champions, and a crushing 26–9 defeat of Bath that year established them as the unofficial club champions of Great Britain.

How to describe Jonathan Davies the player? The Gareth Davies–Malcolm Dacey controversy had renewed a debate within Welsh rugby about the relative merits of a kicking and a running outside-half that went back to the days of Billy Cleaver and Glyn Davies. But Jonathan, supporters pointed out, could do anything. Cliff Morgan described him as a new Barry John, Brian Thomas as a Barry John who could tackle; John Billot of the *Western Mail* saw in him a virtual composite of the great Welsh outside-halves of the past ('the instinctive dodging of Cliff Morgan, the sharp changes of direction that typified Bennett, the sharp acceleration of Watkins, the laid-back confidence of Barry John and the eye for the tactical roller that Gareth Davies perfected'). Jonathan himself politely declined to see himself in these terms: he was simply the first Jonathan Davies.

And it was not only his extraordinary playing skills, the quick thinking, the tactical invention, the startling blast of pace in attack and the happy knack of dropping goals (a record twelve, to add to his five tries, in his international career) at crucial moments, that lit up the rugby field. There was also the style with which he played, the unsettling combination of tactical maturity and impish opportunism, the audacity ('no one was ever dropped for trying') and sheer self-assurance that shone from everything he tried and that made him seem immediately at home on the international pitch. His personality off the field was a disarming combination of modesty and self-belief; on the field he played with the kind of arrogance that stems less from disdain of others than from supreme confidence in one's own abilities. Despite his size (the half-back combination of Davies and Jones must have been one of the physically slightest in the international game), he was impossible to intimidate, not above a touch of gamesmanship, and capable of winding up opposing forwards to frenzy (famously, England flanker Mickey Skinner in that Five Nations encounter at Twickenham in 1988). After a game, his high-pitched and fast spoken post-match interviews were an entertainment in themselves. At Neath these qualities made him the lynchpin of the team's success, sorely missed when not playing and rapidly gaining a following that ranged far beyond Neath itself. For Wales, however, his skills were a source of frustration as much as enjoyment. Partnered by one of the best scrum-halves in the world, with a midfield of young skilful runners, it was his and our misfortune that the team as a whole could not measure up to the sum of its parts.

Yet Jonathan was not short of opportunities to play alongside, as well as against, the best in the world. With the global explosion of interest in Sevens rugby worldwide, his audacious playing style attracted invitations to travel and to mix with the rugby elite unimaginable to previous generations, and that few adventurous young players could have turned down. The frenetic pace of modern top-flight rugby took its toll, as he travelled 75,000 miles in a season to play with the Scottish Co-Optimists in Zimbabwe, the Irish Wolfhounds in the Hong Kong Sevens, as well as the Wales Sevens side in the Sydney Sevens (where he scored three tries in fourteen minutes against New Zealand) and the Wales touring team in Fiji, Tonga and Western Samoa. A succession of injuries that forced him to drop out of the British Lions side that played the Rest of the World at Twickenham in 1986 brought accusations of selfishness from fans and warnings from former players that he should learn to say no sometimes. The pressures of rugby also had an effect on his private life – a trial separation, a much-publicized drink-driving conviction – although hardly the hell-raising a few press articles strained to uncover.

But the basic contradiction at the heart of Davies's rugby was, on the one hand, his sheer enjoyment of playing, whenever and wherever possible, and on the other his hard-headed attitude to the game itself, and the rewards it could – or could not but arguably should – offer. Davies was neither the first nor the only player in Wales to whom appeals to the amateur spirit seemed increasingly hypocritical and outdated. 'Boot money' allegations and players' revelations of a British Lions 'tour fund' in the 1970s undermined official attempts to uphold the pretence of amateurism. By the mid-1980s the looser definition of 'amateurism' in rugby union outside the four home countries was notorious, and British players increasingly mixed with overseas stars whose financial security for their retirement had already been openly assured. But it was not simply internal factors that were fatally undermining amateurism in northern hemisphere rugby union. The world was changing. Across the whole of international sport the amateur ethos was becoming redefined, from the sanctioning of trust funds in athletics to the question of professional participation in the Olympics themselves. Rugby union was a lone (and divided) voice against change.

To an extent, rugby in Wales still looked after its own. Brian Thomas's contacts had brought Davies financial security in the short term with an employer who was happy, in effect, to subsidize his rugby-playing. Although rumours about club back-handers (always hotly denied) abounded with Jonathan as with every other top player (for it was undeniably true that his presence on the field visibly increased club gates), there were other well-known 'unofficial' means to supplement incomes (notably through appearance and hospitality work), to which the game's administrators turned a blind eye even as they sought to defend the narrowest definitions of amateurism at the International Rugby Board. But what of the future? Terry Holmes's decision to turn professional at the age of twenty-eight, with a damaged shoulder and no other clear prospect of financial security before him, was an early warning. Rugby league teams had already noted Davies's talent (how could they not?), and in 1986 Leeds offered Jonathan a record £100,000 to sign for them, an offer which he did not lightly reject.

In January 1987 (barely a week after being hailed as 'A god to rouse the valleys' in a full-length *Times* feature), Davies provoked less favourable headlines with an interview in a short-lived sports magazine, *Sportsweek*, during which he was reported as saying it was '99 per cent certain' that he would move to rugby league after that summer's inaugural World Cup. Claiming he had been quoted out of context, Davies apologized publicly to the Welsh Rugby Union, but if the details were contested, the point of view expressed ('We are expected to behave like professionals but we are treated like amateurs') was increasingly hard to refute. When one put so much into a sport (and his commitment to rugby, both on and off the field, was unquestioned), might not one expect, at some point, something back in return?

The *Sportsweek* article probably cost Davies an early chance at the Welsh captaincy; it almost certainly cost him his place at Neath. When Brian Thomas requested he commit himself to Neath for the 1987–8 season, Davies refused. If it was inconceivable to Thomas that Davies could not see the need for such an assurance, it was equally inconceivable to Davies that Thomas could not see why it was impossible. Injured and clubless in the 1987 World Cup, he still helped Wales to confound expectations by first reaching the semi-finals then, after a crushing defeat by New Zealand, rallying to beat Australia for third place. Although it was his half-back partner who returned with his reputation most enhanced, Davies was nominated to the 'team of teams' selected by Gerald Davies (as rugby correspondent of *The Times*, one of Jonathan's keenest advocates and most incisive critics). He returned to take up a place, not in rugby league, but with Llanelli, six years after they had turned him down.

The backlash had already begun. The young tyro was now established as the key player in the team: this position of responsibility brought with it different expectations and demands. What had seemed instinctive brilliance in previous seasons was increasingly criticised as selfishness, arrogance, tactical error. Persistent injury restricted his appearances for Llanelli, and Jonathan began the 1988 Five Nations campaign with his very place in the team under question. 'Jonathan's main asset is his unpredictability,' a selector was rumoured to have said, 'but once that is predicted is it any longer an asset?'

Yet 1988, Triple Crown year, saw Jonathan's two most spectacular displays in the Five Nations for Wales and his naming as Whitbread Rugby World Player of the Year. He was inspirational against England at Twickenham, where the look of blank incredulity on his face when brought down just short of a certain score by England full-back Jon Webb's despairing tap is as vivid in many memories as the exhilarating fifty-yard run from deep in his own half that launched Wales's match-turning second try. His performance against Scotland at Cardiff, where he dropped two goals in the last eight minutes to secure a 25–20 victory, was widely hailed as the best in his Wales career, and featured his most celebrated international try, a well-fielded looping pass from Robert Jones some twenty yards from the Scottish line, an instinctive low grubber-kick and a heartstopping burst through the Scottish forwards to score.

But although he helped meld Llanelli's squad of brilliant individuals into an effective team unit, he was again criticized for his absences through injury, and victory over Neath in the Schweppes Cup Final was overshadowed by the spiteful behaviour of some of his former colleagues. The Triple Crown triumph proved one of many false dawns, as Wales's disastrous tour of New Zealand that summer summed up all that was wrong with the Welsh game. Although Davies himself played some of the best and most desperate rugby of his career (including a breathtaking solo try in the Second Test), the team that had ended the Five Nations with such optimism was systematically destroyed, both physically and mentally, over the course of an itinerary that the New Zealand coach himself said he would have refused to accept. Drained by defeats, injuries, sub-standard accommodation and poor transportation arrangements, the Welsh players were confronted at first hand with a rugby nation where All Blacks maintained 'amateur' status while openly earning money through endorsements and sponsorship, where a players' liaison committee co-ordinated with the New Zealand Rugby Union, where players even received expenses for their wives to see the games. On their return, Jonathan asked to address the WRU's annual general meeting, to present the players' views of the tour and their suggestions as to the way forward; his letter did not even receive an acknowledgement. Coach Tony Gray was sacked before his own report could be submitted. When finally announced, the WRU's recommendations included a unanimous appeal for the laws of the game to be more consistently interpreted worldwide; however, a recommendation that touring players be permitted to travel club class was not unanimous.

Relations between squad and officials worsened throughout the autumn. After an unconvincing victory over Western Samoa several leading players were peremptorily dropped and Triple Crown captain Bleddyn Bowen inexplicably sidelined. Wales lost 9–15 to Romania before a small and derisive crowd on 12 December – the first premier rugby nation to lose to an emerging national side. To those watching it appeared that Davies, captaining a weary and unhappy side, was trying too hard to win it by himself; his tactical judgment seemed strained and his kicking poor. 'Rwy wedi danto', Gerald Davies heard him sigh at the end of the post-match press conference, an exhausted player nearing the end of his tether. In the next few weeks he was ignored by WRU officials, cold-shouldered by coach John Ryan and treated like a scapegoat by the selectors. Over Christmas Doug Laughton, the Widnes coach, made his move and on 5 January 1989 Jonathan Davies became the 154th Wales player to go North.

The news put Davies on front pages across Britain. The record fee (around £150,000) was widely rumoured to be as high as £240,000. At a triumphant press conference Widnes showed Davies off to sports journalists from across the rugby-playing world. Within the rugby union world the cries of 'traitor' were inevitable. When Terry Holmes had moved North he was nearing the end of a valiant career and in dubious playing health; his move had been generally recognized as a wise investment. Jonathan Davies was only twenty-six, with his best still before him, turning his back not only on a desperately low Wales team but on an assured British Lions place. In *The Sun* Bobby Windsor (a veteran of boot money and tour fund stories) pronounced that Wales would do better without him. Frank Keating of *The Guardian* dourly predicted that Davies was too small to make his mark in rugby league. But despite the inevitable accusations of greed and disloyalty, the groundswell of feeling – particularly among former and current players – was less hostile than might have once been supposed. It was so clearly not the lack of money as much as the lack of respect that had provided the final push into League, but it so happened that in sport as elsewhere by the late 1980s respect was most clearly measured in money. Several leading Welsh players followed Davies's example over the next few months. The WRU made a few more enemies by denying the BBC permission to interview Davies on the Cardiff pitch before the Wales–England game, citing 'IRB regulations', though they could not prevent him being interviewed in the analysts' box instead.

In a country where rugby union has always got far more press and television coverage than its professional counterpart, it is sometimes hard to recall just how good a rugby league player Jonathan Davies was. With Widnes and then Warrington he was given the opportunity to fulfil his potential, and he found a game that suited his talents and temperament even more than rugby union. He went North burdened with a huge weight of expectation, but Widnes took care of their new investment. After a demoralizing physical examination – at which he was told to go away and put on a stone in weight – he was introduced into the team with a promising though for once unspectacular twenty-seven minutes as replacement in a game Widnes already had under control, a reassuring experience for both himself and the expectant crowds (twice the normal gate, including television crews from France and Australia, several coachloads from Trimsaran and – a rugby league scout's dream – six Welsh internationals for moral support). Playing as utility back, he helped Widnes to win every trophy in the game except the Challenge Cup (they were runners-up). Playing centre for Warrington after a cash-strapped Widnes were forced to transfer him in 1993, he was instrumental in transforming a middling side into championship contenders. In two summers in Australia, with Canterbury-Bankstown and North Queensland Cowboys, he more than held his own in the most competitive rugby league environment in the world. Only a few code-breakers make the step from club rugby league to international level, but Jonathan Davies did so with ease, touring with the 'Lions' in New Zealand in 1990, making eleven appearances for Great Britain between 1990 and 1994, and nine for Wales between 1991 and 1995.

In a code where the players' roles and responsibilities are more evenly shared, and where individual breaks count as much as team play, Davies found a game in which effort was clearly rewarded, and which enabled him to shine without having also to assume responsibility for his team's success or failure. Heavier and more powerful, his defensive and tackling skills took on a new dimension, while his running skills, especially his speed off the mark, became his trademark. He scored the fastest 1,000 points in league history. He was named Player of the Season by his fellow professionals in 1991 and again in 1994. This was his best year in rugby league: he also won the game's highest individual accolade, the Man of Steel award, and was man of the match when the Great Britain team, with only twelve men for most of the match, tore up the form book in sensational style to defeat Australia 8–4 at Wembley. His spectacular fifty-yard try, dummying past two players and beating a third to a diving touchdown in the corner, brought thoughts of what might have been had Davies stayed in Wales. So did the astonishing success of the revitalized Wales rugby league team (under Davies's captaincy and featuring a squad largely made up of former rugby union stars) the following year. While the Wales rugby union team won the wooden spoon in the Five Nations, their league counterparts became

European Champions (beating England for the first time since 1977), and after a storming victory over Western Samoa (itself a bitter irony for rugby union fans) reached the semi-finals of the Rugby League World Cup. Jonathan Davies's last game for Wales was the semi-final defeat against England before a crowd of 30,000 at Old Trafford. He left the pitch in tears, with the crowd still singing 'Bread of Heaven', after what he later described as the most emotional fortnight of his career.

Above all, Davies's enjoyment of rugby league shone through. If the game itself appealed to his physical skills, the hard professional training and the shared professional commitment provided a job satisfaction untainted by the ambiguity with which rugby union had become riven. However, as rugby union rules regarding payments began finally to crack, he admitted that had such conditions existed when he was playing he never would have left. When the IRB finally acknowledged that rugby league players might be permitted after a century's prohibition to make the transfer to rugby union, Davies was the first man people thought of. It was widely known that he hankered to play out his career in Wales, and that he saw his long-term future in terms of rugby union not league; it was less well known how ill his wife was and how important it was to be near family once more.

Jonathan Davies's historic move from Warrington RLC to Cardiff RFC exposed the uneasy new world of professional rugby union, as his erstwhile predecessor Gareth Davies (now Cardiff chief executive) and the Cardiff management secured a secret financial and employment package that involved at various levels Cardiff sponsors Jewson's, at least two millionaire backers, the WRU and BBC Wales. But the undignified rush to cash in on professionalism took its toll here as elsewhere in the British game. Although much was made publicly of Davies's future role as mentor to the younger Cardiff players, to many outsiders Cardiff's actions seemed to represent a publicity coup: a gesture of intent, but without clear strategic purpose. To a successful and settled Cardiff team, Davies seemed an intruder. He was rushed into his debut for Cardiff after just one training session, in the unfamiliar position of full-back, in a match rescheduled from Saturday to Sunday in order to facilitate live television coverage. An unexpectedly small crowd saw him apparently cold-shouldered by the other players; soon the joke went round that he had more chance of winning the lottery than of being passed the ball by his own side. Once restored to the outside-half position in the following season, Davies showed that, despite being slower than of old, his tactical acumen and brilliant improvization could still turn a game. He was instrumental in the club's successful Heineken Cup run (dropping, as of old, the clinching goal against the much-fancied Wasps), and found himself once more in the running as a candidate for a Wales cap.

Nothing perhaps sums up the parlous state of Welsh rugby in the 1990s than that the idea of recalling a 33-year-old veteran uncapped for eight years was seriously entertained – nor that, in many experienced eyes (including those of Gerald Davies, J. P. R. Williams and David Campese) the idea had clear merits. Davies's last caps for Wales, however, were surely anticlimactic. Against Australia in December 1996 (Campese's muted farewell to international rugby) he was clearly not the same player as before: he was stronger, his kicking and tactical sense were as sharp as before, but while the Welsh pack still could not get enough ball, the blistering acceleration that had allowed Davies to make breaks where no one else could had gone. To a player who had expressed concern at the devaluation of the international cap, his six minutes as a blood-replacement against the USA and his final-minute appearance against Scotland (marking his first appearance in the Five Nations for nine years) were almost derisory. His last game against England, twelve years after his debut against the same team on the same ground, was a sad farewell; he had not experienced Wales so comprehensively outplayed by England before. But even here, he was in the thick of the action, his performance in defence was robust and by converting Howley's late try he made a little bit more history as the last player to score in an international at the National Stadium. Such was his grip on the rugby imagination that he was even being spoken of in connection with a place on the 1997 Lions tour to South Africa when his wife's death from cancer, leaving him with three small children, prompted his final retirement from the game.

Jonathan Davies's career revealed the self-assurance of a man who served no ordinary apprenticeship in the game, whose career was not constrained by the game's traditions (traditions that were in themselves fatally weakening), and who as a player sought to control the game rather than let the game control him. His playing style uniquely reflected this attitude. His position, the mythic one of outside-half, brought him both high praise and the highest expectations, but unlike previous players it was not so much the expectations that wore him down as the assumptions, in particular the assumption that an international cap was reward enough in itself. In rugby league he found an environment that was more sympathetic to his character, less dependent on him as the sole matchwinner, and that rewarded his talents openly, not secretly. Once back in 'professional' rugby union, however, he demonstrated how little had changed for the better in the Welsh game in his absence.

After his retirement he finally received the sympathy that he had never courted as a player, as the emotional burden under which he had played his last few seasons became publicly known. But his always uncomfortable relationship with the WRU did not long outlast his retirement, and his media interests now predominate. As an analyst for both rugby union and rugby league on the BBC and for the *Independent on Sunday*, he has attracted respect and something of a following for his unassuming manner and trenchant comments. He has also appeared on the S4C soap *Pobol y Cwm* (as himself) – though the prospect of his following Ray Gravell into an acting career seems unlikely.

What does his career show about Welsh rugby and Welsh society? That Welsh villages could still produce, as if out of nowhere, players with outstanding natural talent, able to adapt to any level – even any code – of rugby at the highest level. That the outside-half position remains, as well as the most glamorous position, also the most thankless, and that not even the best outside-half can – or can be expected to – win games without a pack able to win the ball. That amateurism in rugby union dug its own grave by refusing to acknowledge the world around it: a world where players in all sports seek to be rewarded for their talents with financial security, and where management skills are the first essential, not the last consideration. Finally, that to call Davies an unfulfilled talent reveals the narrowness of a nation's sporting horizons. In a country where rugby league and rugby union had a more equal status, Davies's extraordinary achievement in reaching the heights of both would have received the recognition it merited. But not even the most exciting player of his generation could break the union stranglehold on the Welsh imagination.

What did Jonathan Davies bring to rugby in Wales? The pleasure of instinctive, enterprising running rugby. The frustration that there were not more around him to fashion a team worthy of his, and others', talents. But always, the joy of sheer ability. The last sight of him on the international field, the broad smile amid a sea of defeated Welsh faces on the soon-to-be-demolished National Stadium pitch as he embraced his long-time opposite number Rob Andrew, summed up a career. If one Welsh player of recent times could be said to have exemplified both the most consummate professionalism and the true amateur spirit, Jonathan Davies was that player.

NIGEL WALKER

Rhodri Morgan

'Well done! Want to swap?' Those were the somewhat terse words with which Jeff Wilson, All Black Player of the Year, congratulated his opponent Nigel Walker after the New Zealanders had once again crushed Wales 42–7 at the first ever home rugby union international that Wales or anyone else for that matter had played at Wembley Stadium. Apart from scoring Wales's only try under the posts, Walker had given one of the finest defensive performances ever seen by any player in the red jersey of Wales. It was the only redeeming aspect of Wales's subjugation by the world's number-one team. Nigel Walker had played against 'their' top player and he had come off best.

What was extraordinary about it was that when Walker came back to rugby union at the age of twenty-nine, eleven years after he had given the game up in disillusionment after failing to get picked for the Wales under-19s team, and after putting the Indian sign on his opposite number in the final trial, he had come back in as a track athlete known for his speed. He was picked for his value in attack, with his obvious defensive frailties a handicap with which whoever selected him at club or international level would have to live. You obviously could not expect somebody to come back into rugby after such a long break to pick up the subtleties of defensive alignment, let alone the timing of how to make a tackle.

Walker's method was really pretty simple against Jeff Wilson, but it was risky. Jeff Wilson has power, speed and a devastating sidestep. So you show him the outside and you force him to take the outside. Jeff Wilson is also as fast as a greyhound and big and strong with it. Nigel Walker had to take a risk on that side. What he did was to force him out on to the touchline and let him go past, say half a yard or so, and then when Wilson put his head back and headed for the corner, Walker would chase after him, catch him from the back and yank him down by the shirt collar, shoulders or the waist. Wilson had three opportunities for a clear run to the corner and they all resulted in Nigel Walker bringing off superb tackles from behind. What gave those of us watching the game on the television set such satisfaction was that when late in the second half Jeff Wilson had a fourth opportunity to pass

Walker, his nerve had gone and he tried to chip over his head, having failed to figure a way around him. Coming off the field, Jeff Wilson's brief but respectful five words were the second sign of respect for Nigel Walker that day. The first was when Walker scored Wales's only try, shooting in under the posts. When Justin Marshall, New Zealand's beefy scrum-half, all fourteen stones of him, realized that Walker had actually scored and had planted the ball firmly on the ground under the posts and that he was too late with his tackle to stop him, he also showed Nigel Walker the ultimate respect that any All Black can show an opponent. He belted him on the head, a late punch for which he certainly should have been penalized, and a mark of how all New Zealand teams hate to have their line crossed.

In the next game against England Walker was injured again and missed the other Five Nations matches in the 1997–8 season. He retired at the end of the season and so we have lost an opportunity to see him play in the 1999 World Cup. Yet, what does this man's astonishing return to rugby at almost thirty years of age tell us? The first thing was that he was getting no faster in athletics. His peak had come and gone in the mid-1980s. He had won a World Indoor bronze medal in the 60-metres hurdles. He had reached the semi-finals of the 110-metres hurdles in the Los Angeles Olympics of 1984, and had finished an unlucky fourth by a fractional two hundredths of a second in the 110-metres hurdles in the European Athletics Championships in Stuttgart in 1986. By 1994 his athletic time had come and gone. Far from being British champion at his favourite event, he was only the third fastest 110-metres hurdler in Cardiff, behind Colin Jackson and Paul Gray. His back was hurting from the constant stress on the spine of that peculiar moment in the hurdles when you throw your lead leg over the top of the 3′ 6″ hurdle and you bring your chin down almost so as to make contact with your knee, to help to force that lead leg straight back down on to the ground to recommence sprinting with the minimum delay. What was he to do with his sporting career? Retire gracefully? Take up commentating? No, instead he decided to do something that only a script writer for a rugby equivalent of Roy of the Rovers comic could have written. He decided to return to a much harder physical game of rugby than the one that he had given up more than ten years earlier.

In the 1960s and 1970s it was quite common to combine rugby and athletics, since the seasons did not overlap. Gareth Edwards carried on with his athletics until the end of his days at Cardiff Training College, although he never did it in his post-College career. J. J. Williams went one better and enjoyed a very distinguished athletics career in which he represented Great Britain and Wales in the 400 metres and the 4 × 400 relay even at Olympic level. Allan Martin put the shot and threw the discus for Wales over a long period of his career as a rugby international. It was simply good summer training, good for developing speed and strength. With the development of year-round athletics with the indoor season, and with the almost unfailing supplementing of the rugby season by a summer tour to Namibia or Canada or wherever, combining rugby and athletics has now become impossible, unless you do it the Nigel Walker way. When you stop being fast enough for athletics, at least at Olympic level, then you can take up rugby instead. Even 5 per cent slower than you once were, you are still going to be the fastest player on the field. The problem is not your speed, but tackling and being tackled.

Fitness standards are higher in athletics than in rugby union. When Nigel Walker joined Cardiff and took part in the weight-training sessions with the other players in the squad, the big beefy forwards were quite staggered at the poundages that this relatively skinny figure, barely over thirteen stone, could shift. In a sport like athletics you have to have the constant discipline to shift those weights and to accept that there is simply no room for the booze up and no room for the missed training session.

Even as an athlete, Nigel Walker needed to be totally dedicated to his training, because by Colin Jackson-type standards, he was not an outstandingly naturally gifted athlete. He was an athlete who had to work at it. I actually went to Stuttgart to watch the European Athletics Championships in 1986. Jackson was the man expected to carry Britain's hopes in the 110-metres hurdles final. In the previous year he had won the World Junior Championships by a street. He was a couple of yards faster than Nigel Walker and always seemed to look as smooth as silk over the hurdles. By contrast, Nigel Walker was a worker. He did not have an outstanding hurdling technique, and was not outstandingly fast by world track and field standards. I have to admit, therefore, that I had one thing in mind in buying a very expensive ticket for that day, absolutely bang on the finish line. It was in order to shout 'come on Wales!' as Colin Jackson romped home with the gold medal. However, Colin Jackson pulled a muscle warming up that morning, just before the qualifying heats and did not run. It was Nigel Walker who was the only British and the only Welsh representative in the final. When the gun went I was looking down the track seeing these athletes coming towards me. I think Nigel Walker was in lane 2 or 3. I have never seen so much clattering of wood in my life. There seemed to be hurdles flying every-where. Nigel Walker hit seven out of the ten hurdles, but somehow he did not let it completely throw him off balance. He was still in medal contention on the run-in, producing one of those trademark very low dips for the line that he and Jackson used when in contention. These dips always annoyed the photo-finish judges, since it frequently took them below the photograph. However, when the photograph was finally produced it was Enrique Sala of Spain who had just got the bronze medal by two hundredths of a second from Walker.

Finishing fourth in a European Athletics Championship Final is good, but perhaps not all that much to write home about. What struck me was the sheer determination of somebody who is having an appalling race and whose technique on the day has let him down badly and who is spraying the hurdles all over the track. Nevertheless he did not give up. He must have been thinking 'I have come all this way. I have reached the final. My racing technique has completely gone to pot, but I am damned if I am going to give up now, without giving it everything I have got'. He had enough discipline to keep himself in contention, in spite of probably doing the worst 110-metres hurdles in the technical sense he had ever run.

It was that sense of self-discipline and determination which Nigel Walker brought to his late conversion back to rugby. It was that willingness to pick himself up that sustained him even after a whole series of injuries, especially to his shoulder prevented him from holding down a regular place in the Welsh team. At the end of his first season, and after some wonderful displays in the talented Cardiff three-quarter line of Mark Ring, Mike Hall and Mike Rayer, he was picked for the Welsh team for the match against Ireland.

I think his biggest disappointment must have been the 1995 World Cup in South Africa. During most of Nigel Walker's curious career in international rugby, Wales has been at panic stations, swapping team selection, captaincy and coaches and finally even stadia, like most people change shirts. The coach during the 1995 season was Alan Davies. Davies had arrived just before the 1991 World Cup as a last-minute panic measure. Just before the 1995 World Cup he was sacked in yet another panic measure, but because Wales had had a rather grim season that year. Alan Davies had discussed Nigel Walker's dodgy shoulder with him right throughout that season. He had told Walker that he would be going to South Africa with the Welsh squad and that he should not have an operation on his shoulder, noting that Walker's speed would be a huge asset and a major threat on the hard grounds of South Africa. When Alan Davies got the chop at the end of that disappointing season, Cardiff's Australian coach Alec Evans was appointed, and there followed a change of policy on Walker's shoulder operation. He was now told that he would not be going to South Africa for the World Cup and that he should have the operation during the summer, as there was too much of a risk that he might be injured on the hard grounds of South Africa. This was a pretty cruel fate. Just think about it. For any rugby player to return to rugby union at Walker's age and then to establish himself, at least when fit, as one of Wales's most dangerous attacking players and with increasingly sound defence as well, it must be a huge bonus in your career to get the chance to play in a World Cup, particularly in such a historic and emotional setting as the newly emerging South Africa under Nelson Mandela's government.

For a black player, one of the very small handful of black players who have ever represented Wales, to have the opportunity to go to a country like South Africa where rugby was almost entirely a white man's game was bound to be an incredible dream come true. With Nelson Mandela using the Springboks and the World Cup as a uniting force this was well beyond the realms of schoolboy dreams. Not to play in South Africa because Wales changed its coach just before the World Cup must have been a shattering disappointment and one which must have tested Nigel Walker's self-discipline to the limits.

Of course his rugby career has had its up-moments too. Leaving aside the game against New Zealand in November 1997, he also took part in the famous victory against France in 1994 and showed that startling turn of speed right at the end of the game when he took a one-yard pass from Scott Quinnell on the halfway line, and was just simply 'off'. The acceleration away and his seemingly effortless ability to sustain that speed over fifty yards without any sweat whatsoever was enough to make any thought of a covering tackle out of the question. It put the lid on one of the finest Welsh performances of what has been a notoriously barren period.

That was a favourite try, even though he scored another in the next game against England at Twickenham. His strike record for Wales was to be a remarkable twelve tries in seventeen internationals, and one is left to reflect on how many more there could have been had it not been for misguided selection policies and cruel injuries. On several frustrating occasions he was badly injured and substituted early in games in which subsequent tries were scored from the wing. There was no sadder sight in Welsh rugby than his premature departure from the field of play as at Twickenham in 1998.

In Cardiff's European adventure in 1996–7, he was to score a wonderful try in the Cardiff v. Bath quarter-final at Cardiff Arms Park, coming in on the short ball from Jonathan Davies. This was the try which turned the game in Cardiff's favour after Bath had been doing all of the pressing, and it was that try which saw Nigel Walker uncharacteristically lose his usual self-discipline. After he had scored it, he bounced the ball down on the turf in the manner favoured by American footballers after they have reached the end zone to celebrate the touchdown. On television afterwards, Jonathan Davies laconically remarked, 'Actually I thought Nigel made a bit of a meal of it!' There was something very special about that day. I have been a Cardiff supporter for fifty years now, but that was the first time I have ever heard a Cardiff rugby crowd break into *Cwm Rhondda* and *Hymns and Arias*. We all knew in our heart of hearts that this was not just Cardiff v. Bath, but rather Wales v. England and the emotional tension could be cut with a knife.

Perhaps, however, the moment for which Nigel Walker will always be remembered in Welsh rugby history was not one of his international tries, but the try which he scored during the last game played at the National Stadium before it was closed for demolition. It was Cardiff v. Swansea. It was the ultimate East v. West dream Swalec Cup Final.

Defences were dominant. It was not so much drift defence as drift net defence. Everybody was swallowed up. The ball reached Nigel Walker on the halfway line. Not quite a hospital pass but certainly he was well covered. There were two Swansea tacklers shepherding him out towards the touchline. He came inside the first one, zigzagged outside the second one, hurdled over a third one and set off for the posts. In a classic number-8 covering move, Stuart Davies went thundering across and made a lunging aerial dive at where Nigel Walker should have been, if he had been just a 'normal' left-winger. If he had connected with him, he would have knocked Walker into the fifth row of seats in the North Stand, and they would be picking bits of his ribs out of the stand even to this day. But Walker had already gone and Davies could only make a slight contact of his hand on Walker's ankles, Seconds later Nigel Walker touched down under the posts having scored one of the outstanding tries of the season, if not of the decade and one worthy to grace the very last day of rugby at the National Stadium. It may not have been the last try scored at the National Stadium, since that honour went to Stuart Davies, but it made the day. It secured Nigel Walker's place in rugby history. You could play it on your video machine till the cows come home and never get tired of watching it. In a way it was the classic hurdler's try. I often think of it in comparison with seeing Nigel clattering the woodwork on the way up the straight in Stuttgart eleven years previously. You just must not let little things like hitting hurdles or Swansea players' ankle-taps put you off your purpose of reaching the line.

Some people might say that Nigel Walker, as he prepares to make that well-trodden conversion from player to commentator and professional man of business, will be a superb role-model for young black athletes in all sports. Forget the black bit. Nigel Walker is one of the finest role models you could find for any young athlete, white, black, rugby, athletics, any sport, any country, any race. He is, of course, a true Cardiffian, born in St David's Hospital and brought up by his Jamaican parents in Rumney. He learned his rugby at Rumney High School where he was taught by David Williams. That early failure to make the Welsh Schools side led to his opting for athletics, a sport in which he found that assessments were patently objective, unlike those in the subjective world of Welsh rugby. Over a decade later, however, he was happy to join a Cardiff team that he had supported as a youngster when his heroes had been P. L. Jones and Gerald Davies, and where now his great friend was to be the future Welsh captain, Jonathan Humphreys. Remarkably, Rumney High School and Cardiff are the only club sides for which he has played. As youngsters he and his brother had also put on their red-and-white scarves to support Wales. Later he was to develop his Welsh in a BBC radio series for learners and contribute to programmes on the well-being and future of the language and Welsh culture generally. Often in situations of great pressure Nigel Walker has graced the Welsh shirt, but his contribution to the life of his country is far from over.

SCOTT GIBBS

Huw Richards

Not since Jonathan Davies has a Welsh player enjoyed so formidable an international reputation as Scott Gibbs. By the end of 1997, Gibbs, at the age of twenty-six, was recognized not only in Wales but across the whole world of rugby union as one of the game's outstanding contemporary practitioners. The one British player habitually selected for notional World XVs, he was hailed by All Black winger Jonah Lomu – widely seen as the hardest man in the world to tackle – as the game's best tackler.

His reputation had reached new heights following a spectacular series of defensive efforts for the 1997 British and Irish Lions team in South Africa. While the Springboks threw the Test series away by myopically over-physical tactics and atrocious goal-kicking, their onslaught still had to be resisted. Gibbs became the symbol of a team who defied all expectations to become only the second Lions team this century to win a series in South Africa. The defining moment of the series came shortly after half-time in the Second Test at Durban. Gibbs broke through in midfield. Confronted by giant South African prop Os du Randt, a good fifty pounds heavier than himself, he rejected the options of swerve or sidestep in favour of direct physical confrontation. Dropping his shoulder, he drove straight through du Randt, leaving him a forlorn and shaken pile on the floor. In that moment Gibbs did more than merely panic South Africa into conceding a penalty that Neil Jenkins converted to keep the Lions within striking distance. His demolition of du Randt was a resounding affirmation that, far from being cowed by South African physicality, the Lions could and would respond in kind. Gibbs was voted Man of the Series. When a press panel chose an ideal Lions team from every squad since 1971, he was the only member of the 1997 party to make the XV. In most years boxer Joe Calzaghe would have been an obvious Welsh Sports Personality of the Year. Such events inevitably favour the individual sportsman over the team player and Calzaghe is personable, charismatic and a recently crowned world champion. But not in 1997. Gibbs won that too.

Coming within a year of his return to union after two seasons in rugby league, his efforts in South Africa continued a career of almost ceaseless personal success. Capped at nineteen, he was Welsh Player of the Year at twenty, a British and Irish Lion who displaced the game's biggest name – England captain Will Carling – from the Test side at twenty-two, and an expensive rugby league capture at twenty-three. Allowed, when union went open in 1995, to return from league, his reappearance in 1996 was followed in rapid succession by an international recall, the captaincy of Wales and a Lions place. If the 1997–8 season checked that apparently inexorable progress – he was swamped with the rest of the Wales XV in the débâcle at Twickenham, inconspicuous in the defeat of Scotland and injured for the rest of the international season – this was a fate common to most of the Lions Test team, drained by non-stop international rugby.

It is a remarkable, unprecedented career. Wales has always cherished its rugby heroes, and in the late 1990s is shorter of them than at most times in the last century. Yet the public response to Gibbs remains ambivalent. He commands unlimited respect and admiration, but not the unconditional affection accorded contemporaries like Ieuan Evans, Nigel Walker and Robert Howley. His chances of attaining the supreme Welsh accolade of recognition by christian name alone are diminished by the presence of Scott Quinnell – it certainly helps to be a comparative rarity, a Ieuan or a Garin – but it is notable that he remains, rather curtly, 'Gibbs' in supporters' vernacular.

This reserve is rooted to a great extent in the circumstances surrounding his transfer from St Helens, Swansea to St Helens, Lancashire in 1994 and some of the comments he made about Wales during his period as a league player. But it goes rather deeper than that. Welsh rugby's ambivalence about Scott Gibbs reflects a discomfort with what the game has become in the 1990s.

He has been described, by *Sunday Times* rugby correspondent Stephen Jones, as 'the prototype of the twenty-first century rugby player'. It is equally possible to see him as a successor to a classic line of rugged Welsh centres who have terrorized imposing opponents by sheer physical dynamism. To read in Welsh rugby's fundamental text, Gareth Williams and Dai Smith's *Fields of Praise*, of Claude Davey 'thundering through like an angry bison' to score for Wales against New Zealand in 1935 or Dr Jack Matthews in the immediate post-war years: 'While his tackling was in itself a considerable offensive weapon, particularly as a demoralizing and ball-loosening tactic, Matthews in possession was an attacking player of speed and substance', is to visualize Gibbs in flickering black-and-white newsreel.

His career is characterized by apparent paradox. He is a publicity-shunner whose wedding, two weeks after the Lions tour, was covered in *Hello*-style detail by the Welsh press. A sublimely gifted player of rugby union, he would rather play rugby league, watch football or talk about jazz. A self-effacing team man on the field, he has been pursued by accusations of self-seeking egotism. Described as a 'rugby prostitute' and banned from the Swansea clubhouse when he left for rugby league in 1994, he rejected offers from other clubs in England and Wales to return to Swansea a little over two years later. Some of this is a matter of personal temperament and preference. Yet the accusations of greed and his uncomfortable relationship with club and country are a direct consequence of the times in which he lives and plays his rugby. The 1990s have been a time of unprecedented change for the game, the first half of the decade dominated by the final decay of amateurism, culminating in the International Board decision of 27 August 1995 to accept open professionalism, the second half by a painful adjustment at times redolent of the post-Communist transition in Russia – a highly regulated society replaced by one with few rules save those of the jungle.

The change is as much psychological as financial. There is an inherent mismatch between the outlook and priorities of the followers of any sport and of its professional players. The fans see the game, and may well play it, as a means of entertainment and enjoyment. Their commitment is emotional. However exasperated – and few followers have been more exasperated than Welsh rugby union fans since the early 1980s – their identification with the team they follow is unconditional. For many the weekend game is a relief from mundane reality, and this applies as much to the keyboard or telephone workers of the 1990s as to their predecessors whose daily battle was with a coalface or blast furnace. But for the professional player the game is their reality, their equivalent of the coalface or keyboard. Enjoyable or not, it is before anything a business, their means of making a living. The club or national team whose fortunes command the emotional involvement of a city or country is to the player an employer with a far more prosaic leverage – the contract which defines his duties, pay and conditions. For Powell Dyffryn or the Driver and Vehicle Licensing Centre, read Swansea Cricket and Football Club and the Welsh Rugby Union. The mismatch is particularly marked when a game is undergoing the transition to full professionalism. Rugby union may have accepted professionalism, but its ideology remains firmly rooted in the older values of emotional commitment and enjoyment – camaraderie, fellowship, loyalty and the game for its own sake. It is uncomfortable with what it has become – the whole new world of transfer fees, top players with six-figure salaries, investor clubs and rows over television contracts – and not just because it is still a long way from generating the income needed to match its new outgoings. Scott Gibbs has done nothing to alleviate that discomfort. He has not merely accepted professional values, but embraced them openly and wholeheartedly. Little he has said or done would even have occasioned comment in business or a longer-established professional sport, but rugby has still to come to terms with the way it has changed.

Some sportsmen are expert in cloaking acquisitive motives in more acceptable terms. The transfer that offers them 'a great new challenge' at a club with 'great fans' and the coach of their dreams is only incidentally much more lucrative than their previous contract. Gibbs has never bothered to dissemble. *Wales on Sunday* rugby writer Paul Rees, a consistent admirer, has been led to compare him with Meursault, the protagonist of Albert Camus' novel *L'Etranger*: 'He had one major weakness in the eyes of society: he appeared to lack the basic emotions and reactions, including hypocrisy, that were required of him.'

In examining Gibbs's remorseless pursuit of rugby fortune, it is tempting to echo John Maynard Keynes's famous misreading of Lloyd George, that he was 'rooted in nothing', if only because 'goat-footed bard' is one of the few epithets not to have been tossed at him. But like Lloyd George, Gibbs is firmly rooted in Wales. While his contract with Swansea is a lucrative one, and he showed some symptoms of itchy feet when Northampton made a mammoth offer immediately after the Lions tour, his decision to return to Swansea rather than join any of the English clubs prepared to pay heavily for him in 1996 was evidence of firm attachment.

In one respect, that of coming from, but not playing for, Bridgend he is highly typical of leading Welsh players of the 1990s. Five of the twenty-one who played against England at Twickenham in 1998 were born in Bridgend, but only one, replacement lock Chris Stephens, plays at the Brewery Field. Gibbs differed from the bulk in going west rather than east, joining first Neath then Swansea, rather than forming part of the ceaseless stream to Cardiff. He captained Wales Youth as a Pencoed player and has throughout his career turned for advice to his father Graham, a former international gymnast and pole-vaulter whom he consistently cites as the main influence upon him.

If place matters, time has been even more important. The changes of the 1990s offered rugby union players unprecedented financial opportunities, first as the game tried to fight off league predators then as, in the wake of open professionalism, it allowed league players previously banned *sine die* to resume their union careers. Scott Gibbs was perfectly placed by virtue of age, talent, temperament and background to take full advantage of those opportunities. As W. S. Gilbert might have put it, he is the very model of a modern rugby mercenary.

His first season in senior rugby was 1990–1, the first year of the Heineken Leagues, whose introduction of regular competition for leading clubs was one of the decisive rites of passage in the game's progress towards full professionalism. His opportunity was provided by rugby league, which had taken Neath and Wales centre Allan Bateman – seven seasons later to be his Welsh centre partner – to Warrington in the close season. Neath took the first title and national coach Ron Waldron, in a doomed attempt to reproduce their rumbustious style at international level, scattered caps by the handful at the Gnoll. Neither the system nor several of the players made the transition to top level. Gibbs, chosen for Wales a week before his twentieth birthday after only fifteen first-class appearances, was a conspicuous exception. His efforts in a miserable season for Wales – the 28-year-old unbeaten run at home to England was smashed on his debut, only a manic 21–21 draw with Ireland prevented a Five Nations whitewash and the tour of Australia, culminating in the concession of 134 points to New South Wales and the Wallabies and an intra-squad brawl, was probably the lowest of Welsh rugby's depressingly large collection of late-century low points – won him selection as Welsh Player of the Year. The *Welsh Brewers*

Rugby Annual, noting his 'strength to surge through the half-gap' had no doubt that he was 'one of those players to brighten our darkness, provided he is not seduced by the rugby league code'. The proviso was well made. No league courtship of a union star was ever more public.

Wigan had already made one offer for him, and would bid again in May 1992. In early 1992 he was on his way to sign for Hull, but changed his mind during an interminable motorway journey. The likelihood that he would eventually go was clear. It was not just that his combination of hard straight running and watertight defence were exactly the qualities league most prizes. His background too made him a promising target. Paul Thorburn later regretted the slight implied when he told the Wigan chairman that as a graduate he was in a different category to most league recruits, but he hit on a sociological reality. Thorburn's education greatly enhanced his prospects of a decent job alongside, and then after, his rugby career – hence less pressure to cash in on his rugby skills. Gibbs, who left his Welsh-medium comprehensive school at sixteen to become a glazier, had much more limited prospects. In the past unions, hamstrung by their own regulations on amateurism, had been unable to do much more than hope that players would not go. In the 1990s, though, the rules had been loosened. Direct payment for playing was still ruled out but, with the rules encompassing more grey areas than Cardiff on a foggy night, other forms of earning were not.

The second Wigan bid – reported as being a £35,000 signing-on fee plus £200,000 over four years, was beaten off by a concerted WRU effort making use of a 'player welfare programme' explicitly aimed at countering league predators. The *Daily Mail* reported: 'Prospects for better jobs, sponsored cars and promotional work were outlined to the Swansea centre in a series of meetings with [WRU commercial executive Jonathan] Price, coach Alan Davies, Swansea chairman Mike James and other leading figures.' A fresh bid, worth around £330,000, by St Helens in late 1993 brought further enhancements. The 'Save Scott Gibbs' appeal was beginning to rival the Swalec Cup Final as the Welsh game's most watched domestic annual event. A few years later Gibbs would confess to a lingering ambition to study music at an American university. He would undoubtedly be at home with North American academics, for whom getting an offer from a rival institution is a recognized means of getting a better deal without moving on.

In March 1994 Gibbs, out of action with an injury since the previous December, added a post with the Swansea computer company MicroCompass to existing contracts with Welsh Water and the St Pierre Golf and Country Club. He said: 'This job is a great opportunity for me to build a serious career and I'm very much looking forward to doing this . . . I'm sure I will be the first of many players who get the chance to learn a new career and it could mean an end to the need to look at the option of turning professional.' Six weeks later he signed for St Helens.

This sequence of events, and the timing of his decision – so soon after he appeared to have committed himself to Swansea and Wales, and without warning to club or employer – ensured a furious reaction in Wales. Other players who had gone North, however much regretted by club and country, did so with the personal good wishes of both. Immense loss though he was, Gibbs was not necessarily more significant a departure than Jonathan Davies or the props Dai Young and Stuart Evans. He went when both club and country might have felt it could spare him – without him Wales won its first Five Nations title since 1988 and Swansea clinched its first Heineken championship only three days after he left.

Reactions combined exasperation with feelings of betrayal. Swansea chairman Mike James was famously quoted as calling him 'a rugby prostitute', adding: 'I feel he has abused everything that has been done for him by a lot of people who had his interest at heart. I find his behaviour appalling . . . he gave us an absolute assurance that he would not consider doing anything like this. He's been a very naughty boy and I'm just appalled . . . Over the years we have lost many players to other Welsh teams as well as rugby league and to a man they have all been welcomed back. But I never want to see Gibbs again.' Ieuan Evans, then captain of Wales, put his condemnation in business rather than moral terms: 'Scott is a very silly boy. He had a wonderful opportunity to capitalise on his high profile in Wales.' Evans, Robert Jones, Mike Hall and Tony Clement dropped Gibbs from their recently formed Just Players management group with Evans saying: 'We don't need him. In fact I think we will be better off without him.' Stung by allegations of ill-faith, Gibbs said he had not told his family or club because they would dissuade him again, as they had done with previous offers: 'There would have been another load of fuss and I didn't want to go through it all again. I knew everyone would turn against me when they found out, but it was time to look after number one.'

That attitude was entirely consistent with an unsentimentally businesslike approach to the game. Only three weeks earlier he had regaled readers of his *South Wales Evening Post* column, aptly titled *In a League of his Own* and enabled by loosening amateur regulations, with details of a visit to former Swansea and Wales colleague Richard Webster, who had signed for Salford: 'The lifestyle of a pro league player is one to relish. His only objective now is to profit from the game and that is no bad thing.' He cited with approval Webster's desperate desire to get on for the last two minutes of a Wales v. France league international: 'What did you say to coach Clive Griffiths with two minutes to go? Was it "get me on Clive and I'll score the winner"?' 'No!', Webby replied. 'Let me on Clive, I want my international bonus from Salford as well as my win bonus.' It was, argued Gibbs, 'a good honest attitude'.

Interviewed during his spell at St Helens he would comment that 'You can't measure winning and losing on the enjoyment factor alone: it comes in the number of pound notes', and that 'no decisions can be made on sentimental grounds. We are professionals. The bottom line is money. Your shelf life as a player is limited and you have to make the most of it.' Recalled by Wales, the first of the league returnees to make the team when he played against Italy in late 1996, he said: 'When you pull on the red jersey you feel a lot better, but history doesn't mean that much. I want the win bonus on Saturday.'

Those *Evening Post* columns also proffered a justification for such attitudes. In the last three months before joining St Helens he argued: 'Rugby union is a ruthless game and I may not always be wanted' and that 'The word that always crops up is "loyalty". We see and hear it regularly in rugby, but who really cares? In this modern day you have to look after number one.' Little he saw on returning to union is likely to have disabused him. He saw the WRU axe the squad contracts of Andy Moore and Emyr Lewis – one injured, the other dropped – and Swansea tear up eight contracts when hit by cash-flow problems. One reason for those problems was Gibbs's own salary, but it confirmed that there is little loyalty to anyone at the vulnerable end of professional rugby's food chain.

His own experience of injury shows how even the most vivid talents may become vulnerable. The severed ligaments suffered against the All Blacks in December 1993 may have stimulated his decision to cash in on rugby league interest – and undoubtedly cost him money as he accepted an offer estimated around £100,000 less than the one he had rejected the previous autumn. A rugby league injury cost him a £2,000 per match contract to play for Manly in Australia.

Gibbs also illustrates one of the basic rules of professional sport's labour market – that exceptions will be made for the truly outstanding. The managements of Wigan RLFC and Great Britain never pretended much affection for Ellery Hanley, who in the 1980s exasperated a publicity-conscious game by cutting off relations with the press, but they recognized that as player and captain he was essential to creating winning teams. Gibbs's dealings with Swansea and the WRU in 1992–4, and their desperation to reclaim him in 1996 underline that lesson. He shares a wariness of the media with Hanley, although for different reasons. Hanley was angered by the retailing of incidents from a chequered youth. Gibbs's one notable off-field indiscretion, the taking and driving away of a taxi in 1994, an incident which emphasized the 'small world' aspects of Welsh life when the arresting officer was a fellow international, lock forward Steve Sutton, created no problems of this sort.

His reticence is rather the consequence of personal preference. He is not reclusive or antisocial – he would hardly have been a member of the Lions entertainment committee if he were. Jeremy Guscott, his Lions Test partner at centre on both the 1993 and 1997 tours, has written that he 'enjoys a good night out . . . but he also likes his own space'. Rugby remains a gregarious, clubbable world but Swansea team-mates reckon to have seen him matchdays apart, only once in their clubhouse during the 1996–7 season. The game finished, he is not interested in talking about rugby, telling Paul Rees: 'I see no point. Rugby is about the taking part. After that I just want to get away from it all and go home.' Returning from Wales's win at Murrayfield in 1997 he told interviewers that he would not be watching a recording of the match as he had seen enough rugby recently and would rather watch football on television. *Daily Telegraph* writer Robert Philip conjured a hugely entertaining column from a weekend failing to track him down in Wales. Yet this has not been every journalist's experience – Welsh-language journalists, short-handed and limited in their choice of interviewees during the Lions tour, found him invariably ready to emerge towel-clad after exhausting matches to talk at length.

He has compelled attention rather than sought it. Allan Bateman, a shrewd observer of his international partner, has said: 'He would rather sit in the corner and watch what is going on than be the centre of attention.' In a revealing interview with Paul Rees, Gibbs, who subscribes to an American magazine called *Modern Drummer,* explained his preference for that role in a band: 'The drummer is the most understated member of a band: while others cavort and show off, he gets on with his job and crowds relate to that. That is how I see myself, getting on with it in the background.' Logical enough, one might say, for a player who undoubtedly marches to his own beat. But that self-image is valid. The surest ways to capture attention on a rugby field are captaincy and scoring tries. Gibbs has shown little taste for either. He has every credential for captaincy except desire. It was Gibbs who, with more experienced league players silent as St Helens fell fourteen points behind Bradford in the almost absurdly dramatic 1996 Rugby League Challenge Cup Final, rounded on his team-mates and reminded them that the match was still there for the winning, and who talked and cajoled non-stop through the last fifteen minutes of the First Test between the Lions and South Africa at Cape Town a year later. His self-assessment as 'not a group leader' is belied by the evidence of the *Life with the Lions* film documentary of the Lions tour.

He is a confirmed try-maker rather than taker. A record of four tries in his first thirty-two Welsh internationals compares with twenty-one in fifty-nine for a player of comparable style and gifts, Frank Bunce, admittedly in a much better team, or Will Carling's twelve in seventy-two matches. His one truly memorable union try was not for Wales or the Lions, but in Swansea's comprehensive defeat of the 1992 Australians. The action recorded in the *Rugby Leaguer*'s account of the first score in the 1996 Rugby League Cup final epitomizes his approach near the opposition line: 'For a moment it looked as if Gibbs had a chance to become the first Welshman in 11 years to score a try in a Wembley final, but he offloaded a gem of an inside pass for Prescott to score his first try.' Playing outside him, St Helens wings Alan Hunte and Danny Arnold enjoyed spectacularly prolific seasons.

There is little doubt that he sees his sporting life in directly opposite terms to those of Danny Blanchflower, a professional footballer who contrived to epitomize the amateur ideal by arguing that the game was about glory rather than money. Still, if Gibbs is more openly interested in money than conventional rugby opinion regards as being in good taste, few doubt that he justifies his salary. Few players have matched a remarkable talent for adjusting instantaneously to new levels of the game and, in the case of rugby league, to a new game. On entering senior rugby he was at once the best inside-centre in Wales, and winning his first cap after only a handful of games he was at once the most effective player in the national team. His best international games have been the most demanding, playing for the Lions in New Zealand and South Africa – although this is also symptomatic of the general decline in the Welsh game in the 1980s and 1990s, meaning that the best Welsh players may, like many Irish stars across the years, have to wait for Lions tours to play in teams capable of making the best use of their talents. The adjustment to rugby league is notoriously tough, yet within weeks of his debut for St Helens *Open Rugby* magazine, never an enthusiast for expensive union signings, was proclaiming 'Its OK – Gibbs can play!' and St Helens coach Eric Hughes was seriously advocating his inclusion in the Great Britain squad.

This demonstrates not an immense natural talent, but the ability to adjust to new demands – most notably the physical demands of league. Stephen Jones captured the essence of the early Gibbs in 1992: 'He may be smaller than most centres but he is a relentless physical presence in midfield, with a razor-sharp break. He is also, pound for pound, one of the game's most thumping tacklers.' Some players reckon to have come back from league with a new mental attitude. Gibbs, who already had the mental attitudes of professionalism, came back with a new physique. Recognizing that league required extra power and bulk he put in the hours in the weight room and with boxing gloves, developing the shape that led Jeremy Guscott to label him 'the world's fastest prop'.

Weighing less than thirteen stone when first capped, Gibbs has added more than thirty pounds in weight, four inches to his waist and chest measurement and two inches to his neck. Frank Bunce, reminded in 1997 of the way he had shaken the young Gibbs with ferocious tackles during the 1991 World Cup, said half-jokingly: 'I gather he's a lot bigger now. I hope he's not looking for revenge.' In the unlikely event of Bunce being afraid of anything on two feet, the implication was that it might be Gibbs. He knows how to use that physique too. Kingsley Ogedengbe, an athletics coach interviewed by *Rugby News*, pointed out that this was mental as much as physical: 'People think Scott Gibbs is an awesome tackler because of his size. Wrong. If that were the case why aren't props and locks tackling with the same power he demonstrates? It's down to speed and timing. If you watch Gibbs closely it doesn't matter whether he's tackling a big guy or a small guy, he hits them at pace and more often than not above the centre of gravity above the waist. It's a devastating combination that shows he's mentally focused.'

Focused. Motivated – as in Jeremy Guscott's comment that Gibbs is 'Totally motivated. Very focused when playing or training, so much so that he can be a little over-exuberant. He's so physically strong he was capable of doing real damage in training sessions'. In a period in which the language as well as the practice of sport and business have become increasingly intertwined, the terminology naturally attaches itself to Gibbs, fluent in both idioms, as when he explained his potentially fraught return to Swansea as 'This is business. A simple case of supply and demand.'

This is the modern world. Whether one likes or dislikes Scott Gibbs depends to a great extent on whether one likes what rugby has become. The hurt tone of some of his responses to criticism suggests that Gibbs cares more than he might want to admit about being liked. Like him or not, all the evidence from other professional sports is that his attitudes are merely ahead of their time and will increasingly become the norm. All that Wales can hope is that his imitators are half as talented, focused and motivated. If we have seen the future, it seems to work.

NEIL JENKINS

Tim Williams

Imagine the past, remember the future. So advised that great historian Lewis Namier. The Neil Jenkins story is to a large extent about how even if a whole nation imagined a glorious rugby past and in that process forgot about the future, there was one outside-half who did not. It is also about how that outside-half inherited a clapped-out rugby tradition and set about trying to re-invent it for the modern era.

I would have had this view of the noble Neil Jenkins even if I did not come from the same area, go to the same school and support Pontypridd RFC, for whom he plays so magnificently. That he is *paisano* does no harm mind. Nor does the fact that wherever he has played and however he has performed – for Wales or the British Lions – he has given not only a good account of himself, both as a player and as a person, but also of the people from whom he springs, a people who see in him a mirror to their best selves. He is the boy next door who just happened to win the Test series for the British Lions in South Africa (notwithstanding the claims of that fancy-dan Guscott). The fact that I cannot write 'just happened to win the Five Nations for Wales' is largely because even his genius has been unable to turn a sow's ear into a silk purse: unusually for a Welsh back, but all too typical of the condition in which we as a rugby nation find ourselves, his single most significant performance has been in the red shirt of Britain and not of Wales.

For a Pontypriddian, one image stands out from all the rest from the video of the Lions on tour to South Africa in 1997. It is from the Second Test. It is of Jason Leonard, the English prop, and the Lions' medic, James Robson, getting ever more excited – and respectful – as it dawns on them that, while the Springbok place-kicking is way off target, Ponty's Neil Jenkins is simply never going to miss. Inexorably, remorselessly, fearlessly Jenkins was kicking the Lions to victory in a game in which his team had been beaten in every other department. The response on the bench each time the ball sailed exactly through the middle of the posts was the mantra: 'awesome f****g awesome'. Watching the game live in a London pub filled with Englishmen who found themselves in the unusual position of chanting a Welsh rugby player's name I thought it something more than an irony – the words crime, scandal and outrage came to mind – that whereas Jenkins was undoubtedly one of the first names to go down on the Lions Test team sheet he had always been a controversial choice for Wales and had in fact been forced to cede his chosen role as outside-half to – pause – Arwel Thomas. Work that one out if you can. As Dic Penderyn said in somewhat similar circumstances: 'Oh Lord, what an injustice!'

Now, there will be many in Wales who will conclude all too hastily that Pontypriddians have a rather over-developed sense of injustice as far as their rugby players are concerned. It is our metier, it seems. But to be fair, we have had a lot of practice. Even Pontypridd's contribution as one of the founding clubs of the Welsh Rugby Union has been air-brushed from history – for although Pontypridd was one of the clubs which met at Tenby in March 1880 to discuss forming a national union by the time the formal meeting took place in Neath in March 1881 the club had been 'disinvited'. Chilling don't you think? And as far back as we can remember there are players who have been ignored or misused by the national selectors. It would not be difficult to put together a team (including subs) of 'The Best Players Never to Have Played, Played only Once or Twice or Had to Move to More Fashionable Clubs to Play for Wales'. A short selection from a very long list would include hooker Jock Watkins who never got the cap he deserved, locks Bob Penberthy and Danny Harris, hooker Phil John, winger David Manley, and then flanker Tommy David and utility forward Andrew Lamerton both of whom infamously had to pretend that they were Scarlets in order to wear the other red jersey.

So there. Pontypriddians are not paranoid. We are actually persecuted (and indeed, post-Brive, prosecuted). Neil Jenkins's treatment at the hands of an ungrateful nation simply comes at the end of a long tradition. It also comes at the end, one hopes, of a period which has seen a decline in the town's fortunes since the 1920s. By which I mean to suggest that insofar as there is any basis to the charge that Pontypriddians have 'over-reacted' to their effective exclusion from the top table of Welsh rugby it is likely to lie in the sense that is not just the Welsh Rugby Union which has passed by on the other side of Ponty – so too has that economic and social dynamism which, in the words of the *Glamorgan Free Press* of 15 August 1891, made the town the 'internal capital of the coalfield' at the end of the nineteenth century, when it was the fulcrum of the world's premier coal-producing area. For a town ('a town mind you, not a mere colliery village . . . Yes a town, which aims at the position of a country town and metropolis of the coalfield', *Pontypridd Church Shield*, August 1903) which has had such a deflating twentieth century, such treatment of the local heroes in a bastion of the national sport is very hard to take.

The difference of course is that whereas in the past those who failed to select Ponty players knew about rugby but seemed too blinkered or snobbish to pick the best to play for Wales, today's critics of Neil Jenkins – in and out of the WRU – simply do not know what they are talking about. Rugby knowledge, never that extensive in a nation which can call an era in which it never beat New Zealand the 'Golden Years' – has collapsed in Wales along with the quality of the rugby played. Except possibly in Pontypridd of course and, certainly, in the town's western hinterland where some twenty-six years ago Jenkins was born, grew-up, still lives and learned all the rugby he knows.

Jenkins's home patch, his square mile, is the frankly unromantic stretch of Welsh soil between Llantwit Fardre and Church Village some three miles from Pontypridd itself. Quaint it ain't. In fact, it may be whatever the opposite of quaint is. I can say this with some authority because I know the area very well and because I was born, grew-up and learned all the rugby I know less than two miles away in the even less quaint village of Beddau. In my part of the world 'Beddau man speaks highly of Llantwit Fardre player' would make the local newspaper. To say that there is a rivalry between Beddau RFC and our colleagues down the road is like saying that John Prescott and Peter Mandelson do not get on. It is to understate the matter somewhat. If you have seen the film *Zulu* you will get my drift – this is the local sporting Derby as the continuation of communal conflict by other means. And, to add injury to insult, were it not for a schism in the Beddau ranks in the late 1970s due to some unpleasantness on tour which led to most of the team being banned *sine die* and decamping to Llantwit to play then the latter would probably not have been able to assemble a decent team and possibly Neil would have started his career not with them but with Beddau, the more senior club and one with a fine reputation as a forcing house of talent. It is after all where the great Steve Fenwick said he 'learned all his rugby' when he played for Beddau in the early 1970s.

A Derby game between the mini-rugby teams of Beddau and Llantwit is the first game that Neil Jenkins remembers playing (one suspects partly because of the aggro and the significance of the fixture for the parents). Tellingly, Neil has little to say about the influence of schooling on his rugby development – unlike previous generations of great Welsh players who cloud over at the mention of their respective grammar schools – and focuses instead on the role played by his community and indeed family. Equally tellingly, he was never selected to play for the Welsh Schools side and made his reputation with Wales Youth. Although Neil did play for his secondary school – my old school Bryncelynnog Comprehensive, Beddau – the role played by his family in making this only child into the points-scoring machine he remains cannot be underestimated.

Born into what he says is a rugby-mad family which dealt in scrap metal, he was coached by his father Roger but it was his mother's brothers who actually taught him how to kick: fifty-seven caps in the Welsh shirt, and 594 points later – an average of more than ten points per game – a (sometimes) grateful nation should thank them. But however promising the rugby gene pool, Jenkins the Boot was not in fact created overnight. He barely did any place-kicking for Llantwit Youth or Pontypridd Youth and only really 'took it seriously' in his second year of senior rugby with Pontypridd – one wonders how good he might have been if he had started earlier. For we sometimes forget – no, we always forget – that Neil Jenkins was in only his first full senior season when he was drafted in – no catapulted in – to the Wales ranks not for his place-kicking, which was more than adequately performed by the long-range specialist Paul Thorburn, but as the latest teenage sensation from the infamous Welsh outside-half factory from whose assembly line was expected products in whom place-kicking was optional but genius – especially of the 'leave them for dead' sidestepping kind – an absolute requirement.

In fact Jenkins was, ironically given subsequent selectorial shenanigans which have seen him play eight times at centre and nine at fullback, a beneficiary of the iron rule of WRU selection policy: when the team performs abysmally, as happened in the whitewash year of 1990, change the outside-half. The line-out may be ruled out, the loose forwards may in fact be going backwards and the front row might make Babar the elephant seem aggressive by comparison but, according to the

the Welsh take on the rugby universe, it is not their fault. Blame the outside-half. Replace him. The king is dead. Long live the king. And so, at just nineteen years of age, Neil Jenkins assumed the mantle of Cliff Morgan, David Watkins, Barry John, Phil Bennett and his own hero Jonathan Davies – all dropped after poor team performances by the way – in a country where the position has a unique but disproportionate place in the collective perception of how, in what style, the game is to be played. As Jenkins says, 'I've found that nowhere else gives the No. 10 so much stick as here.' While that tradition, that burden, that challenge, that glamour was the main reason why Jenkins wanted, like most Welsh youngsters of his generation, to wear the number-10 shirt – in the manner of all great outside-halves he craves responsibility, wants to direct the show and is not happy unless in the centre of the action – living up to the inflated expectations of a Welsh public wallowing in ill-informed idolatry for the wearers of that shirt was never going to be easy because never possible. Inflated, ill-informed, idolatry? OK, so I'm being too restrained. This is portentous, ignorant ancestor-worship.

Everywhere else where rugby is taken and played seriously, the game has moved on but Welsh understanding has not. We are still fighting the last war instead of the one we are in. Hence the persistent foolhardy peculiarly Welsh pursuit of that rugby Eldorado, Barry John Land, the land that time forgot. The land where outside-halves, outside breaks, dummies, swerves, sidesteps and downright voodoo, score tries in magic moments which define and determine games. The land where nothing new is learned and nothing forgotten, where young ordinands are selected and made priests of the collective cult, to carry on the ways of their elders and betters, destined to repeat again and again scenes, manoeuvres, and moves from a glorious divinely inspired tradition, like some rugby version of *Last Year at Marienbad*.

Like? Well not very much like, actually. However heavenly Barry John Land was to visit for a short time, to be trapped there for the last generation has been hell on earth for Welsh rugby supporters. Moreover, even though *Marienbad* was a fine film for the era and got the vote of the Left Bank, it never played well in Peoria. Its appeal was limited. The same goes for the Welsh obsession with outside-half play. It never played well in Pretoria, Perth, Christchurch or Ponty for that matter. This is something Neil Jenkins realized when a youth player –

and it is a vision for which he has never received the support he deserves or indeed been given the players with whom he might work to achieve the vision. He has been a modern player in a backward-looking culture.

'We are a nation of lookers back basically; we don't look to the future. The 70s was 20 years ago; we had a great side but we have to move on.' The voice is that of Neil Jenkins and his actions have spoken louder than even his own eloquent – and he is that – words have done. Moving on has meant, essentially, recognizing that classic Welsh outside-half play has had its day at the highest levels. The time and space required for such wizardry simply no longer exists at international level in the era of flatter, fitter, faster, properly marshalled 'blanket ' defences – and of indulgent referees allowing defenders to live offside (particularly when back-row forwards were allowed to detach themselves from the scrum before the opposing ball was out).

At the same time as the rules have changed (or been disregarded) and turnovers have become more frequent, the dangers of the lone player attempting a break without support are more apparent. More positively, the attacking options diversify as the role of back rows in breaking through defences and the need for phases or waves of attack – with forwards interchanging with backs – are recognized. This is the general climate in which Neil Jenkins's style at international level has emerged, as did that of Rob Andrew, a similar kind of player. This is a climate in which the outside-half retains a strategic role linking backs with forwards but makes fewer heroic *sorties* into No Man's Land and uses the boot to break through tight defences or simply to force opponents to attack from deep positions; a climate in which outside-halves, like all backs, have to show a higher order defensive capacity than that previously required or even dreamed of by players in our so-called golden era.

Moreover, the nature and quality of the Wales teams in which Neil Jenkins has played have also dictated a conservative style of play. It is difficult to attack without the ball, and it is also difficult, even if possession is yours, to attack from your own 22-metre line from a line-out under pressure or a scrum going backwards. With Welsh forward play on the whole so feeble since the late 1970s, the opportunity to take risks is reduced. Indeed, it is often forgotten that the platform on which those 'golden' Welsh backs could perform was provided by an unusually good batch of forwards the like of which Welsh rugby rarely enjoyed before and never since. No longer can we have the confidence that a ball taken into the tackle by a back will be retained and recycled by the Welsh forwards. Yet, at club level where Jenkins has found more space and time and is confident that he has backs and forwards capable of sustaining an expansive and interactive game, he has been less conservative and more ready to take risks. Together, Pontypridd play what Jenkins calls 'the best style of rugby in Wales – another reason they don't like us'.

The Jenkins style and genius were celebrated by coach Alan Davies in the match programme for the Wales–England clash of 1993. His endorsement came with an implied warning, however, which would prove all too prophetic. 'Neil is a player of amazing talent', he wrote. 'What we must do is find ways of unleashing his full potential on the international stage. He is a classic example of the modern school of outside-halves, whose goal-kicking style is modelled on that of New Zealand's Grant Fox. What I hope and expect is that people will be emulating Neil Jenkins in the not too distant future.' That, incidentally, was a year, when against all expectations, Wales beat England. Yet, generally, since Neil Jenkins was recruited as the latest outside-half saviour, the Welsh team has struggled to survive let alone find a decent style of play that would 'unleash his full potential'. At the same time of course, Pontypridd have become the champions of Welsh rugby, the slayers of Bath, the equal of Brive and all in all one of the best sides in Britain, if not Europe, playing a modern style of rugby in the process. But for Wales, Jenkins has been lumbered with forwards without any pace or penetration and thus deprived of good fast ball in attacking positions he has been forced to become – with exceptional games proving the rule – Jenkins the Boot if Wales were to get any points on the board at all. For most of his time in the Welsh shirt the only Welsh 'attacking tactic' of any substance seemingly approved by the management has been to secure penalties and toss the ball to Neil.

That he obliged and kept us in games which were otherwise out of sight is an understatement: he almost single-handedly kept Welsh rugby afloat in the 1990s. That he has done so while being subject to deselection, repositioning, near-constant questioning of his credentials in the Welsh press and serious injury is remarkable, and a tribute to his mental toughness which is seldom commented on. This outstanding toughness – a characteristic associated with few recent Welsh players apart from Jonathan Davies and himself – is central to his character and to why I admire him so much. He represents for me the welcome triumph of character, determination and application over mere personality in a culture which worships the latter and finds the former concepts – although infinitely more useful and purposeful – pedestrian and actually rather plebeian, our self-image and our notion of what virtues backs should possess being rather more elevated. Kings after all should not get their hands dirty, Merlins do not need to practice their tricks, and geniuses do not need to have grit. What Neil Jenkins has – say it loud, say it proud – is the right stuff. This is recognized wherever good rugby is played, from Ponty to South Africa. The fact that there is even a question mark about him in Wales, says more about the abject state of the game in his homeland than it does about him.

He is the come-back kid for a start. First selected at outside-half in the 1991 Five Nations Championship, he was dropped for the ill-fated Brisbane Test and never played in the 1991 World Cup. He returned at centre for the 1992 campaign, except for the last game against Scotland where he scored eleven points at outside-half out of Wales's winning tally of fifteen points. Then he was injured and did not play in the Australian game at Cardiff that year. Next, he was selected at outside-half for the whole of the 1993 Five Nations – then moved to centre and full-back for the Zimbabwe tour before returning to outside-half in the Namibia Test. In his next game he was moved back to centre for the Japan Test at home and again for the game which Wales lost to Canada, though he scored all of Wales's twenty-four points that day. For a change, he was moved back to outside-half for the whole of the 1994 Five Nations, which Wales won. And once more he scored all Wales's points in an international game, against Ireland at Lansdowne Road (where he has never lost: he has scored ninety-three points against Ireland alone). He has, by the way, scored all of Wales's points on no fewer than eleven occasions and the Welsh team almost never performs well or indeed scores very much if his kicking is not on song.

He stayed at outside-half until the 1995 World Cup when he was moved to centre again. After playing twice in that position he was moved back to outside-half for the game with Ireland at Johannesburg.

After a couple more games at outside-half he broke his collar bone and was unavailable to play against Italy in January 1996. He then only made it to the bench for the first three games in the Five Nations, the new 'Barry John', west Walian Arwel Thomas being preferred. After that retro-indulgence (part 1) he returned to the number-10 position for the French game, the first and only game Wales won in that campaign. For the rest of 1996 he played at outside-half, until politely informed as it were that he has only been keeping the berth warm for Jonathan Davies's return to international rugby union (retro-indulgence part 2) and that he is really a full-back. Not picked for the game against the USA in January 1997, he spent the 1997 Five Nations championship at full-back even though Jonathan Davies was replaced by Arwel Thomas until the final game against England, when Jonathan Davies took Thomas's place. It was in this game that Jenkins broke his arm. He then recovered to play for the Lions, returned to the number-10 spot for the November games against Tonga and New Zealand before giving way yet again to Arwel Thomas for the Italy and England games. After telling the selectors than he will never again play for Wales at full-back after the England *débâcle*, he is selected at outside-half for the rest of the 1998 season. He yet again plays a blinder in Dublin, scoring a try, three penalties and three conversions.

The message? Do not be misled by this young man's transparent decency and somewhat bucolic demeanour. He is one tough boyo. But then as he said after the Brive game, 'we don't come from the valleys for nothing'. And like all good valleys' boys he thanks his parents for the gifts they have given him, in this case an unfailing toughness and self-belief, which has allowed him so impressively, to survive setbacks and insults which would have undermined lesser players, lesser men. 'Ever since I was young, my father has told me that you've just got to go out and make your own living because if you don't do it no-one's going to help you. And when I was growing up he used to say: don't worry about anyone; just get on with your own life; anybody give you any gyp just ignore it and move on and don't worry; thick-skinned, like.'

I should say. You see Jenkins at his toughest when taking a crucial kick in front of a baying away crowd. Four steps back, two steps to the left, ball pointed forward, look up at the posts, pause, pause, pause again, drive the crowd mad, step up, kick the ball between the posts. (A routine which, although it has got slightly quicker, has not varied.) And you realize that he is not only fearless: he likes the theatre of it all. As he says of a hostile crowd, 'The crowd? It makes things easier when you know you are annoying someone; especially the opposition fans; hopefully you put it straight through the posts.'

The measure of this man is that he enjoyed playing at Brive. It was a suitable amphitheatre for him with a hostile and knowledgeable home crowd right in his face as he played for the club that is the passion of his life, a club which, with its passionate, partisan and rugby-wise supporters is probably closer in spirit to a French club than any other in Wales. Neither he nor Ponty gave an inch in that awe-inspiring game when, although Ponty cut-up Brive behind the scrum like no French side has ever been thus cut up, duff refereeing robbed the club, the town, Wales, me, of an extravagantly earned victory. But whatever the result the way Ponty played, the way that they showed that Welsh rugby still has bottle and class, at least in one of its unfashionable last redoubts, was a great source of pride to this Pontypriddian – and to the man who marshalled his troops so superbly that day. As Jenkins puts it: 'They just thought they could head-butt us; kick us, stamp us and walk all over us and beat us by 30 points and we are going to smile and go home nicely; we don't come from the valleys for nothing; the boys ain't going to take any messing and lie down. We got stuck in and they didn't like it.'

Jenkins's delight in playing for his home-town team – his neighbours, friends and family – at the highest level suffuses his being. The fact that they return the compliment – even if it takes the form of the gentle satire of hundreds in the crowd wearing 'Ginger Monster' wigs and stick-out ears not unlike their hero – gives him immense confidence and helps make Sardis Road such a formidable place for visiting teams. 'Playing for the club, believe you me is special. It's like it's your family. Here,' he adds, 'is an atmosphere I like and enjoy.' (One team who obviously did not enjoy Sardis Road was Bath who expected to waltz around their opponents. On a massive day for the club, the Bath team underestimated its opposition and was destroyed. Jenkins remembers seeing their faces before the game, laughing, assuming that it would be easy. They were never in the game.)

The way in which he handled the smashing defeat by England in 1998 is evidence enough of his toughness and brutal honesty. It was reported after that game that he was too depressed to go out of his house. While recognizing that Welsh rugby simply is not good enough he accepts his own role in that defeat. 'It was my fault. I messed up badly. I didn't want to play full-back. I had a bollocking from my mother for accepting it when I should have stayed on the bench rather than be what I'm not.' His honesty about the disaster against France is also impressive and his analysis persuasive. Personally he says he was 'skinned' by Castaignède – the first time it had ever happened, he notes, and the last, he promises. He is convinced that like most of the Lions he performed indifferently for some of last season because of fatigue and a sense of anti-climax. He knows that Welsh club rugby is no longer a good preparation for the demands of modern international rugby. It is not surprising that he says that he did not enjoy playing for Wales in 1998, apart from against the New Zealanders, whom he admires so much.

By contrast, he enjoyed playing for the Lions not least because 'it's great to be part of a good side', one which is talented and well-trained, motivated and managed – so much so that it gives a player the confidence to 'have a go when you want'. His ambition is to play for the Lions again in the 2000 tour to New Zealand – and for Pontypridd to flourish, to carry on besting more fashionable Welsh clubs and to achieve a consistently high class of rugby so as to prepare more and more Ponty players for the demands of international rugby. Amen to that.

What is not so clear is what are his remaining ambitions for Wales. In between getting my photograph taken with him and asking him to sign a match programme, I asked him how he wished to be remembered. His answer, typically modest and honest, supports the view that the experience of being the Ponty man who became a Lion and played such a significant role in their success, has become central to his assessment of his own standing in the game, indeed of his understanding of himself. Quietly, but significantly, his words also convey with characteristic dignity and politeness some of the wounds of playing at number 10 in this traumatized rugby culture where brilliance and commitment are deemed insufficient in the face of the required myth and miracles. Initially stressing that it would be nice after a period of intense interest in him in Wales, if after he retired no one remembered him – 'To be honest, no disrespect, but I'd be happy to walk down the street and no one recognizes me (they'd recognize me by my hair and my years mind)!' He then opened up. 'It would be nice to be remembered', he remarked, 'as a half tidy player: He wasn't bad; he had a lot of criticism but he wasn't a bad player; he gave his all for his country and his club.'

A half-tidy player? Not bad? He does not protest enough. For me, Neil Jenkins is the best Welsh player of the 1990s bar none and one of the finest all-round British backs of the era. Ask the Lions, ask the Boks, ask the bob-bank at Sardis Road. Ask people who know. And ask Neil Jenkins, Welsh outside-half prophet without sufficient honour in his own country, what his response is to the doubting Thomases, Bowrings and Cobners, and how he sees his own international record: 'I'm just happy I was a Lion and I don't care, they can slag me but they can't take that away from me.'

A man walks these mean streets, who is himself not mean. His name is Neil Jenkins. The nation never deserved him. His critics were not fit to tie his boot laces.

The analysis of Welsh rugby presented here was developed in an all-night session at Café Alberto Madrid, 7 July 1998, by myself and Simon Cookson. All quotes are taken from an interview with Neil Jenkins carried out at Sardis Road by myself and Mr Cookson, whom I thank for his help in researching this piece. My chapter is dedicated to the memory of the late Jon Vaughn Jones, a great Welshman, socialist, rugby critic and friend. He was wrong about Neil mind.

AFTERWORD

Huw Richards and Peter Stead

It was only a game that men played until they grew up, and she could not understand what all the fuss was about. Ronnie tried to explain, but the problem defeated him. If the Welsh language was threatened, the coal industry staggering under-manned on its last legs, the Methodist chapels boarded up, the town Fifteen *still retained the elan of old. They were the supreme in-group and the kudos that attached to them was in no way diminished by the ravages of the sixties. Pop groups and cinema stars were outside figures, but the* Fifteen, *the boys, as Ronnie called them, remained local property and were regarded with tribal affection.*

The immediate reaction on reading this passage from Alun Richards's short story *The Drop-Out* (1973) is to wonder whether the *Fifteen* of his fictional town – the creation of his own mind, of course, but nevertheless a reflection of real Valleys communities – still retains its status a quarter of a century later. Or has it joined those other once unassailable features of south Wales life on the spoil-heap of history? One has to fear the latter.

One of the risks of attempting to assess the state of any sport in any country is that of assuming the role of that Lord Derby, who was memorably said to 'bear the imprint of the last person to have sat upon him'. The most recent event to have sat upon the battered spirits of Welsh rugby union is the 96–13 beating by South Africa in the summer of 1998, a defeat which looms sufficiently large to block out any other thoughts – unless it be the reflection first inspired by the Springboks 1994 demolition of Swansea by 78–7: 'We didn't isolate this lot for long enough.'

South Africa always has been bad news for Wales, and not only as a source of political dissension. The last significant Welsh victory in South Africa was Rorke's Drift, and our national XVs have yet to triumph, home or away, in eleven meetings. The difference nowadays is that we are reminded of the gulf between the northern and southern

218

hemispheres much more frequently. The first four meetings between Wales and South Africa were spread over forty-five years. The last four have taken place in the space of forty-three months. As we contemplate the 1999 World Cup and try not to shudder, it is a worthwhile exercise in perspective to wonder whether Wales would ever have won the competition even if it had being going as long as the football version, which started in 1930. Welsh eras of dominance, even of the European game, are crammed into two spells – twelve of Wales's seventeen Triple Crowns were won either between 1900 and 1911 or from 1969 to 1979. The 1950 and 1952 Triple Crowns break up a fallow period between 1911 and 1965.

Wales would certainly have challenged strongly for the trophy in the 1970s. But as Clem Thomas, never one to duck unpleasant realities, was wont to point out, Wales failed to beat New Zealand in four meetings (five counting the 1974 match at Cardiff, a Test in all but official status) between 1969 and 1978. Victories by the British Lions in New Zealand in 1971 and the Barbarians at the Arms Park in 1973 were Welsh coached and led, but required Irish, Scottish and English assistance. Unaided, our best team in living memory, many of its members celebrated in this book, could not beat New Zealand in a fair to good era.

For better, for worse, rugby has been central both to Welsh, at least south Welsh, popular culture and to external perceptions of Wales. New Zealand journalist, Warwick Roger, quotes a former Springbok as saying: 'A South African rugby player has really only got two places to tour – New Zealand and Wales. In other countries you were there, but nobody knew you were there: you played the game and experienced the enthusiasm of the rugby community, but nobody else knew you.' England wing David Duckham found in the 1970s that he could walk unrecognized near his office in Birmingham, but would be spotted within moments of stepping on to the street in Cardiff, Swansea or Llanelli, a difference he acknowledged in the title of his autobiography *Dai for England*.

An even more potent acknowledgement of Wales's importance to the game, and its central importance to Wales, is its role as host nation of the 1999 World Cup. Yet this threatens to be a distinctly mixed blessing – and not only for the embarrassment that threatens on the field. It is hard to escape the feeling that the £121 million to be spent on the Millennium Stadium might have been better spent on almost any other project in Wales. That the project was capable of attracting £47 million of lottery money testifies to the political power of the Welsh Rugby Union. That they have chosen to devote a further £70 million and more to a prestige building project, demolishing a perfectly adequate ground in the process, shows a bizarre sense of priorities at a time when the game on the field is in unquestioned crisis.

It must be admitted that one problem that the Union faces as it tries to address the game's decline is that no two Welsh observers, and few outsiders, can agree on its causes. A number have presented themselves. One possible explanation is that we were spoilt by the simultaneous development of a number of remarkable talents in the 1960s and 1970s, and that a crash was inevitable once they had retired. It is tempting, for instance, to date decline to the retirement of Gareth Edwards in 1978. Gareth's mere presence conferred a sense of security – that if all else failed, against British opposition at least, he would probably find a way of winning the match. Yet the succession of Terry Holmes, Robert Jones and Robert Howley at scrum-half has meant that Gareth is the only one of the 1970s greats whose place has consistently been filled by world-class players.

One can point to a variety of 'what if' questions. What if Carwyn James had not died prematurely, and the Welsh Rugby Union had had the sense to turn to him as decline set in the late 1980s? Or what if the WRU had recognized that the disastrous 1988 tour of New Zealand was their fault, and not that of Tony Gray and Derek Quinnell, and kept faith with the management team that had delivered a thrilling Triple Crown during the domestic season?

A book dealing with the character of rugby is the last place where the importance of the individual can be denied. But, as this book also shows, even the greatest players and coaches are the prisoners of their times. The decline in the first seventeen years of Welsh rugby's second century has been too deep to be ascribed to, or prevented by, the actions of any individual. A variety of theories have been posited. Rugby league, always a popular villain, was blamed for slicing off a layer of talent in the late 1980s and early 1990s. But most of those players have now returned to union, and results have not improved. And the improvement shown by some players induces regret that rather more were not tempted North for two or three years. Nor can schools, and specifically comprehensivization in the state system, be blamed. The decline in playing standards has been most dramatic among tight forwards, not normally the positions aspired to by grammar school products. And if comprehensivization were so damaging, the English game would hardly be enjoying its most fruitful period since the 1920s, built in part on players from unpretentious backgrounds like prop-forward Jason Leonard. A far more convincing explanation is provided by changes in employment patterns. And not just the oft-noted disappearance of coal and steel. Rugby also relied heavily on public service employees – policemen, teachers and doctors. A few policemen are still to be found in Premier League action, but the other groups are all but extinct. Welsh rugby, with its reliance on heavy industry and the public services, might be seen as one of the, presumably unintended, victims of Thatcherism.

There is little doubt that professionalism, initially welcomed because it would allow league exiles to return, has been disastrous for Wales. It was always a puzzle why Max Boyce, generally an astute observer of human behaviour as most successful comedians are, should have characterized rugby league directors as 'plastic e-type Englishmen'. Whatever their limitations, the men who ran St Helens or Bradford Northern were rarely either plastic or e-type. But maybe Max was simply ahead of his time. The league scout has been replaced by someone much closer to his archetype, and twice as menacing – the man with the chequebook marked 'Newcastle', 'Harlequins' or 'Saracens'. There is a real danger that the Welsh game, lacking millionaires of the sort who have funded the top English clubs, will like Scottish football become a mere feeder to a rich, dominant English league. Some countervailing financial weight must be found – which makes it doubly deplorable that the WRU should have devoted its financial resources to the Millennium Stadium while carrying on guerrilla warfare with the, scarcely blameless, clubs. It could be said of Cardiff RFC and the WRU that they regard each other with mutual contempt – and that they are both right.

The secession of Cardiff and Swansea from the domestic structure, after weeks of wrangling from which nobody emerged with much credit, achieved the minor miracle of sending the Welsh game into the 1998–9 season in even lower spirits than it had finished in 1997–8. The domestic game, in which Neath's close-season near collapse was a reminder of chronic insolvency, was decapitated as Swansea and Cardiff gambled on the goodwill of the capricious and self-interested English clubs. The proposed British league, reconnecting Swansea and Cardiff and offering other Welsh clubs an escape from the destructive intro-spection of recent years, remained the best, perhaps the last, hope for the game in Wales.

So where do we go from here? It is instructive to compare and contrast reactions to two previous disastrous tours. Failure in New Zealand in 1988 was greeted by the sacking of the management team and a refusal to listen to players, led by Jonathan Davies, who had constructive suggestions to make about the future of the game. Failure in South Africa in 1964 brought about a basic rethink and the foundations of the coaching revolution which ensured the best was made of the extraordinary talent of the 1970s.

Committees of inquiry make dull reading alongside calls to 'sack the lot of them' or 'bring them all home'. Yet it has to be said that arresting the decline of Welsh rugby has so far proved well beyond the wit of any one individual, or the Welsh Rugby Union as a whole. One of the problems besetting the game in recent years has been chronic short-termism, with vital decisions like league restructuring taking place at short notice and with little forethought. Nor should it just be an internal WRU matter. We should not be ashamed to seek outside expertise, any more than Australia were when they hit the depths in the 1970s and called in people like WRU coaching organizer Ray Williams to help. So the appointment of New Zealand coach, Graham Henry, if not the unholy shambles preceding it, is welcome. Outsiders, albeit captains rather than coaches, have often had an impact on the Welsh team: Watcyn Thomas, John Gwilliam and John Dawes come to mind. The one previous overseas coaching appointment, that of Alec Evans in 1995, looked too much like a Cardiff takeover to produce any of the advantages associated with bringing in an outsider. Goodwill outside Wales is not lacking – little would delight New Zealanders more than for Wales to be worth beating again, while rugby's cardinal weakness as an aspirant world game is that it has so few major nations. It simply cannot afford to allow them to slip away into chronic uncompetitiveness. Nor should any such inquiry draw solely on the rugby world – business, sports science, and perhaps even a historian to explain how things have got as they are, could all offer important expertise. The alternatives? To carry on as we are and hope that some as yet unsuspected seam of massive natural talent will show itself. It cannot be ruled out. But the longer Wales goes on suffering colossal hammerings, the thinner will be the voice of optimism which still speaks to most fans at the start of each season – the hope that this year will be different and the glory days will return.

Meanwhile nostalgia remains our favourite mode. Treasured memories, however, need always to be harnessed to both loyalty and constructive criticism. As we add the prefix 'long' to our suffering we must note the example of the Chicago Cubs and the Boston Red Sox who last won baseball's World Series in 1908 and 1918 respectively and yet who generate tremendous support and fanatical loyalty as well as fierce debate. Those two historic clubs are owned by wealthy tycoons, but the billionaires in the hospitality suites are never allowed to forget that their franchises essentially belong to fans who, more than ever before, fill the stands, buy official merchandise and expect to see every play analysed on television and in the press. The lesson for rugby is that if the game is to be recast it must be done according to the entertainment and emotional needs of its true supporters.

Rugby is a team game and, accordingly, what we treasure most are victories, those moments when the final whistle occasions real joy, big hugs and perhaps a tear. Club victories over the All Blacks, away wins in Edinburgh, Paris and Dublin, and real drubbings of the English as in 1967 and 1976 all jostle for pride of place in the album of memories. But perhaps even more we dwell on those personalities who made victory possible and who, even at less exalted times, seemed to be giving our game its character, its heart and soul.

Gareth Edwards was arguably the greatest player ever to play for Wales and supporters were always fully aware of how keen he was to score in the big games, whether it was the spectacular tries celebrated here or those almost inevitable cheeky five-yard scores. Ambition took many forms. Nobody who saw how anxious Derek Quinnell was to defy the final whistle by getting on to the field as a substitute against France in 1972 could have been left in any doubt as to what playing for Wales meant in that era. There were players who consciously cultivated the mythic, knowing that to be a national predilection. When Clive Rowlands reminded us that winning was more important than losing in style he did so in the spirit of a miners' leader of an earlier era for whom, when all else failed, resort had to be made to class warfare and obduracy. Nobody wore the red shirt with more obvious pride than Ray Gravell whose every appearance sent both him and us back to the history books to check up on Owain Glyndŵr and the Welsh princes.

The singing of *Hen Wlad Fy Nhadau* has often been seen to affect players and none more so than Paul Thorburn whose tears were evidence of a determination that had taken this unlikely star, born to a military family in Germany and educated like Wales's first ever captain of 1881 at Hereford Cathedral School, to the forefront of Welsh rugby. Not inappropriately Thorburn was the last captain of Wales to capture the Triple Crown. There were players like J. P. R. Williams and Bob Norster who recommended themselves to fans by reserving their most masterful efforts for the games against England. Meanwhile, off the field, men like Denzil Williams, Alun Pask and Clem Thomas exuded so much natural dignity and authority that we began to wonder whether we had underestimated our imperial claims. All the while we never doubted that Wales would only win if its players were good and realized why it was that they were playing for Wales, playing for us.

SELECT BIBLIOGRAPHY

Paul Beken and Stephen Jones, *Dragon in Exile: The Centenary History of London Welsh RFC* (London: Springwood, 1985).

John Bentley, *Lions Uncaged: The Lions in South Africa* (London: Chameleon, 1997)

John Billot, *History of Welsh International Rugby* (Ferndale: Ron Jones, 1971).

W. J. Townsend Collins, *Rugby Recollections* (Newport: R. H. Johns, 1948).

Gerald Davies, *An Autobiography* (London: Allen and Unwin, 1979).

Gerald Davies, *Welsh Rugby Scrapbook* (London: Souvenir, 1983).

Jonathan Davies, with Peter Corrigan, *Codebreaker* (London: Bloomsbury, 1996).

Mervyn Davies, with David Parry-Jones, *Number 8* (London: Pelham, 1977).

Edward Donovan and others, *Pontypool's Pride: The Official History of Pontypool Rugby Football Club 1868–1988* (Abertillery: The Old Bakehouse, 1988).

Gareth Edwards, *Gareth* (London: Stanley Paul, 1978).

Gareth Edwards (ed. David Parry-Jones), *The Golden Years of Welsh Rugby* (London: Harrap, 1982).

Gareth Edwards, *Rugby* (London: Partridge, 1986).

Barbara M. Evans, *Blaina Rugby Football Club 1875–1975* (Risca: Starling, 1976).

Ieuan Evans, with Peter Jackson, *Bread of Heaven* (Edinburgh: Mainstream, 1995).

David Farmer, *The Life and Times of Swansea RFC: The All Whites* (Swansea: DEPS, 1995).

Dave Gallaher and W. J. Stead, *The Complete Rugby Footballer* (London: Methuen, 1906).

Robert Gate, *Gone North: Welshmen in Rugby League*, 2 vols (Sowerby Bridge: Gate, 1986, 1988).

Rowe Harding, *Rugby Reminiscences and Opinions* (London: Eyre and Spottiswoode, 1929).

Gareth Hughes, *The Scarlets: A History of Llanelli Rugby Football Club* (Llanelli: Llanelli RFC, 1988).

Carwyn James, *Focus on Rugby* (London: Stanley Paul, 1983).

Garry Jenkins, *The Beautiful Team* (London: Simon & Schuster, 1998).

John Jenkins (ed.), *Carwyn: Un o 'Fois y Pentre'* (Llandysul: Gomer, 1983).

John Jenkins, Duncan Pierce and Timothy Auty, *Who's Who of Welsh International Rugby Players* (Wrexham: Bridge Books, 1991).

Vivian Jenkins, *Lions Rampant: The British Isles Rugby Tour of South Africa 1955* (London: Cassell, 1956).

Barry John, *The Barry John Story* (London: Collins, 1973).

Stephen Jones, *Endless Winter* (Edinburgh: Mainstream, 1993).

Frank Keating, *The Great Number Tens* (London: Partridge, 1993).

Peter Lush and Dave Farrar (eds), *Tries in the Valleys: a History of Rugby League in Wales* (London: London League Publications, 1998).

Ian Malin, *Rugby, Blood and Money: English Rugby Union Goes Professional* (Edinburgh: Mainstream, 1997).

T. P. McLean, *Red Dragons of Rugby: Welsh-All Blacks Encounters 1905–1969* (Wellington: A. H. and A. W. Reed, 1969).

T. P. McLean, *Lions Rampant: the Lions Tour in New Zealand 1971* (Wellington: A. H. and A. W. Reed, 1971).

P. Melling, *Man of Amman: The Life of Dai Davies* (Llandysul: Gomer, 1994).

Geoffrey Moorhouse, *At The George and other essays on Rugby League* (London: Hodder and Stoughton, 1989).

Cliff Morgan, with Geoffrey Nicholson, *Cliff Morgan: The Autobiography: Beyond the Fields of Play* (London: Hodder and Stoughton, 1996).

John Morgan, *John Morgan's Wales* (Swansea: Christopher Davies, 1993).

W. John Morgan and Geoffrey Nicholson, *Report on Rugby* (London: Heinemann, 1959).

Terry O'Connor, *How the Lions Won* (London: Collins, 1975).

Graham Price, *Price of Wales* (London: Willow, 1984).

John Reason, *The Victorious Lions* (London: Rugby Books, 1971).

John Reason (ed.), *The Lions Speak* (London: Rugby Books, 1972).

John Reason, *The Unbeaten Lions* (London: Rugby Books, 1974).

John Reason and Carwyn James, *The World of Rugby* (London: BBC, 1979).

Alun Richards, *A Touch of Glory* (London: Michael Joseph, 1980).

Alun Richards, *Carwyn: A Personal Memoir* (London: Michael Joseph, 1984).

Warwick Roger, *Old Heroes: 1956 Springbok tour and the lives beyond* (Auckland: Hodder and Stoughton, 1991).

Bill Samuel, *Rugby: Body and Soul* (Llandysul: Gomer, 1986).

David Smith and Gareth Williams, *Fields of Praise* (Cardiff: University of Wales Press, 1980).

John Taylor, *Decade of the Dragon: a celebration of Welsh rugby 1969–1979* (London: Hodder and Stoughton, 1980).

Clem Thomas and Geoffrey Nicholson, *Welsh Rugby: The Crowning Years 1968–80* (London: Collins, 1980).

Clem Thomas, *The History of the British Lions* (Edinburgh: Mainstream, 1996).

J. B. G. Thomas, *The Lions on Trek* (London: Stanley Paul, 1956).

J. B. G. Thomas, *Rugger in the Blood* (London: Pelham, 1985).

David Watkins and Brian Dobbs, *The David Watkins Story* (London: Pelham, 1971).

David Watkins (ed. David Parry-Jones), *An Autobiography* (London: Cassell, 1980).

Bleddyn Williams, *Rugger My Life* (London: Stanley Paul, 1956).

Gareth Williams, *1905 And All That: essays on rugby football, sport and Welsh society* (Llandysul: Gomer, 1991).

J. P. R. Williams, *JPR: An Autobiography* (London: Collins, 1979).

Jack Winstanley, *The Billy Boston Story* (Wigan: The Wigan Observer, 1963).

INDEX

Aberavon 4, 67, 99, 112, 132, 153, 165
Abergavenny 127
Abertillery 4, 5, 77, 112
Aberystwyth 34, 164
Aitken, George 37
All Blacks, the *see* New Zealand
Amman United 35
Andrew, Rob 157, 177, 210
Arkwright, Jack 51
Arms Park (Cardiff) 4, 9, 22, 61, 67, 68,
    70, 77, 81, 82, 83, 84, 95, 97, 101, 102,
    103, 105, 106, 110, 111, 141, 186, 219
    see also National Stadium
Armstrong, Gary 151
Arnold, Danny 200
Ashton, Cliff 67, 99
Ashton, Eric 50, 57
Athletic Park (Wellington) 87
Auckland 50, 71, 88
Australia (rugby league) 49–50, 173
Australia (Wallabies) 36, 70, 72, 100, 110,
    117, 133, 134, 139, 149, 156–7, 159,
    170, 175, 195, 200, 212, 222

Baker, William J. 8
Bannerman, John 12
Barbarians, the 67, 88, 97, 157, 159, 219
Barnes, Stuart 158, 159
Barton, Frank 55
Bastiat, Jean-Pierre 103
Bateman, Allan 140, 195, 200
Bath 127, 141, 158, 167, 186, 211, 214
Beautiful Team, The 13
Beckingham, Geoff 22
Beddau 207
Bennett, George 53
Bennett, Phil 28, 72, 88, 89, 98, 103, 104,
    105, 137, 140, 167, 209
Bergiers, Roy 42
Berry Hill 127, 132
Bevan, Brian 49, 50
Bevan, John 89
Beyond the Fields of Play 18
Bidgood, Roger 133
Billot, John 20, 167

Billy Boston Story, The 58
Bish, Roy 80
Bishop, David 132–3, 134, 150–1
Blaenavon 126, 127
Blaina 62–3
Blanco, Serge 154
Blundells 34
Boland 82
Bonymaen 5
Boston, Billy 45–58
Boucher, Arthur 11
Bourgarel, Roger 85
Bowcott, H. M. 110
Bowen, Bleddyn 154, 156, 171
Boyce, Max 221
Boys of Summer, The 13
Brace, John ('Alfie') 34
Brace, Onllwyn 34, 35, 77, 152
Bradford Northern (later Bradford Bulls)
    166, 200
Bradshaw, Keith 69, 99
Brescia 130
Brewery Field (Bridgend) 195
Bridgeman, Sempronius 64
Bridgend 194
Bridgend RFC 68, 70, 99, 133, 154, 195
Brisbane 50, 139, 212
Bristol 152, 159, 160
British Lions 11, 21, 26–7, 28, 32, 37,
    38–41, 70–1, 82, 83, 84, 85–8, 89, 98,
    99, 101, 102, 105, 112, 113, 114, 116,
    118, 119, 125, 128, 138, 141, 153, 154,
    156–7, 163, 168, 175, 191, 199, 200,
    201, 205, 215, 219
Britton, Gordon 66
Brive 206, 211, 213, 214
Brown, Mark 131
Brynaman 34
Bunce, Frank 200, 201–2
Burgess, Bob 87
Burnett, Roy 23, 66, 67
Bush, Percy 12
Butler, Edward 131

Campbell-Lamerton, Michael 70, 71

Campese, David 144, 156, 173
Canada 139, 212
Canterbury 40
Canterbury-Bankstown (Australia) 173
Cape Town 200
Carbonneau, Philippe 156
Cardiff 4, 5, 22, 28, 47, 54, 78, 95, 96–7,
    124, 133, 166, 187, 219
Cardiff Blue Dragons 73
Cardiff Internationals (CIACs) 50, 53, 55
Cardiff RFC 4, 11, 21, 22, 23, 67, 77, 80,
    81, 99, 100, 114, 132, 141, 151, 154,
    165, 174, 183, 184, 185, 186–7, 195,
    221, 222
Cardiff Rugby Club: The Greatest 81
Cardus, Neville 13
Carisbrook Park (Dunedin) 32, 86
Carling, Will 143, 192, 200
Carmarthen 35, 38, 140
Carmarthen Athletic 141
Carmichael, Sandy 40
Castaignède, Thomas 215
Cefneithin 31, 32, 44, 95, 101, 106
Central Park (Wigan) 50, 52, 53
Chalmers, Craig 157
Charlton, Paul 73
Christchurch 87
Clarke, Don 14, 68
Cleaver, Billy 21, 23, 167
Cleaver, Hylton 10
Clement, Bill 84
Clement, Tony 197
Clinch, James 12
Cobner, Terry 89, 126, 127, 128, 130, 131
Coles, Fenton 123
Collier, Frank 53
Collins, W. J. Townsend 11, 152
Compleat Angler, The 9
Complete Rugby Footballer, The 9
Cooke, Geoff 143
Cooper, Russell 64
Corbett, Len 12
Coulman, Mike 73
Cove-Smith, R. 10
Coventry RFC 81
Crauste, Michael 12
Crawford, Ernie 12
Cresswell, Brian 66
Cross Hands 33

Cross Keys 11, 128
Cwmcelyn 64, 65

Dacey, Malcolm 155, 165, 166, 167
Dai For England 219
Daily Mail, The 196
Daily Telegraph 199
Dauga, Benoit 85
Davey, Claude 192
David, Tom 42, 89, 206
Davidge, Glyn 66
Davies, Alan 158, 185, 196, 211
Davies, Cliff 21, 77
Davies, Cyril 140
Davies, Dai 51
Davies, Danny 27, 81
Davies, Gareth 100, 119, 140, 164, 165,
    166, 167, 174
Davies, Gerald 35, 72, 77, 82, 87, 89, 91,
    105, 110, 111, 113, 116, 126, 130, 150,
    151, 170, 171, 175, 188
Davies, Glyn 23, 167
Davies, Goff 131, 154
Davies, Jonathan 100, 140, 150, 156, 158,
    161–77, 186, 191, 197, 209, 212, 213,
    222
Davies, Leighton 80
Davies, Mervyn 41, 82, 89, 105, 111, 114,
    115, 116, 118, 119
Davies, Stuart 187
Davies, Willie 23
Davies, W. J. A. 10
Dawes, John 38, 39, 84, 85, 88, 89, 105,
    114, 118, 119, 222
Dean, Paul 157
Dempsey, Jack 8
Dixon, Colin 53, 73
Drop-Out, The 218
Dublin 26, 70, 82, 88, 213
Duckham, David 219
Dunedin 86, 87
Dunvant 5
du Randt, Os 191
Durban 191
Dwyer, Bob 149

Eastbourne 41
Ebbw Vale 65, 77
Eden Park (Auckland) 32

Edinburgh 3
Edwards, Gareth 72, 75–92, 96, 98, 100, 101, 102, 103, 105, 111, 116, 126, 151, 152, 154, 158, 160, 183, 220, 223
Egan, Joe 56
Ellis Park (Johannesburg) 26, 27
Ellis, William Webb 37
England (rugby league) 174
England (rugby union) 10, 67, 69, 72, 77, 82, 83, 84, 88, 101, 102, 111, 143, 144, 156, 157, 158, 160, 166, 167, 170, 172, 175, 186, 195, 211, 213, 214, 224
Evans, Alec (Alexander) 158, 185, 222
Evans, Bill 127
Evans, Bob 66
Evans, Caradoc 31
Evans, Cliff 52
Evans, Colin 123
Evans, Ieuan (Llanelli coach) 38
Evans, Ieuan 135–45, 150, 160, 192, 197
Evans, Roddy 99
Evans, Ron 99
Evans, Stuart 197
Evans, Wynne 36

Famous Flankers 12
Famous Full-backs 12
Farr, Tommy 8
Farr-Jones, Nick 156
Faulkner, Lyndon 132
Faulkner, Tony 'Charlie' 128, 129, 130, 131
Fenwick, Steve 207
Ferguson, John 47, 56
Fielding, Keith 73
Fields of Praise 192
Fiji 69, 158, 166, 168
Flimby 48
Floyd, Ron 127
Football – The Rugby Union Game 8, 9
Ford, Ian 66
Ford, Trevor 12, 97
Forest of Dean 126
Fox, Grant 211
France (rugby league) 198
France (rugby union) 11, 36, 68, 69, 70, 72, 82, 83, 85, 88, 89, 102, 103, 117, 139, 142, 149, 166, 185–6, 213, 215, 224
France B 127, 166

Francis, Roy 53
Freeman, Johnny 53
Frost, David 38

Gabe, R. T. 103
Gale, Norman 116
Gallaher, Dave 9, 39
Gallico, Paul 13
Gannett, Lewis 13
Garndiffaith 2
Gate, Robert 48
Gent, D. R. 10
Geoghegan, Simon 157
Giants of South African Rugby 12
Gibbs, Scott 6, 140, 159, 189–202
Gibson, Michael 39, 40, 69, 71, 98, 160
Gill, Henderson 56
Gill, Ken 73
Givvens, Alec 53
Glamorgan Free Press 206
Gloucester 126, 131, 133, 166
Gnoll, the (Neath) 4, 11, 111, 167, 195
Going, Sid 39, 85
Goldsworthy, Mike 132
Gould, Arthur 11, 12, 142, 152
Graham, Tom 11
Gravell, Ray 140, 176, 224
Gray, Tony 112, 114, 115, 157, 171, 220
Great Britain (rugby league) 49–50, 72, 73, 173, 199, 201
Great Number Tens, The 12
Great Rugger Players 1900–1954 12
Greenslade, Des 66
Griffiths, Clive 198
Griffiths, Jonathan 157
Griffiths, Ron 155
Guardian, The 38, 172
Guscott, Jeremy 137, 157, 199, 201, 202, 205
Gwauncaegurwen 78, 90
Gwilliam, John 222
Gwynn, W. H. 8

Haden, Andy 90
Halberstam, David 13
Halifax 48, 53
Hall, Mike 157, 184, 197
Hanley, Ellery 55–7, 199
Harding, John 8

Harding, Rowe 10–11
Harris, Danny 206
Hastings, Gavin 144
Hastings, Scott 157
Hawke's Bay 105
Hayward, Dai 77, 114
Hendy 11
Henry, Graham 222
Hesketh, Chris 73
Hiddlestone, Dai 11
Hignell, Andrew 8
Hill, Andy 141
Hinshelwood, Sandy 61
Hipwell, Mick 77
Holmes, Terry 81, 119, 151, 156, 158, 165, 166, 169, 172, 220
Hopkins, Kevin 155
Hopkins, Raymond 'Chico' 42, 86
Howley, Robert 154, 159, 175, 192, 220
Howley, Tommy 50
Hughes, Dennis 112
Hughes, Eric 201
Hughes, Maurice 52
Hull 196
Hull Kingston Rovers 133
Hullin, Billy 77
Humphreys, Jonathan 188
Hunte, Alan 200
Hurcome, Danny 50

I Lead the Attack 12
Independent on Sunday 176
International Rugby Board (IRB) 174, 193
Ireland 68, 69, 72, 84, 110, 144, 160, 166, 195, 212
Irish Wolfhounds 168
Irvine, Andy 89
Italy 142, 198, 213

James, C. L. R. 1
James, Carwyn 23, 29–44, 83, 86, 87, 95, 98, 99, 100, 101, 102, 105, 106, 118, 140, 164, 220
James, Mike 196, 197
Japan 212
Jarden, Ron 14
Jarman, Chris 133
Jarrett, Keith 72, 77, 101, 102
Jenkins, Albert 11, 12, 140

Jenkins, Garin 133, 149
Jenkins, Garry 13
Jenkins, Neil 6, 149, 191, 203–16
Jenkins, Vivian 25, 27, 47
Jerram, Sid 50
Johannesburg 26, 27, 212
John, Barry 24, 28, 40, 41, 71–2, 81, 82, 85, 87, 88, 93–106, 110, 116, 118, 126, 138, 140, 164, 167, 209
John, Phil 206
Johnson, Jack 8
Johnson, Tom 'Codger' 11
Jones, Anthony 153
Jones, Benny 123, 124
Jones, Brian 66
Jones, Cliff 23, 37
Jones, D. James (Gwenallt) 31, 34
Jones, D. Ken 61, 70, 140
Jones, Dick 159
Jones, Gwyn 44
Jones, Ken 21, 66, 67, 89, 150
Jones, Lee 132
Jones, Omri 112, 116
Jones, Peter 14
Jones, P. L. 188
Jones, Rhodri 153
Jones, Robert 119, 140, 147–60, 166, 167, 170, 197, 220
Jones, Staff 131
Jones, Stephen 157, 192, 201
Jones, Steve 131

Kahn, Roger 13
Karalius, Vince 48
Karam, Joe 89
Kavanagh, Ronnie 12
Keating, Frank 12, 13, 117, 172
Keillor, Garrison 57
Kingsholm (Gloucester) 127, 131
Kirk, David 152
Kirkpatrick, Ian 41, 88
Kirwan, John 144
Koch, Chris 14
Kyle, Jackie 24

Lagisquet, Patrice 144
Lalanne, Denis 12
Lamerton, Andrew 206
Lansdowne Road (Dublin) 69, 83, 212

Lardner, Ring 13
Laughton, Doug 172
Leeds 169
Leicester 131
Leigh 164
Leonard, Jason 205, 221
Lewis, Allan 61, 69, 70, 77
Lewis, Emyr 143, 198
Lewis, Malcolm 165
Lewis, Peter 130, 131
Life with the Lions 200
Lions Rampant 25, 87
Llandovery College 33, 36, 37
Llanelli 34, 140, 219
Llanelli RFC (the Scarlets) 4, 23, 35, 42,
    43, 80, 81, 96, 100, 109, 130, 138, 141,
    153, 157, 163, 165, 170, 171
Llantwit Fardre 207, 208
Llewellyn, Gareth 160
Lloyd, John 99
Lochore, Brian 81
Loftus Versfeld (Pretoria) 27
Lomu, Jonah 191
London Welsh 109, 110, 111, 112,
    113–14, 115, 116, 118, 119, 130
Long, Sean 55
Lonkhurst, Bob 8
Loughborough College 111, 113
Loveridge, Dave 151
Lowe, Graham 56
Lynagh, Michael 12

McCormick, Fergie 40, 85, 98, 105
McDermott, Barrie 55
McIlvanney, Hugh 13
Maclaren, Bill 117, 142
McLean, Terry 87
McLoughlin, Ray 39, 40
Macpherson, G. P. S. 37
Maesteg 4, 42, 67, 86, 109
Mail on Sunday, The 119
Manley, David 206
Manly (Australia) 199
Mantle, John 72
Marriott, C. J. B. 10
Marshall, Frank 8
Marshall, Justin 182
Martin, Allan 183
Martin, Chris 166

Mathias, Roy 96
Matthews, Jack 21, 192–3
Meads, Colin 38, 85
Meredith, Billy 8
Meredith, Bryn 66
Merthyr Tydfil 5
Millennium Stadium 159, 219
Millfield 79, 80
Modern Rugby Game, The 9
Moon, Rupert 158, 160
Moore, Andy 198
Moore, Brian 137
Moorhouse, Geoffrey 13, 48
Morgan, Cliff 6, 12, 15–28, 36, 62, 64, 69,
    80, 89, 99, 154, 167, 209
Morgan, Haydn 112
Morgan, Teddy 9
Morris, Dai 82, 111, 114, 115, 116, 119
Morris, Dewi 158
Morris, Haydn 21, 27
Morris, Steve 11
Moseley 100
Moseley, Kevin 133
Mountain Ash 3, 50
Mountford, Cec 53
Muller, Hennie 97
Mulligan, Andrew 12
Murphy, Alex 48, 50
Murrayfield 67, 98, 100, 110, 111, 113,
    117, 131, 153, 199

Namibia 158, 212
National Stadium 142, 143, 164, 175, 177,
    186 *see also* Arms Park
Nant-y-glo 62
Neath RFC 4, 67, 82, 111, 150, 153, 159,
    165, 166, 167, 168, 170, 171, 195, 222
Newbridge RFC 4, 64, 109, 112, 131, 133
Newport 126, 128, 132, 133
Newport RFC 4, 11, 23, 66–7, 68, 69, 70,
    72, 73, 99, 126, 165
News of the World, The 47
New South Wales (Australia) 70, 195
New Zealand (rugby league) 50
New Zealand (rugby union) 5, 9, 21, 23,
    38–42, 68, 70–1, 72, 81, 83, 85, 88, 98,
    105, 118, 125, 130, 139, 142, 149, 156,
    157, 159, 170, 171, 181–2, 185, 192,
    199, 207, 213, 215, 219

Nicholls, Gwyn 9, 22, 152, 160
Nicholson, Geoffrey 18
Norster, Robert 140, 153, 156, 224
Northampton 194
North Queensland Cowboys (Australia) 173

O'Brien, Des 70
Odsal Stadium (Bradford) 50
Offiah, Martin 49, 55
Ogedengbe, Kingsley 202
Old Deer Park (London Welsh) 114, 115
Oldham 50, 73
Oldham Rugby League 37
Old Heroes 14
Old Trafford 174
Open Rugby 201
Orrell 131
Otago 130
Owen, Dickie 152, 159
Owens, George 'Dodger' 50
Owens, Jesse 8

Parc des Princes (Paris) 149
Paris 3, 5, 68, 70, 82, 144
Parker, A. C. 12
Parker, Tom 11
Parry-Williams, T. H. 34
Pask, Alun 71, 111, 224
Penarth 66, 132, 153
Penberthy, Bob 206
Penclawdd 3
Pencoed 195
Perkins, John 124, 127, 131
Philip, Robert 199
Pontarddulais 132, 140
Pontypool Park 123, 124, 127, 133, 134
Pontypool RFC 119, 121–34, 150
Pontypridd 12, 206–7
Pontypridd Church Shield 207
Pontypridd RFC 23, 42, 109, 150, 165, 205, 206, 208, 211, 214, 215
Powell, Wick 81
Prescott, Steve 200
Pretoria 27
Price, Brian 66, 69, 83
Price, Graham 127, 128, 130, 131, 153
Price, Jonathan 196
Price, Malcolm 123

Prosser, Bob 67, 68, 73
Prosser, Ray 124–31, 133, 134
Protheroe, Gary 99
Pullin, John 89

Queensland 70
Quinnell, Derek 39, 89, 157, 220, 224
Quinnell, Scott 186, 192
Quittenton, Roger 133

Raphael, J. E. 10
Raybould, Billy 96
Rayer, Mike 184
Reason, John 43
Rees, Alan 67
Rees, Joe 11
Rees, Paul (Pontypool) 133
Rees, Paul 152, 155, 194, 199, 200
Rees, Peter 66
Rhondda, the 25
Rhydlewis 31, 32
Rice, Grantland 13
Richards, Alun 23, 24, 31, 41, 43, 218
Richards, Bryan 23, 99
Richards, David 155, 156
Richards, Dean 156
Richards, Ken 99
Richards, Maurice 73, 102
Ring, Johnny 49
Ring, Mark 133, 142, 184
Roberts, Randy 8
Robins, John 113
Robinson, Jackie 13
Robson, James 205
Rodney Parade (Newport) 5, 11, 68, 111
Roger, Warwick 14, 219
Romania 131, 139, 152, 171
Romanos, Joseph 12
Rovigo 43
Rowlands, Clive 38, 42, 67, 69, 153, 156, 224
rugby league 37, 45–58, 72–3, 81, 160, 163, 164, 166, 169, 172, 173, 174, 176, 192, 193, 195, 196, 197, 198, 199, 200, 201, 220, 221
Rugby News 202
Rugby Recollections 11
Rugby Reminiscences and Opinions 10
Rugby: The Great Ones 12

Rugby World 158
Rugger: the Greatest Game 10
Rugger My Life 12
Runyon, Damon 13
Rutherford, Don 38
Ryan, John 172
Ryan, Martin 54, 55, 56

Sailor, Wendell 54
St Helens (Swansea) 4, 192
St Helens (rugby league) 48, 51, 72, 192, 196, 197, 198, 200, 201
Salford 51, 53, 72, 73, 81, 160, 198
Samuel, Gary 77
Samuel, Bill 78, 83, 85, 154
Saracens, the 133
Sardis Road (Pontypridd) 214
Scotland 10, 12, 42, 61, 67, 69, 70, 82, 84, 88, 131, 142, 153, 166, 170, 175, 192, 212
Scott, J. M. B. 10
Scottish Co-Optimists 168
Seeling, Charlie 47
Seven Sisters 2
Shelford, Wayne 131
Skinner, Mickey 167
Slattery, Fergus 118
Smith, Dai 22, 24, 26, 115, 154, 192
Smith, Doug 85, 86
Smith, Ian 11, 37
Smith, Pat 25
Sole, David 142
South Africa (Springboks) 14, 27, 38, 69, 82, 83, 89, 97, 102, 103, 149, 157, 159, 185, 191, 200, 205, 218, 219
South Australia, 70
Southland 70
South Wales Argus 11, 72, 152
South Wales Evening Post 155, 198
South Wales Police 155
Spain 141
Springboks *see* South Africa
Sportsweek 169, 170
Squire, Jeff 131, 132
Stade Colombes 77, 84, 102
Stead, W. J. 9, 39
Stephens, Chris 195
Stephenson, George 11
Stoop, Adrian 12

Stopford, John 49, 51, 52, 56
Stradey Park (Llanelli) 5, 11, 34, 109, 111, 138, 140, 141
Stransky, Joel 149
Stuart, I. M. B. 10
Sullivan, Jim 47, 48, 50, 51, 54
Summer of '49 13
Sun, The 172
Sunday Times 157, 192
Sutton, Roy 154
Sutton, Steve 199
Swansea 159, 219
Swansea (the All Whites) 4, 8, 11, 23, 26, 80, 99, 130, 132, 133, 149, 150, 152, 153, 154, 155, 159, 160, 163, 165, 166, 186–7, 192, 193, 194, 195, 197, 198, 199, 200, 202, 218, 221, 222
Swinton 52, 73

Talbot Athletic Ground (Aberavon) 132, 133
Tanner, Haydn 22, 23, 64, 77, 81
Taylor, Bleddyn 132, 133
Taylor, Ivor 126, 132
Taylor, John 82, 105, 107–20
Telfer, Jim 125
Thomas, Arwel 154, 156, 206, 213
Thomas, Brian 4, 165, 167, 169, 170
Thomas, Clem 26, 34, 82, 89, 219, 224
Thomas, Delme 110
Thomas, Graham 51
Thomas, Gwyn 21, 24
Thomas, J. B. G. 12, 38, 61, 67, 109, 165
Thomas, Johnny 50
Thomas, Malcolm 66
Thomas, Watcyn 222
Thompson, Cec 53
Thorburn, Paul 166, 196, 208, 224
Tiger Bay 47, 54
Times, The 170
Tondu 3
Tonga 164, 168, 213
Tosswill, L. R. 10
Trebanog 25
Trebanos 153, 154
Tredegar 129
Tremain, Kel 82
Trevor, P. C. 10
Trimsaran 163, 164, 173